AF623855

Ladakh Then and Now

Zain-ul-Aabedin Aabedi

ATLANTIC
PUBLISHERS & DISTRIBUTORS (P) LTD

Published by
ATLANTIC
PUBLISHERS & DISTRIBUTORS (P) LTD
7/22, Ansari Road, Darya Ganj,
New Delhi-110002
Phones : +91-11-40775252, 23273880, 23275880, 23280451
Fax : +91-11-23285873
Web : www.atlanticbooks.com
E-mail : orders@atlanticbooks.com

Branch Office
5, Nallathambi Street, Wallajah Road,
Chennai-600002
Phones : +91-44-64611085, 32413319
E-mail : chennai@atlanticbooks.com

Copyright © The Author, 2015

ISBN: 978-81-269-2002-0

All rights reserved. No part of this publication may be reproduced, stored in a retrieval system, transmitted or utilized in any form or by any means, electronic, mechanical, photocopying, recording or otherwise, without the prior permission of the copyright owner. Application for such permission should be addressed to the publisher.

Disclaimer

The author and the publisher have taken every effort to the maximum of their skill, expertise and knowledge to provide correct material in the book. Even then if some mistakes persist in the content of the book the publisher does not take responsibility for the same. The publisher shall have no liability to any person or entity with respect to any loss or damage caused, or alleged to have been caused directly or indirectly, by the information contained in this book. Hence, the book should be taken as a general guide only.

The publisher has fully tried to follow the copyright law. However, if any work is found to be similar, it is unintentional and the same should not be used as defamatory or to file legal suit against the author/publisher.

If the readers find any mistakes we shall be grateful to them for pointing out those to us so that they can be corrected in the next edition.

All disputes are subject to the jurisdiction of Delhi court only.

Printed in India at Nice Printing Press, A-33/3A, Site-IV, Industrial Area, Sahibabad, Ghaziabad, U.P

NAWANG RIGZIN

Minister for
Urban Development and
Urban Local Bodies
Government of Jammu & Kashmir

DO No. : PS/HM/UD&ULB/..........

Dated : 29. 10. 2013

Message

I am pleased that Mr. Zain-ul-Aabedi has come up with a book on the history of Ladakh under the title *Ladakh Then and Now*. As the title itself suggests, the book touches the history as well as the present state of life in Ladakh. It briefly covers the two very important dynasties of Ladakh—Lachen Dynasty and Namgyal Dynasty. Due space is also given to the Dogra invasion of Ladakh which in itself was a very crucial phase of political transition in Ladakh.

The book also covers the cotemporary history of Ladakh with a special reference to the contribution of the contemporary leaders, right from Kushok Bakula to present-day leaders, in various facets of development. The author also makes an attempt to discuss different layers of social change in Ladakh—socio-political, cultural, spiritual, and economic.

Given the paucity of literary information on Ladakh, the book is a welcome addition to the scarce literature on Ladakh. I do hope that the author will not stop his endeavor here but will try to explore various other facets of Ladakh in the future.

I am sure the book would prove to be a handy compendium of past-and-present Ladakh not only for the students and teachers, but also for researchers/scholars and all other Ladakh enthusiasts. My best wishes are with him.

(Nawang Rigzin Jora)

LAHDC LEH
རིག་འཛིན་དཔལ་འབར།
RIGZIN SPALBAR

སྤྱི་དཔོན།
ལ་དྭགས་རང་སྐྱོང་རི་སྒྲོང་ས་ཡར་རྒྱས་ལྷན་ཚོགས། སླེ།
Chairman / Chief Executive Councillor
LADAKH AUTONOMOUS HILL DEVELOPMENT COUNCIL LEH
LEH LADAKH - 194101 (INDIA)
TEL. : (O) 01982-252212 FAX : 257187
E-mail : cec_lahdc@yahoo.co.in www.leh.nic.in

Foreword

It gives me pleasure that Mr. Zain-ul-Aabedin Aabedi is bringing the title *Ladakh Then and Now* to present precisely the essential information regarding the history of Ladakh. The book covers the brief history of Lachen dynasty, Namgyal dynasty, Dogra's invasion to Ladakh and the great and unforgettable contribution of contemporary leaders of Ladakh, right from K.G. Bakula Rinpochey to present date, in the development and upliftment of Ladakhi Society.

The author has also reflected how the economic, social, cultural, spiritual, and educational changes are taking place in the region with the passage of time.

I hope this book will help to bridge the gap between the past and present Ladakh and would prove beneficial, informative and educative to the students, teachers, scholars, historians, and researchers.

My best wishes are with him.

2/11/13

(Rigzin Spalbar)

Preface

My purpose of writing this book is to open to the readers the vast field of historical and political knowledge about Ladakh, and to give a brief description of the rulers of Lachen dynasty (1020-1500), Namgyal dynasty (1500-1834), Nominal kings (1835-42), Dogra rulers (1842-1966), and about the political leaders of the post-Independence period.

Ladakh has experienced tremendous changes during the last four decades. The increase in literacy rate, fast growth of employment potential, sharp rise of economic opportunities, inflow of tourists since 1974, adoption of some agriculture innovations, and growth in internal trade and business have opened up new avenues of earning. As a result, there have been profound changes in our economic and social order. Certain issues pertaining to Ladakhi culture, agriculture, society, education, ecology, politics, and religion have been discussed in this book.

Ladakh remained quite isolated in the past for centuries together, except, for a limited number of traders, due to harsh topography and climate, remoteness, and inaccessibility. Efforts have been made to write briefly on the role of eminent political personalities of the post-Independence period who were deeply associated with this region, right from Kushok Gyalrsas Bakula to the present period. Efforts have also been made to mention the socio-cultural developments and events which have occurred in the past few decades.

My thanks are due to all the well wishers and scholars who guided and helped me with their valuable suggestions. I am indebted to Mr. Vilayat Ali Abbasi for patiently and painstakingly going through the whole manuscript. I am also grateful to authors and historians whose thought and literary work helped me to accomplish the task of writing this book. It is hoped that the book will be very useful to the students and teachers of history, historians, and researchers in this field.

Healthy suggestions from historians, academicians and scholars are, however, welcome.

Zain-ul-Aabedin Aabedi

Introduction

Ladakh had been an independent state from 10th century AD to 19th century under the rule of Lachen and Namgyal kings. Lachen Spalgi Nima Gon was the first king who established the Lachen dynasty in 900 AD and ruled over Ladakh from Shay as its capital. Tsephel Tundup Namgyal was the last king who was dethroned by the Dogras. Wazir Zorawar Singh conquered both Ladakh and Baltistan at the command of Maharaja Gulab Singh, and annexed them to Jammu kingdom through a treaty of peace, signed on September 17, 1842. However, the British handed over Kashmir to Maharaja Gulab Singh in 1846 AD by the treaty of Amritsar, which was signed on March 16, 1846. Ladakh became an integral part of J&K State, and eventually of the Republic of India in the wake of India's Independence in 1947. After three years in 1950, the People's Republic of China brought Tibet and Xinjiang under its control, and the age-old trade relations between Ladakh and central Asia got terminated. Trade with Tibet came to an end in 1960. Thereby Ladakh lost its importance as a trade centre and ceased to receive information and trade goods from these countries. Ladakhi people depended for many things on their neighbours. Whenever trade was disrupted on account of disturbances in neighbouring states, shortage of general goods occurred in Ladakh and this led to hardships. Moreover, the region suffered a lot spiritually, because of prohibition on entry into Tibet.

Consequent upon the annexation of Ladakh to the State of J&K in 1842 during the reign of Maharaja Gulab Singh, the Dogras took steps to administer the region through an administrative head known as "Thanedar". The first such functionary was Magna Thanedar. The Thanedars enjoyed both the civil and military powers. Post-Independence Ladakh consists of the two districts of Leh and Kargil, whereas Skardo and Gilgit, which were parts of pre-Independence Wazarat of Ladakh, are now parts of Pakistan's northern area. Once Leh was the summer capital and Skardo was the winter capital of Ladakh. Ladakh is surrounded by important nations of central Asia. It touches the borders of China and Pakistan. Thus, it is an important region from defence and strategic point of view as well. The town of Leh is situated at an altitude of 11,500 ft. above sea level. The highest road and highest airfield in the world are also located in Ladakh.

The climate of Ladakh is severe with aridity as its essential feature and is caused by the Himalayan Wall which prevents moisture-laden clouds of the Indian monsoon from entering there. That is why the climate of the region is extremely dry. The climate of the region was not so rigorous thousands of years ago, when its substantial part was covered with lakes and the quantity of rainfall was much higher than the present three or four inches annually. Ladakh's landscape would have naturally been different then with plenty of water around, which was subsequently drained off by the geological phenomena like earthquakes and flash floods. Now we experience intense heat under direct sunshine and biting cold after the sunset. The forbidding climate, remoteness, and inaccessibility kept the region isolated except for traders for centuries, especially during winter, when due to heavy snowfall, both Zojila and Ratangla are closed for about six months.

Ladakh forms one of the most elevated areas of the world and there are human habitations ranging from 9,000 to about 15,000 feet above sea level. The great River of Ladakh is the Indus and its principal tributaries are Zanskar, Daras, Shayok, and Shigar. The Indus has given India its name. It is called "Sindhu" in India. The word 'Sindhu' emerged from Sindh, then became Hindu, and finally Hindustan, which is the name of our beloved country. The source of the river is at Kailash-Mansarovar and the water of the Indus is considered sacred both for the Buddhists and the Hindus, and especially for the Sindhis. The Sindhu-Darshan, Singgay-Khababs festival is being celebrated annually at Shay Manla for the last 15 years since 1997, and besides the Ladakhis, many pilgrims and tourists from adjoining areas attend the festival. The traditional Ladakhi belief held that the source of the river at Mansarovar is like a "lion's mouth", therefore, they call it Singgay Khabab, which means "lion's mouth". Some of the prominent lakes of Ladakh are situated in Changthang region. They are Pangong Lake, Khumdan Lake, Tsomoriri Lake, Yunamtso Lake, Hanley Lake, Kyagartso Lake, and Tsorul Lake. There is heavier snowfall around Pangong Lake because of intense humidity.

Ladakh attracts a host of expeditionists, writers, poets, saints, and scholars. Volumes of books have been devoted to highlight the uniqueness of its history and cultural heritage. Thousands of tourists from all over the world have been visiting this place for many decades. The heavy influx of visitors in summer has transformed Ladakh, especially Leh town, into a busy and crowded place. During the summer season, the local population is outnumbered in the crowd of visitors and labourers from outside Ladakh. However, some factors such as the growing influence of Western culture and changing social attitudes of the people are worrying. It would be unfortunate if in the grab of development and modernization we abandon our traditional lifestyle, customs, and ethical and aesthetic values. Hence, there is an urgent need for introspection and make the people aware of the consequences of such unhealthy trends.

The present Ladakhi races are a combination of three ethnic groups, viz. Mon, Dard and Mongol. It is believed that the Mon tribe was the first ethnic group to settle in Ladakh. They migrated from north India via Kullu and Manali. Some historians are of the opinion that the Mons came from Monhali. They came here hundred years before the Christian era. Thus, early civilization began in Ladakh through them. Basically, they were not Buddhist, but due to interaction with the Buddhist missionaries who visited Ladakh in 3rd century BC, they were influenced by Buddhism. They established Mon colonies at Gia, Miroo, Martselang, Chemday, Shara, Igoo,

Hemya, Zangskar, etc. According to Francke, they had colonies upto Rudok. This shows that they did a wonderful job for the upliftment of society and development of the present civilization. Upper Ladakh was then ruled by a Mon chief called Gyapa Cho, while the lower Ladakh was divided into small chiefdom, with the Dard chief Cho Baqdoor Skyap as the most prominent ruler. According to Gergan, the last name of the 'Mon' village ends with "chay", such as Tangchay, Terchay, Phukchay, Likchay, etc., whereas the first name of 'Dard' village starts with "Ha, He or Hi" like Hanu, Hembabs, Henasku, Hemya, Hipti, Hemis and Himaling, etc. Before the advent of Tibetan Buddhism in the region, the inhabitants of Spiti and nearby regions were said to be 'Mon' or Monpa. According to the Indian historians (Handa 2001, Tibetan Rgyalpo 2006, and local Tobdan 1984), although locals in Spiti today use the word 'Mon' for Indians, Tobdan states that Mons were a mixed Indo-Tibetan race, who lived between the Indian plains and the Tibetan plateau. Today there are 'Mon' or Monpa in Bhutan and eastern India.

The Dards were the other Indo-Aryan tribe who probably migrated to Ladakh from Afghanistan, Gilgit, and Hunzanagar, etc. just after the Mons. They settled in lower Ladakh, right from Daras, Dah-Hanu, Batalik, Garkon, Tagmachik, Domkhar, Khalsey and other areas, and established their colonies. They had their castles at many places like Gya-Miroo, Hemya, Khalatsey, Nyarma, and Tsemo hill at Leh, called Brokpa Khar. The interaction between the Dards and Mons turned out to be hostile. The Dards gradually subdued the Mons. The process had a social implication. It led to the reduction of Mons to a lower status in the society. The process had its parallel with the reduction of Dravidian tribe in India, when they were subdued by the Aryans.

Later, at the invitation of the Gyapa Cho, a Tibetan prince Skid-de-Nimagon reached Ladakh alongwith a hundred horsemen. He chose Shay as his capital and extended his kingdom. It is said that the Tibetans were much arrogant who ill-treated the Mons.

The introduction of Buddhism in Ladakh and Tibet can be traced back to early 3rd century BC, when emperor Ashoka sent Buddhist missionaries there for the propagation of Buddhism. It is said that Ladakh got its Buddhism earlier than Tibet did. The Chinese pilgrim Fa-hien observes the presence of Buddhism in Ladakh. Many historians believed that some Ladakhis and Kashmiris spread Buddhist faith in Tibet. Even though Buddhism entered Tibet from Ladakh and Kashmir, it was the Lamaist Buddhism which later came to Ladakh from Tibet after 7th century, and spread in Ladakh. As far as Tibet is concerned, Buddhism flourished there in 7th century during the reign of king Hrong-tsan Gampo. He made Buddhism a state religion but there were language problems. Till then the Tibetans were not having any written script to record the things and communicate. Therefore, the king sent a group of sixteen people to Kashmir, headed by Sambota, to learn Sanskrit language in which Buddhist text could be translated. Accordingly, Sambota and some others learned Sanskrit language in Kashmir, and after returning from Kashmir he composed grammar for the Tibetan language. He is considered the father of the present Bhoti language and the script. Today this language is being spoken in one way or the other, right from Baltistan to Arunachal Pradesh and Tibet in the Himalayan belt. Now the people from different states and regions are pressing hard to include the language in the 8th schedule of the Indian Constitution. Many useful books from Sanskrit were translated into Tibetan language by Sambota.

Similarly, Lha Lama Yeshes Sod sent twenty-one young men to Kashmir to learn and study Buddhism deeply under Pandit Saradhakara Verma, but except Rinchen Zangpo and Legspa Sharab, all of them died without achieving the goal. Rinchen Zangpo studied under the learned Buddhist scholar, Pandit S.K. Verma and got translated 161 books. He also got constructed a few dozens of shrines in many parts of Ladakh. Among them Alchi is very popular and is in a good condition even today. He honestly and wholeheartedly devoted himself to the propagation of Buddhism. He founded a monastic university at Nyarma Thiksay; today its ruins lie scattered there in a deplorable condition. There was a time when the people of entire region, right from Ladakh to Gilgit and Baltistan, followed the religion of "Bon" prior to Buddhism. The stone inscriptions and statues of Lord Buddha in Mulbek, Suru Kartsey, Daras, Sod and even in Baltistan reveal the fact that once Buddhism was a popular religion in this area after Bon. The eternal Bon signs of *swastika* and other images on rocks and caves appear to be remainders of the older Zhang-Zhung kingdom (Petech 1997). In the 10th century, a powerful kingdom was formed in western Tibet, known as Guge, covering Guge, Purang, Ladakh, Zangskar, and Spiti (Petech 1997). Guge's Buddhist king sponsored the propagation of Buddhism by constructing temples and monasteries and sponsoring scholarly activities. As a result, indigenous 'Bon' practitioners were converted to Tibetan Buddhism.

After the emergence of Islam in Kashmir and owing to mass conversion of Kashmiri pandits to Islam, under the aegis of Bulbul Shah and Shah Hamdan in 14th century, its neighbouring regions like Gilgit, Baltistan, Zangskar, Nubra, Purik, Daras, and Leh could not save themselves from its influence. As Petech explains, "The conversion of Kashmir brought a new instability to western Tibet". Ladakh stands on the old central Asian trade route and has been a halting place since ancient days, both for the trading caravans and mighty armies. Traders from Baltistan, Kashmir, central Asian Countries, Tibet, China, Punjab, etc. used to come here for trade purposes. It was Hazrat Shah Hamdan, Syed Mohammad Noor-Bakhsh, and Meer Shamsud-din Araqi who got converted the whole area of Baltistan to Islam. Moreover the Yarkendi Hajjis proceeded to Mecca for Hajj through Ladakh. Its location on the route to Mecca brought elements of influence from Islam. This facilitated the entry of all the religions which came here.

Several geological events had many implications for the socio-cultural set up in the region. One such event is the flooding of Shayok river, which was caused by the breakage of Khumdan lake. The flooding of Shayok was responsible for the arrival of Balti Muslims of Chaythang (Khapulo) in Leh, during the reign of Takpa Bum Ldey during 1730-70 AD. The flood eventually destroyed the Chaythang town, and the Balti Muslims were forced to migrate to Leh. King Takpa Bum Ldey was so generous and kind that he not only allowed the Balti Muslims to settle in the Chuchot area but also never pressurized them to convert to Buddhism. He further provided relief to them. The Muslim population in Chuchot constructed mosques and Imambarahs at various places and strictly followed their own religion. Later, under an agreement between the Mughal commander Fidai Khan and Raja Delek Namgyal in 1680 AD, many Kashmiri Muslims came to Leh to trade in wool and pashmina. Most of them settled here and married local women. Some literate persons of Tak and Radhu families were appointed as Munshis by the Raja to make correspondence in Urdu and Persian with the Mughals. Since the Mughals wanted an uninterrupted flow of pashmina to Kashmir, they sustained a balanced control over both Baltistan and Ladakh. The Mughal Emperor sent decrees to the Ladakhi kings to be loyal and sincere, and conferred the robe of honour, the sword and title to them. This practice continued until the rule of Muhammad Shah in the mid 18th century. By that time the Mughal dynasty was on the verge of collapse. In a way, Muslim travellers, Saints, Sufis, and traders played a very important role in the introduction of Islam in Ladakh.

Wazir Zorawar Singh Kalohria invaded Ladakh thrice in 1833, 1834 and 1839 AD, and Ladakh faced a new enemy, different from the past invaders. This was the Dogra force of Raja Gulab Singh of Jammu. In the past, invaders had withdrawn after receiving handsome booty as tribute. But this time the Dogras came to take the possession of Ladakh permanently. Zorawar Singh was the man who annexed both Baltistan and Ladakh with the Jammu kingdom through a treaty of peace signed on September 17, 1842. Before that, Ladakh was an independent state, and Raja Tundup Namgyal was the last ruler of independent Ladakh. However, when the British handed over Kashmir to Maharaja Gulab Singh in 1846 by the treaty of Amritsar, Ladakh became an integral part of Jammu and Kashmir State, and eventually of the Republic of

India in the wake of India's Independence in 1947. After hearing the news of the advance of the Dogras under Zorawar Singh, Raja Tundup Namgyal sent a huge army to Purig to stop the Dogras, under the command of Stokpa Kalon Dorjay Namgyal, Leh Lonpo Mourup Stanzin and Kalon Pankhapa, but they failed to stop them. The Dogras captured Leh and the Raja was dethroned. Later on, the Dogras invaded Baltistan and Raja Tundup Namgyal was forced to accompany them to Baltistan where he died of small pox at Khapulo, and his body was brought to Stok for cremation. After the capture of Baltistan, Zorawar Singh invaded Tibet and while fighting with the Tibetans, he died at Toyu Purang on 12th of December 1841. Similarly, Dogra commanders Dewan Hari Chand and Wazir Ratnu invaded Ladakh and Tibet in 1842 AD, to take the revenge of the defeat and assassination of General Zorawar Singh Kalohria.

In the light of wide context of this book, the brief history of Tibet—formation of Lachen dynasty, transfer of capital from Shay to Leh in 1500 AD, establishment of Namgyal dynasty and its end in 1842, the annexation of Ladakh with J&K State and finally with Republic of India in 1947, etc. and all other subjective contents are included in this book. The contribution of the contemporary leaders from the pre-and post-Independence period, right from Kushok Bakula to present date, is also briefly discussed.

Contents

The Lachen Dynasty of Ladakh (900-1400)

1

Skit-Ldey-Nima Gon was the first king who ruled over Ladakh during the 9th century. The Ladakhi kings considered themselves the descendants of Nyathri Tsanpo the first king of Tibet, whose date is about 200 or 300 BC. Although these kings are very proud of being the offsprings of the great kings of Tibet, but they do not wish to be reminded the fact that

Genealogical Table of Lachen Kingdom of Ladakh

1.	Skit Ldey Nima Gon (Yathi Keeda) 975-990, AD. King of Kugay, Purang and Ladakh		
2.	Spalgi Gon (990-1020) King Ladakh, Zangskar and Spltl	Tashi Gon (Purang)	Ldey Sog Gon (Kugay)
3.	Chhosgon (1020-1050)	Dagon	
4.	Lachen Takspa Ldey	1050-1075 AD	
5.	Lachen Chang Chhub Semspa	1075-1100 AD	
6.	Lachen Gyalpo	1100-1125 AD	
7.	Lachen Otpala	1125-1150 AD	
8.	Lachen Naghlog	1150-1175 AD	
9.	Lachen Gaybum	1175-1200 AD	Lachen Gaibay
10.	Lachen Joldor	1200-1230 AD	
11.	Lachen Tashi Gon	1230-1265 AD	
12.	Lachen Chhospail	1265-1290 AD	
13.	Lachen Mourup Gon	1290-1340 AD	
14.	Gyalbu RInchen (Malik SadruddIn Shah, King of Kashmir, who died In Kashmir In the Year 1327 AD		
15.	Lachen Sherab	1340-1430 AD	
16.	Lachen Thisog Ldey	1400-1430 AD	
17.	Lachen Malik Bum Ldey Raja Shey	1430-1470 AD	Lachen Takpa Bum Raja Tingmogang
18.	Lachen Lotus Chhogdan Tongpa Ali Brother	1470-1534 AD	Lapstan Sherab Brother
19.	Lachen Bara	1430-1455 AD	
20.	Lachen Bhagon	1475-1500 AD	
21.	Lachen Tashi Gon	1500-1532 AD	

Lachen Lahwang Gon brother of Lachen Tashi Gon was made blind and Imprisoned.

their special ancestor after whom their dynasty branched off from the central Tibetan dynasty, was Langdharma, the famous apostate of Buddhism. Although Buddhism had been introduced into Central Tibet around 400 AD, it did not become a great religion until King Shrong Tsan Gampo openly accepted it and made it a state religion and used his influence to let it spread over the whole of Tibet. It is said that he married with two Buddhist princesses, one from Nepal and another from China. These two queens persuaded Srong-Tsan-Gampo to introduce Buddhism in Tibet. Consequently he decided to give his full support in the propagation of Buddhism in Tibet. But again there was language problem, as there was no written language in Tibet. Therefore for the upliftment of Buddhism he sent Sambhuta along with sixteen other companions to Kashmir to learn Sanskrit language and compose such a language in which Buddhist texts from Sanskrit can be translated. Sambhuta went to Kashmir. He studied Sanskrit language, and after returning from Kashmir he composed grammar for Tibetan language. He is considered the father of this language. The king asked the people in general and the intelligent people in particular to learn Tibetan language and help in translation work. He in this way first time laid the foundation of Buddhism in Tibet. Still, for about two more centuries, it had to fight for its existence, as the supporters of the ancient Bon Chos of Tibet were not willing to give up their national creed for one introduced from a foreign country. About 900 AD the hope of the friends of the Bon Chos was centred in prince Langdharma. Although he was older than his brother Ralpachan but he was excluded from the succession on the ground that he was inimical and unfriendly to Buddhism. However, he got a chance when his brother was killed by the enemies of Buddhism. His first measure was to deprive the monasteries of the conditions of tenure, and, in consequence of this, many Indian Pandits left Tibet. But the King found that these had not sufficient effect, and he began to persecute Buddhism openly. Many Buddhists monks had to become butchers and the other half hunters. Whoever did not show a liking for his new profession was beheaded. But when Langdharma thought that he was succeeded in annihilating

Buddhism, the snake which he thought he had crushed bit him. A Buddhist monk put on a robe, black on the outside and white inside, because only the black clothing, the favourite colour of the Bon Chos was allowed to be worn in those days. But underneath his dress he kept a bow and arrow in ready all the time. He approached the King, if he were a suppliant, and threw himself down on the floor. When Langdharma walked up to him, he suddenly rose and shot the King through his heart. Then, in order not to recognize by those who had seen him enter in black, he put on his dress with the white outside and escaped. This Langdharma is the special ancestor of the Ladakhi Kings. Langdharma had a legitimate son from the lesser queen, called Odshrung (about 925-950). But there was also an illegitimate son of the great queen, called Yumstan and it was the latter that seized the Government of Central Tibet.

Odshung's Son was Ldepalkhor-Tsan (About 950-975)

Ldepal Khortsan had two sons—Skit Lde Nima gon and Tashi Tsegspal (about 975-1000). Both were robbed of all their possessions in Central Tibet by Yumstan the illegitimate son of the great queen, and fled to western Tibet (called Ngaris in those days). Trashi Segspal became king of the most western portion of western Tibet, called Yarlung. But Skit Lde Nima Gon conquered western Tibet completely, although at the outset his army numbered only 300 horsemen. On his way to western Tibet, he was once in such a horrible situation that he had nothing to eat but eggs and fish. Ngaris is also known as Maryul, which consist of two parts. The region ahead of Ladags Kongka is called Stot Maryul whereas the region below Ladags Kongka is known as Sham Maryul. Probably Ladakh has got this name because of its reddish soil. It is combination of two words mar and yul, 'mar' means red and 'yul' means region. At that time the Dard tribe was ruling over the Sham Maryul and Cho Bagdur Skyab was their ruler. He was from the Thata Khan's family. It is said that there was not a single habitation right from Ladags Kongka to Martselang, at that time. The main villages of Stot Maryul were Martselang, Gia, Miru, Sakti, Chemdey, Tangtse, Durbuk, Shayok and Rong area. It is said that the people of "Mon" tribe migrated from

Himachal and other plain areas and first came in Gia, later gradually settled in the Stot Maryul. One prominent person among them was Gyapa cho, who became the ruler and was ruling over Stot Maryul. And Gya was his capital. The ruins of the Mon palaces and forts are still existing in many places of Rong region, Gia, Sakti, Tangtse and Shayok and is known as Monkhar. Tibetan Buddhism and its monastic education system came to Spiti more than a thousand years ago as part of an important development in the history of Tibetan Buddhism known as bstan pa phyi dar (later diffusion of Buddhism) Tucci 1933; Klimburg-salter 1997. Before the advent of Tibetan Buddhism in the region, the inhabitants of Spiti and nearby regions were said to be 'Mon' or Mon pa, although locals in Spiti today use the word 'Mon' for Indians. Tobdan states that Mon were a mixed Indo-Tibetan race, which lived between the Indian plains and the Tibetan plateau. Today there are 'Mon' or Mon pa in Bhutan and eastern India. There was not a consolidated government in the Sham and Stot Maryul. Hence, it was a very easy task for Nima Gon to capture them. Once the inhabitants of Khotan invaded Stot Maryul, they reached upto Shayok. When Gyapa cho came to know about this invasion, he was not in a position to defend his country, so he approached the Nima Gon at Purang and requested for military help. Nima Gon easily agreed and both Gyapa cho and Nima Gon jointly attacked the people of Khotani invaders and defeated them. Gyapa cho became very happy and presented the Indus belt right from Martselang and Sham Maryul to Nima gon as a reward. Thus, Nima gon built a fort at Shey, constructed irrigation canals and started farming. Gradually the position of Nima Gon became so strong and captured the whole area of Stot and Sham Maryul and consolidated the Government and Gyapa cho's position was reduced, just as a "Kalon". That is why, he is considered the first Lha Chen king of Western Tibet or Ladakh. According to Wazir Hashmatullah, Rafstan Kalon Mulbe, Heraman Zildar Tangtse, Jigsmat Nambardar Mulbe and Kacho Haider Khan Tambis were the descendents of Gyapa cho's family. The principal towns and castles said to have been built by Nima Gon are; Kharmar in Rudog in the horse year; Tseshogyari in the sheep year; several villages in Dam and Lag and Nyilza zong in Purang and made it his seat. At that time Lama Geshes chan was an influential person in Purang. He arranged the marriage of Nima Gon with Doza Khorskyong, a lady from Purang. He was too much inclined towards Buddhism and ordered the principal sculptures at Shey, which is popularly known as Smanla. In an inscription, he says that he had made them for the religious benefit of the Tsanpo dynasty (his ancestors) and the people of Ngaris (Western Tibet). This shows that already in this generation Langdharma's opposition to Buddhism had disappesred.

Lha Chen Spalgi gon, (About 1000-1025)

Lha Chen Nima Gon had three sons, among whom he divided his kingdom. The eldest son Lha Chen Spalgi gon received Ladakh proper, from the Zojila to Rudog and the gold mine of Gog. Situated in the east of Rudog, his portion was not only the largest, but certainly the most beautiful part of the empire. Trashis gon; the second received a long and narrow strip of country along the northern slope of the Himalayas, of which Purang and Guge are the well-known provinces. Lde-tsog gon, the youngest, received the southern provinces of the kingdom, of which Zanskar, Lahoul, and Spiti are best known. His portion was the smallest. Nothing is known about Trashis gon's descendants. Whereas of Lde tsog gon's descendants eight generations are known. This line of kings became famous through its connection with the famous Buddhist teacher Atisha. The best known of its kings are Yeshes od and Jangchub od. Ladakh and Spiti provide evidence of the practice of Bon religion in the region before the advent of Buddhism. These eternal Bon signs of *swastika* and other images on rocks and caves appear to be remnants of the older Zhang zhung kingdom (Petech 1997).

In the 10th century, a powerful kingdom was formed in western Tibet known as Guge, covering Guge, Purang, Ladakh, Zangskar and Spiti (Petech 1997). Gug's Buddhist king sponsored the propagation of Buddhism by constructing temples and monasteries and sponsoring scholarly activities. Tabo monastery in Spiti, regarded as the oldest continuously operating Buddhist monastery in India and the Himalayas was built during this time (Klimburg-salter 1997). As a result indigenous 'Bon' practitioners were converted to Tibetan Buddhism (*Ibid.*). Whilst the Bon culture declined to extinction in Spiti and Ladakh, scholarships in Buddhist studies were supported by the rulers of Guge, Ladakh and Tibet. Some of the notable scholars and spiritual adepts produced during these periods include a throne holder of Gaden monastery; Dhangkar Paldan Gyaltsan, Rangrik Rechen Kungga Gyatso, Lopon Yeshe Tsettan, Khenpo Gyatso and many others who earned the title of Kachen and Geshe, which is considered to be equivalent to a Doctorate in Buddhist philosophy (Tsering 2000). There are five monasteries in Spiti. Tabo, Dhangkar, Kee, Tengyud and Gungri. The first three monasteries Tabo, Kee and Dhangkar, belong to the Gelug school of Tibetan Buddhism. Tengyud monastery belongs to the Sakya School and Gungri monastery belongs to the Nyingma School.

Drogon and Chhosgon, About (1025-1050)

They were the two sons of Lha Chen Spalgi gon. As in several other cases, nothing besides the names is as yet known. Lha Chen Dragspa Lde, about 1050-1075, was the son of Drogon. Lha chhen Jang chub Semba, about 1075-1100, was the son of Lha chhen Dragspa Lde.

Lha Chen Rgyalpo, About (1100-1125)

He was the son of Lha Chen Jang chub Semba. He built the first real monastery at Likir in the Sham Maryul with the colaboration of Lama Lha-bang Chosjey or Duwang Chosjey a disciple of Lama Tsongkhapa. He asked the Lamas to settle down there in the monastery, which later adopted and reformed the doctrine of Gelugspa order. This is certainly one of the ancient monasteries in Ladakh. Once, in the past 7 households had to sponsor a Lama through the year but presently Likir Gonpa is having shopping complex and other source of income in Leh. According to Francke, below the monastery of Likir there is a large Chortain which contains frescoes inside. They represent Tsongkapa and other Lamas of his time. Its foundation, wood work and pictures are certainly old. But it is unfortunate that instead of renovating the old monuments in its own shape the ruined materials have been shifted few years back to some other place to construct a new chortain. A beautiful pencil-cedar close to the monastery is said to have been planted by Lha Chen Rgyalpo, which is still there. Presently the younger brother of H.H. the Dalai Lama, namely Naris Tsewang is the Head of Likir Gonpa and all transaction is being made in his name and seven other Gonpas are affiliated with Likir Targyas-ling monastery. According to a senior Lama of Likir, the Gonpa owns approximately 3000 Kanals of land. Out of it 50 per cent of land is registered in the name of Gonpa whereas the rest is on Lagan system. Likir looks a little out of the way; but in the past Likir was a town on the great trade route. Before the present road along the Indus was constructed, the ordinary route to Leh was by Tingmogang, Hemis, and Likir.

Lha Chen Utpala (1125-1150)

He was the son of Lha Chen Rgyalpo and ruled over Ladakh for about twenty-five years from 1125 to 1150 AD. His main contribution was to unite all vassal chiefs under one umbrella without disturbing the activities of Buddhist monasteries in Ladakh. All the vassal chiefs had to pay tribute and attend the annual council. He even conquered a new province, lowo, east of Purang and invaded Kullu and the king of Kullu bound himself by oath, "So long as the glaciers of the Kailash do not melt away, or the Mansarowar lake dry up, to pay his tribute to the king of Ladakh". This treaty remained in force for a long time.

Lha Chen Naglug (About 1150-1175)

He was the son of Lha Chen Utpala. He built two palaces in the Sham Maryul. The first in the Wanla in the Tiger year and the second in the Khalatsey in the dragon year. It is said that before the advent of the Lha Chen kings, there used to be a Dard colony at Khalatsey. These Dard had their stronghold in a castle about a mile above the present village. The local Dard chieftains of Khalatsey had their castle on the bank of the Indus, to guard a bridge. This bridge was built in opposition to the Balu Khar Bridge, three miles off, probably to draw the trade to their own territories. King Naglug has built the Bragnag castle on the rock towering above Khalatsey and it is considered the first castle in that area. Besides king Naglug has constructed the first bridge across the Indus in the very same place where the present bridge is. The reason was certainly to draw the trade to his new bridge and thus secure the taxes. There still exist stone inscriptions in close vicinity to the present bridge, which records the first construction of a bridge in this place and gives the Dragon year as the date of construction of the bridge. But the proper name of the king is not given. The inscription simply speaks of "the great king". The edict ends up with a threat to "all who might feel inclined to damage the new bridge. And it was necessary, that the Dard people of Khalatsey may not have wished to see it exclusively used. The threat runs as follows: Whoever thinks evil of it in his heart, Let his heart rot. Whoever stretches his hand towards it, Let his hand be cut off. Whoever harms it with his eye, May his eye become blind? Whoever does any harm to the bridge, may that creature be born in hell. Lha Chen Naglug, was equally interested in the propagation of Buddhism. In 1215 AD, he patronized "Jigsten Gonbo", thus Ladakh came under the influence of Drigungpa order. He started a tradition to send Ladakhi novices to Tibet for higher studies. It is unfortunate that the king failed to strengthen and maintain the status of Nyarma University at Thiksay because of the ideological differences otherwise he must have obtained the objective here in Ladakh itself. Moreover the said university must have become a Buddhist centre of knowledge for the whole region. Thereafter the tradition of preceding the novices to Tibet for higher studies continued till independence for about nine centuries. Lha Chen Gebhe and Gebum (1175-1200), were the sons of Lha Chen Naglug.

Lha Chen Joldor (1200-1225). He was the son of Lha Chen Gebhe. Lha Chen Trashis gon, about 1225-1250 was the son of Lha Chen Joldor, who got copied many religious books in gold.

Lha Chen Lhargyal (1250-1275). He was the son of Trashis gon. According to Francke, the full name of this king was Lha Chen Kunga Namgyal, as he found the name on an ancient sculpture near the village of Taru. During his period a great yogi Urgyanpa visited Ladakh and unveiled the eight miracle rock statues in Nubra valley, locally known as "Gonbos". Besides he also renovated Padma Sambhava caves in Sakti. King Largyal then ordered to copy Kangyur and Stangyur in gold on indigo-tinted paper. This was the first attempt to enrich the Buddhist literature in Ladakh.

Lha Chen Jopal (1275-1300). He was the son of king Largyal. This king performed royal as well as clerical duties in a very efficient manner. He maintained religious and social rules and regulation in the country. In a local song the peaceful and happy days under king Jopal are described. During his time the people were very prosperous with masters and servants alike used to spend their days in a peaceful manner.

Lha Chen Mourup gon (1300-1325). He was the son of Lha Chen Jopal, and was a religious minded king. Like Lha Chen Naglug, he ordered to send novices to Tibet for higher studies of Buddhism. He also got copied Kangyur in two times and sacred books in many times. He got repaired the monasteries which had been built by his ancestors and offered gold, silver, copper, coral beads, pearls, etc. to Buddha in Likir and other monasteries and also sent the valuable goods to the monasteries of Lhasa, through Lama Chhosgi jai jigstain-Sumgi Gonbo of Degungpa sect.

Rgyalbu Rinchen (Malik Sadriddin Shah of Kashmir) 1324-1327

He was the son of Lha Chen Mourup gon. That is all that we learn about him from the Ladakhi chronicles, and it is strange that no more is said about him. It is also remarkable that he is called "gyalbu", prince. It indicates that he could not become a king in his home country Ladakh and left the country during princehood, because of the differences with his father. He did such a wonderful job in wrechedness that nobody can imagine. The following is quoted from Sir Walter Lawrence's account of the history of Kashmir: "At the beginning of the fourteenth century, when Simha Deva was king, Kashmir was a country of drunkards and gamblers. It was a most fitting time for the Tartar king Zulqadar Khan to invade the country. Helpless Simha Deva fled to Kishtawar, and the Tartar slaughtered the people, took slaves, and set fire to the city of Srinager. After an occupation of eight months, the Tartars, who had depopulated the valley, found provisions scarce and tried to get out of Kashmir by the southern passes, but snow overtook them, and Zulqadar Khan and his army and his Kashmiri captives prished "Meanwhile Ram Chand, the commander-in-chief of Simha Deva, had been trying to keep up some semblance of authority in the valley, and when the Tartars departed he moved down and drove out the Gaddis, who had come in on a raid." Ram Chand had with him two men who were destined to play an important part in the history of Kashmir. One was Shah Mirza, from Swat, at whose birth it was prophesied that he would become the king of Kashmir; the other was Rinchen Shah, who having quarreled with his father, the king of Tibet, came as adventurer to the valley. Rinchen Shah seems to be none other than the Ladakhi "Prince Rinchen". It has always been the custom among the Ladakhi kings to make the heir-apparent assistant to his father, when he reached manhood. As regent, Rinchen held different opinions from his father, Rinchen left Ladakh apparently after a son had been born to him, for there is no break in the line of succession. "Before many days passed, Rinchen Shah broke with Ram Chand and with the assistance of his Tibetans "Ladakhies" attacked and killed him. This took place at Lahara Kotta, the present Lar (Ganderbal) in the Sindh valley. He then married Kuta Rani, Ram Chand's daughter and proclaimed himself king, in 1323 AD. He must have been a man of outstanding energy, and great ambition. Rinchen Shah, who had no strong convictions, found it necessary to one or the other forms of faith which existed in Kashmir. He could not become a Hindu, because none of the Hindu castes would admit him to their brotherhood. One morning, he saw a Mohammedan at his prayers, the sight of his worship is said to have inspired in Rinchen the conviction that Islam was the true religion and admiring this form of devotion; he adopted Mohammedanism and took the name of Sadruddin. He built the Jama Masjid Srinager and a great shrine for Bulbul Shah, the man whose devotion he had admired. The shrine is still known by the name Bulbul Lankar. After a short reign of two and a half years Rinchen, the first of the Musalman kings of Kashmir, died. His widow married first a brother of the old king, Simha Deva, and afterwards Shah Mirza, who became the king of Kashmir and thus fulfilled the prophecy about him. It is incredible that the news of Rinchen's accession to the throne of Kashmir was not made known in Ladakh. That no mention is made of this in the Tibetan chronicles may be due to his change of religion. Francke says, "That is the sin which the Ladakhi historians, who wrote the chronicles could not forgive, and we shall meet with a very similar case later on. "It is not out of place to mention here that the credit of being the first Muslim king of Kashmir goes to a Ladakhi prince, "Gyalbu Rinchen" whose Islamic name was Malik Sadruddin Rinchen Shah. In the History of Kashmir, his father's name has been recorded in urdu as "Lagban" or "Bhagin". It may be the first or last name of his father Lha Chen Mourup gon. In Kashmir, Rinchen was having a son with Kota Rani, whose name was Haider Khan. After king Rinchen's death he was brought up under the care of his mother Kota Rani and Shah Meer. Rinchen Shah's grave is in the compound of Bulbul Lankar near the shrine of his pir-e-murshid (spiritual guide) Hazrat Sharifuddin Abdul Rahman Bulbul Shah, on the right side bank of Jhelum River. The grave of Illama Mulla Ahmad Sahib is here along the side of Bulbul Shah's grave. The devotees use to come here daily to recite "Fateha" and Ziarat of the shrine. The Department of Archaeology, Government of Jammu and Kashmir has placed a slab of white marble on Rinchen's grave, which states that he ruled over Kashmir for a brief period of three years, one month and nineteen days. He died in 723 Hijri, according to the year 1323 AD. The grave is on a small platform, covered with white marble stone. Here is a small mosque, on the right bank of the river Jhelum, just adjacent to the Ali Kadal Bridge. It is believed that it was built by Rinchen Shah for his personal prayer. Another bigger mosque just adjacent to the Rinchen's grave, which is presently being used as Jama Masjid of Mohalla Bulbul Lankar, and five time's prayer are being perfomed here. According to the

"Kutba" placed on the wall of the mosque, it is the oldest one in Kashmir constructed for the first time in 720 Hijri/1320 AD, and called Masjide Hanfia. Hence Bulbul Lankar is known as a historical area. It is also said that the Jama Masjid Srinager, situated at Nohata was got constructed by Sultan Sikandar, the father of Sultan Zain-ul-Aabedin Badshah. In the past Nowshahra was the capital of Shahmiri kings. Here was the Zainadub and Zainakadal was the oldest bridge of the city.

Lha Chen Shesrab (1350-1375)

He was the son of Gyalbu Rinchen, since he was married and having a son, before his departure to Kashmir. He ascended the throne in young age, after the death of his grandfather Lha Chen Mourup gon. He built the hamlet Sengge sgang on the top of the Hangtsemo rock, at Saboo. And made it a dependency of the chang castle at Saboo. The local people calls it Sankar castle. The ridges of the mountains west of Saboo are covered with ruined houses and nobody lives there.

Lha Chen Thisog Lde (1375-1400). He was the son of Lha Chen Shesrab. Like his father, he was too much inclined towards Buddhism and built one row of Chortens numbering one hundred and eight (108) at Leh, and two such rows at Sabu. The great reformer Tsongkapa about 1378-1441 AD. During the 15th century, there lived a great Lama in Tibet, whose name was Tsongkapa. Because he was born in village "Tsongkha" of the Kham region and his original name was Lobzang Takpa Spal. He received religious education from the great Lamas of Kadampa, Kargyutpa, and Saskyapa sects and became a very learned person. He found that the monastic life in Tibet is not upto the mark. They are not practicing as per the Buddhist doctrine and principles. Many Lamas are indulged in evil practices. He determined to reform it. He sat down to study writings of the founder of this religion, and soon discovered that there were great discrepancies between what ought to have been and the actual facts. He found that the dress of the Lamas in no way corresponded with that of the early Buddhists. It was red and theirs yellow. He tried to exchange the red dress for the yellow, but the public opinion was against it. Since the people were accustomed to the red garments of the Lamas. Therefore Tsongkapa contented himself with the introduction of yellow caps and scarves only. He set new religious rules and regulation and promoted it among the people. Hundred of people became his disciple and they began to propagate this new reformed Buddhist sect called "Gelukspa". He got constructed a great monastery in Lhasa called Galdan, which is still in a good condition. This sect latter developed very fast throughout Ladakh. King Takpa Bum Lde also patronized it.

Lha Chen Takpa Bum Lde and Lha Chen Takpa Bum (1410-1444)

Lha Chen Thisug Lde had two sons; they were Lha Chen Takpa Bum Lde, popularly called Lde and Lha Chen Takpa Bum, generally known as Takpa. There was a great difference between the ideology and character of these two brothers. Although Takpa Bum Lde was the eldest and ought to have been the king alone. Takpa Bum would not yield, and took possession of part of the kingdom. Lde was of a mild and merciful disposition; Takpa was fierce, gloomy, and inconsiderate. Lde was religiously inclined; Takpa did not care in the least about his future state. Lde was thoughtful about even the downtrodden, weak and needy people among his subjects; Takpa could not bear the idea of having a brother king beside him. Takpa Bum Ldey commenced his career with the erection of a number of religious buildings. First he erected the red college, probably on the Namgyal Tsemo hill perhaps on the same hill, a statue of Maitreya, in a sitting posture, 25 feet high. He also built a triple temple, one surmounting the other, on the pattern of an ancient temple erected by king Yeshes od of Zanskar at Tholing. In the north-west of Leh town, the Teu Serpo hill was considered ill-fated and unlucky. Therefore to remove the fatality and misfortune, he got constructed a temple called "Teu trashi od thu" on the top of this hill, which look like a "Chhorten" from outside, but it is a temple from the inside consisting of 108 small rooms. When king Lde had done all this he believed that he had done virtuous deed and gained enough religious merit. For he said "if I die now it matters not". But there was more in store for him to do. While during this period two disciples Lamas of Tsongkhapa arrived in Ladakh. Carrying a small statue of "Tsepakmed" (eternal life). According to Ladakhi chronicles, the great Tsongkhapa, having in his possession a Tsepagmed about as long as a finger joint, which originated from the blood of his nose, entrusted the same to his disciples and said; "Give it either to Takpa Bum or to Takpa Bum Lde. When the two arrived in Ladakh, the one called Takpa Bum was in Nubra. They went to present the same to him, but he never bothered to look at it. So they went on to Leh. On the morrow the king gave command, "At today's council, whoever attends, be it ascetic or a low caste man, he should not be refused admittance." Now when the two Lamas came into the presence, the king rose and welcomed them. They handed over the present and the king was delighted with it. To keep this sacred present, King Takpa Bum Lde got constructed the Pethub monastery and gave it over to Lama Lawang lotus the first abbot of this monastery, and kept many Lamas of Gelukspa ideology in it. The image of Tsepakmed (Amitayas) was contained in a statue of Shakyamuni, which can now be seen in Tsogchen. This monastery was the first in Ladakh of the Gelukspa sect founded by Tsongkhapa. The other monasteries of the Gelukspa sect in Ladakh, which were constructed later, were Sangkar monastery, Rizong monastery, Thiksay monastery and Diskit monastery. The disciples of Tsongkhapa also did a remarkable work in the propagation of Gelugspa order in Ladakh. The prominent among them was Stot Shesrab Zangpo, who founded a monastery at Stagmo near Thiksay. Later he went to Zanskar and established Gelukspa order at the Karsha monastery, initially this monastery was founded by Phagspa Shesrab during 11th century AD. Shesrab Zangpo also visited Nubra and founded the Diskit monastery there. King Takpa Bum Lde carved an edict on the rock of Mulbe and it was his earnest desire to purify the Buddhism of this country. It runs as follows; "O Lama Tsongkhapa, take notice of this! The king of faith, Bum Lde having seen the fruit of works in the future life, gives order to the people of Mulbe to abolish, above all, the living sacrifices, and greets the Lama. The living sacrifices are abolished." It is considered that the King Takpa Bum Lde would have published this edict in other villages and town also, so as to follow the path of Ahimsa. King Takpa Bum Lde also seems to be influenced by the Sakya order. It is said that Sakya scholar Dorjay Spalzang visited Ladakh and at Mangtro cave meditated for some time. Later the king met the saint and was very much impressed by his meditative ability and saintliness. He donated a large portion of land for the construction of Mangtro monastery of Sakya order. King gave all sort of assistance to Dorjay Spalzang for making the statues of Matreya, Manjushri, and Vajrapani in the monastery and wall paintings like, Dawarpal ratna sutta and lank avatar suttas.

Besides, religious activities the great achievement of king Takpa Bum Lde was the settlement of the Balti migrants in the Indus belt, especially in Chushot probably in 1430-44 AD when Raja Salim Lde was the ruler of Khapolu Baltistan. He not only gave the moral and financial support to these desperate and destitute people but also provided shelter to them in the main Indus belt of Chushot area. He was so passionate, kind and secular king, that he never forced them to embrace Buddhism but also allowed to pray as per their own faith and construct Masjid and Imambarah. The Imambarah Chushot Yokma and Gongma and other Mosques in the Indus belt were built by these early settlers, towards the end of 15th century. The migrant Balties independently followed their own religion of Islam. They were following either Imamia Isne-asharia or Imamia Noorbaksh. Since both these sects of Islam accept Hazrat Ali (AS) son in law of Prophet Muhammad (SAW) as first Caliph in Islam and successor of Prophet (SAW) Moreover, the leader of the faithful Ali (AS) is also considered the first Imam out of the twelfth Imams of the Prophet's progeny. Presently the majority of the populations of the Chushot are Shia Muslims. The main cause of the migration was a flood in the Shayok valley. According to the well-known historian Wazir Hashmatullah, a terrible flood came in the Shayok River during the middle of 15th century. The cause of the flood was blockage of the passage of the Khumdan Lake, from where the source of the Shayok river begins, due to fall of large number of ice boulders in the passage, causing storage of large quantity of water in the lake. During summer, the quantity of water in the lake further increased, because of the melting of snow and ice boulders. As a result the sudden breakage of the passage took place, due to pressure and force generated by the lake water. Consequently, a terrible flood came in the Shayok valley, which not only damaged the canals, Khols, orchards, gardens, and cultivable lands of Nubra valley but also destroyed the Chaythang town of Khapulo along with damage to live stocks, orchards, standing crops and their houses. Consequently a famine like situation occurred in the region. Therefore a section of desperate people migrated to Parkuta and Dogni in Baltistan itself and settled there. But a large number of Balti people migrated to Leh, along with their bag and baggage and settled in the Indus belt. This was the first badge of the Muslims, who laid the foundation of Islam in Leh region. Later, many more joined them from time to time and presently Chushot is the biggest Muslim populated village in the region. The Balti Muslims had made a very great contribution in the evolution of culture and distinct civilization in the region. In the ancient period, as there was no hard and fast rule of passes and passport, etc. for the movements of the people and also people being very innocent and tolerant, they could move freely in absence of any political or cultural barrier. They had linguistic, traditional and cultural similarities which were conducive in their harmonious coexistence. It is not out of place to mention here that one of the sons of Takpa Bum Lde was a Muslim. His name was Tongpa Ali. According to Kashmir chronicles, the king of Kashmir Zain-ul-Aabedin (1423-74) invaded Guge, where from he brought a large number of animals and wealth and had been the royal guest at the Shay palace for a long time. It is said, that Sultan Zain-ul-Aabedin, had pressurized the king Takpa Bum Lde to marry with a Muslim lady of Kashmir. Tongpa Ali might be the son of the Muslim lady. It is also possible that because of the influence of the Muslims, he might have embraced Islam. It is also possible, that his royal status might have reduced from a prince to a "Tongpa" (common man) just to keep him away from the throne. Since after the death of his father Lde, his brother Lotus Chogdan ascended the throne.

As far as his brother Takpa Bum was concerned, he went to Nubra along with his nearest and dearest, in connection with some official work. He stayed there for few months, probably he might have gone there to win the favour of the Chiefs of Nubra over to his side, where from he crossed over to Tingmogang via Largyap and declared himself the king of Sham Maryul. Thereby he divided the Lha Chen kingdom into two parts of Sham Maryul and Stot Maryul. He is considered the builder of the royal town of Tingmogang. Beside Tingmogang one of his principal seats was village Bazgo, where he improved the ancient fortification, so as to make them a stronghold of the first rank. In many inscriptions the castles of Bazgo, Tingmogang, and Leh palace are praised as the most valuable possession of the Ladakhi kings. It is worth mentioning here that the present Namgyal dynasty of Leh had emerged from Takpa Bum's descendants.

Lha Chen Lotus Chhogdan (1440-1470)

He was the elder son of Takpa Bum Lde, who became the supreme king of Stot Maryul and conquered Ngaris Skorsum and all the vassal chiefs were subdued once more. His greatest triumph was the arrival of large quantities of presents, valuable weapons and tribute from Guge in the east. These include a set of precious coats of mail, swords, knives, turquoises, saddles, yak and horses, etc. He sent presents to the first Dalai Lama dGe-dundrub (1391-1474). He also patronized the Gelugspa scholar Lawang Lotus, a pupil of mKas-grub-rje (1385-1438). Lotus Chhogdan's reign seems to have lasted long; for when the blow against the dynasty was struck, it did not come from Takpa's son Bhara, but from his grandson Bhagan. Prince Bhagan formed an alliance with the people of Shay and dethorned the king. One of the great events which took place during the reign of this king was the invasion of Mirza Haider Douglat. According to the "Tarikhe Rashidee Mirza Haider started his journey from yarkend in the last week of Zilhajja and reached in Nubra on first of Safar 938 Hijri (1531 AD). The people of Nubra were subdued but the vassal chiefs fortified themselves, in their respective forts. Hunder fort was the greatest among them and Bu Rafstan (May be Nurboo Rafstan) was the ruler. He struggled for few days and finally was killed in the battle, along with his people and the whole Nubra was conquered. Where from he marched towards Maryul. According to Mirza, he found two rulers in Maryul (Ladakh) at that time, one Lotus Chogdan at Shay and another Tashi Gon at Timisgam. Both came to meet Mirza and presented gifts, etc. When in 1535 a rebellion broke out in Nubra, Tashi Gon failed to support Mirza Haider's officers and was put to death for this." But the chronicals is silent about it. According to Petech, "king Lotus Chhogdan managed to maintain friendly relationship with the invader occupying his country. After some time Mirza Haider invaded Tibet but the tough climate and the terrific difficulties of the terrain stood against the invader. As a barrier, more formidable than any Tibetan army and Mirza had to turn back when he was at eight days march from Ursang (Lhasa). He reached Ladakh safely and retired to Shay, where he stayed for two more years as a royal guest. In 1536 AD, he departed from Badakhshan. After staying a few years in Badakhshan he marched towards Kashmir and became the ruler of Kashmir but did not forget his earlier venture to capture Ladakh and Tibet. Subsequently, in 1545 he invaded Ladakh but could not get a major success. In 1548, he launched a large-scale operation. This time he got success and annexed Ladakh and Baltistan with Kashmir. Mirza appointed his two Governors—Mulla Qasim for Baltistan and Mulla Hassan for Ladakh to look after the administration. Mirza Haider ruled over Kashmir on behalf of Sultan Mohammad Shah for about ten years and died in Kashmir because of deep wound of an arrow, shot by a person by mistake. His grave is in the compound of Mazare-Salateen on the west corner, under a tree. A red slab of stone has been placed over his grave indicating his name, parentage and other details. Here is a big red tomb which was built by Sultan Zain-ul-Aabedin for his mother, the wife of Sultan Sikandar, is raised over stone plenth of an earlier structure. Having five doms with largest in the centre. To the north of this tomb is a stone enclosure wall with gateway on an earlier remains. There are more than 42 graves of the royal families of the Shahmiri clan. One of the graves inside the enclosure is believed to be of Sultan Zain-ul-Aabedin. Lotus Chhogdan's reign seems to have lasted long, for when the blow against the dynasty was struck it neither did nor come from Takpa's son Bhara, but from his grandson Bhagan. Bhara's son, the warlike Bhagan, as said earlier formed an alliance with the people of Shay and dethroned King Lotus Chhogdan along with his brothers Tongpa Ali and Labstan Targais. Thus King Lotus Chhogdan's reign ended disastrously. He was deposed and imprisoned by a prince called Bhagan from a side branch of the family and with him ended the first Ladakhi dynasty.

Lha Chen Bhagan (1470-1500)

Lha Chen Bhagan was a selfish and ambitious man. He plotted against the ruler of Shay. He and the people of Shay having formed an alliance deposed and subjected the King Lotus Chhogdan and his two brothers, Tongpa Ali and Labstan Targyas.

Thus the kingdom of Lotus Chhogdan, which had nothing to fear from external enemies, became an easy prey to its internal foes and nothing is known about the lot of the members of this old dynasty. On the other hand, Bhagan became the ruler of whole Ladakh, and is considered the founder of the the Namgyal dynasty, which lasted in 1834 during the reign of Raja Tundup Namgyal, when the Dogra's captured whole Ladakh and annexed with the Jammu kingdom. Here Namgyal means "Victor" since he combined both the kingdoms once again, by fulfilling the desire of his grandfather.

The word Namgyal is found in the names of all his descendents. The second dynasty descended from the first, i.e. Lha Chen dynasty. According to Wazir Hashmatullah, it was not Bhagan, but his grandson Tsewang Namgyal, who captured the Shay kingdom and ruled over Ladakh. Since the kingdom of Shay and Tingmogang were in tact, during Mirza's departure from Maryul.

PEDEGREE TABLE OF THE NAMGYAL DYNASTY

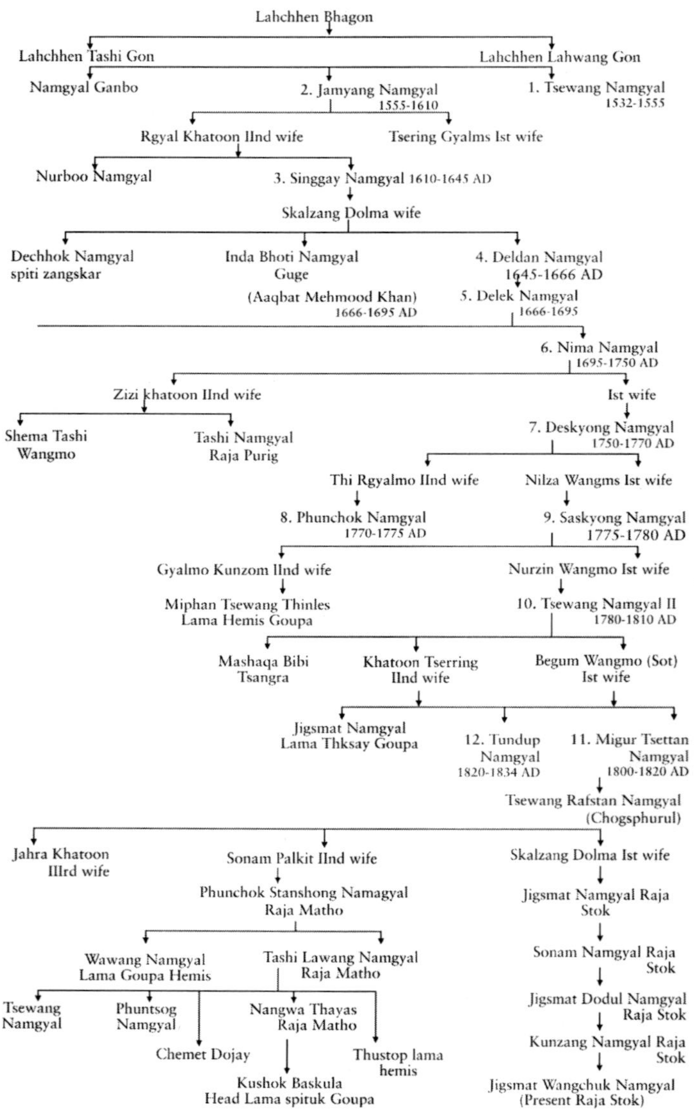

Lhawang Namgyal (1500-1530)

Lha Chen Bhagan had two sons—Lhawang Namgyal and Tashi Namgyal. Lhawang Namgyal was the elder brother and expected to be the crown prince but the bad example set by their father showed its influence on the sons. The younger brother Tashi Namgyal became very ambitious for the crown. Though Lhawang had great bodily strength and was clever at any kind of sport; but Tashi was very crafty, selfish and cruel. He plucked out the eyes of his elder brother and sent him to Lingshed to be kept in prison and himself became the king of Sham Maryul. The first thing that Tashi had to do was to conquer the whole country and subdue the vassal chiefs. He then built the royal palace and some of the watch towers on the top of the Namgyal Tsemo hill, and below it the hamlet of Chhubi. Petech says, "Tashi Namgyal turned out as a very energetic ruler. He conquered all the country from Purig upwards and from Grosod downwards; and since Grosod is the region on the upper tsanpo from the Maryum-la east of lake Mansarovar down to where the Tsa-chu enters the Tsan-po, this implies a temporary imposition of Ladakhi suzerainty over the kingdom of Guge." During the period the Turks invaded Ladakh; he fought against them and killed many Turks. He placed the corpses of the Turks under the image of "Dorjay Jigschat" so as to protect the country from the future invaders and as a mark of thanks offering. Another inscription commemorates repairs carried out by Tashi Namgyal at Alchi and records victories against the Mon (perhaps the people of Kulu and Chamba). After that he turned his attention towards the religious affairs. He convened Chhosjay Ldanma, a great Lama of Degungpa sect from Tibet, who was a pupil of the 18th gdan-rabs Rinchhen Namgyal and according to his advice he built a beautiful monastery of the red sect namely Tashi Chhoszong at Phiyang, which, together with the much older Lamayuru, is now the only Drigungpa centre in Ladakh. He also directed the villagers to be sent at least one of their male children to become Lama. At the spot where from this monastery is seen at the first sight, he placed a long prayer flag. Whosoever, whether thief, robber, liar or anyone guilty of offence, if he escaped and reach at this spot, should be rid of this crime. Moreover, he offered gold water for writing of religious books, prayer flags, cushions, tea, etc. for the famous monasteries of Tibet. He protected clergy and sent precious gifts to the monasteries of Drigung, Saskya, Galdan, Lhasa and Samyas. He even erected many Chhortens in Ladakh. But the judgment of heaven occurred and Tashi remained childless and there was a great danger that the dynasty would die out. Hence, Tashi gave his blind brother a wife and had three sons. They are: Tsewang, Gonbo and Jamyang. According to some historians Tashi Namgyal was assassinated by Sultan Saeed Khan. After the death of their uncle Tashi Namgyal, Lhawang's elder son Tsewang ascended the throne. And shifted his blind father to the capital at Tingmogang, where he received full honors as "father king."

Namgyal Dynasty of Ladakh

2

Lhawang Namgyal who was imprisoned at Lingshed, after plucking the eyes by his younger brother, had three sons; Tsewang Namgyal, Namgyal Gonbo, and Jamyang Namgyal. They all were well-built and tall in stature. After the death of his uncle Tashi Namgyal, Tsewang Namgyal ascended the throne without having any fear of a pretender, because the civil war was now coming to an end. After ascending the throne as a young man Tsewang had to go to war, because the vassal chiefs believed that they had got another chance of making themselves free. They were all subdued and under him the Namgyal kingdom reached at its greatest extension. He appointed his own representatives at the castles of vassal chiefs. Moreover, he was intending to attack Yarkend, but the people of Nubra valley petitioned him to abstain from that war, so that the trade to Yarkend may not be harmed. And he desisted. He received a very great number of tributes from the Changthang region, especially from Guge and Rudok. According to Petech, "A colophone found by Professor Tucci at Bran-kar (Spiti) also mentions king Tsewang Namgyal and his Minister Ga-ga Bumbha-Lde."

Tsewang Namgyal constructed so many roads and bridges in the country, so as to carry on his campaigns easily. The popular among them are; one on the road to Baltistan, near the Hanu gorge, the other on the way to Zanskar, at Hanupata. Tsewang wished to keep the goodwill of people, which he was in danger of losing if he charged them with the construction of the bridge at Hanupata as part of the ordinary forced labour system. He therefore proclaimed that the construction of the bridge was a means for everybody to accumulate religious merit, and that the names of all those who had some share or contribution in the work would be embodied in the inscription. In this way, he made certain arrangements for the goodwill of the people. The Minister who supervised the construction work, was Bumbha Lde. According to the same system, Tsewang's nephew Singgay Namgyal built the Alchi Bridge during his rule. The Lhakhang constructed by Tashi Namgyal, to keep the sacred bones of Buddha's elephant incarnation was defective. It was very small and many people could not come for pilgrimage. Therefore, he planned to construct a grand building in the plain, but he died in his prime youth, without any issue. After his death his younger brother Jamyang Namgyal ascended the throne.

Jamyang Namgyal (1560-1590)

After the death of Tsewang Namgyal, one of his younger brothers had to take up the reins of government. But nothing has been stated in the history about Namgyal Gonbo, instead Jamyang Namgyal became the king of Ladakh. Seeing a good opportunity, all the vassal chiefs revolted against Jamyang and he had to fight them all one after another, and subdued. First of all, he turned his attention to Purig, where great changes were taking place, as the two chiefs of that country, the Raja of Chiktan and Kartse, had adopted Islam and called themselves Sultans. It is said, that Tsering Malik, who then reigned, was the first Muslim chief of Chiktan, who embraced Islam. Fortunately for Jamyang, the two new Sultans of Chiktan and Kartse quarreled with one another, and Jamyang Namgyal decided to go to the assistance of Tsering Malik of Chiktan. Since the Ladakhi new year was approaching soon, and it was not considered lucky to start the campaign before having celebrated the New Year's festival. However, to wait for the New Year would mean a delay of two months. Hence Jamyang decided to celebrate the Losar festival two months before it actually falls. Ever since, *Losar* is being celebrated in Ladakh two months earlier than in Tibet. King Jamyang marched towards Purig, along with a huge army, in the first week of December. After crossing the Fotola pass, he captured Bodh Kharbu. Some of the Balti army was killed and some escaped towards Baltistan to tell the sad story of destruction to their Master. When Ali Sher Khan Anchan came to know about the activities of Jamyang in Purig, he never interfered and kept him busy in Purig and via Chorbatla he directly attacked Ladakh and captured Leh. For the time being the kingdom of Ladakh was under the control of the Balties. Though Jamyang hurriedly came back to Leh, to defend his kingdom, but it was too late and the situation in Leh was totally changed. Nobody was ready to take his side. Jamyang was made prisoner. Later Jamyang petitioned for compromise and it was not the intention of Ali Sher Khan Anchan, to capture permanently and ruled over Ladakh. He easily agreed. According to the agreement, Nala Gurgura had been identified as the border between Skardo and Ladakh. Moreover the Ganokh area and Nala Gurgura had been annexed with the Kartaksha of government of Skardo. The Bodhkharbu region was restored to the government of Ladakh, for which an annual tribute had to pay to the government of Skardo. A Lama of Lama Yuru gonpa was appointed as collector. It is said that this system was continued till the beginning of the Dogra rule in Ladakh. Besides, Jamyang got married his daughter Mendok Gyalmo with Ali Sher Khan. In spite of this agreement, Jamyang was not freed but was taken to Skardo as a prisoner, and a temporary arrangement was made to run the government of Ladakh. When Ali Sher Khan Anchan reached Skardo along with his new queen and father-in-law, he was warmly greeted by the Balties of Skardo, where he got constructed a new palace for the new queen, after her name called Mendok Khar. Since Yabgo Sher Ali Ghazi Raja of Salingkhar Khapulo, was in close relation with Jamyang. He did the job of a mediator and got restored the kingdom of Ladakh to Jamyang and freed from the prison honorably. He also got married Jamyang with his daughter Rgyal Khatoon, who was certainly very beautiful. It is also believed in Ladakh, that Rgyal Khatoon was an incarnation of the white Tara. Now, after Ali Mir had prepared a feast for all the soldiers, and Rgyal Khatoon had put on all her jewels, ornaments and beautiful dress, he invited Jamyang to mount the throne, and then said; "Yesterday I dreamt. I saw a lion emerging from the river in front of the palace and jumping at Rgyal Khatoon; he disappeared into her body. At the very same time also Rgyal Khatoon conceived. Now it is certain, that she will give birth to a male child, whose name you shall call Singgey Namgyal. And the heir to the throne would be none, but Singgey. Having said this, he asked the king Jamyang to return home with the Ladakhi army. When they reached Leh, the Ladakhies warmly welcomed the newly wedded royal couple. Although the Ladakhi Empire was saved but its size was now smaller than it had ever been. Yabgo Ali Mir's main object in marrying Jamyang to his daughter was, to draw him quietly over to Mohammedanism, and it is surprising that this did not happen after all. It is said, that on a rock at Mulbe is carved a weeding congratulation of Jamyang and his new queen. Prior to that Jamyang had already married with Tsering Rgayalmo the daughter of Jigstain Wangchuk and had two sons; Lhawang Namgyal and Stanzin Namgyal and one daughter Mendok Rgyalmo. To set an example to his subjects, Jamyang sent a deputation with costly presents to the principal monasteries of central Tibet, escorted by the sons of his former queen and made them to act as the messenger to the high Lamas. This was a convenient way to get rid of them and facilitate Singgay Namgyal to be the future king, according to the promise made with the Yabgo Ali Mir of Khapulo. They stayed in Lhasa and received religious education from the prominent Lamas of Lhasa. Later Lhawang Namgyal became the Principal Lama of Lahoul. After Jamyang had ordered a number of religious books to be copied in gold, silver, and copper, he got the repair and renovation of the monasteries and Stupas. He was intending to do more service to the Dharma but he died before he had been able to accomplish his purpose.

Petech says, "It was probably under this reign that the first European came to Ladakh. He was the Portuguese merchant Diogo d'Almeida, who stayed in the country for about two years. This happened shortly before 1603, in which year he gave a sworn account of the region to the Archbishop of Goa. Ladakh impressed him as a rich country. Its capital was Basgo. He gives the name of the king as Tammi-guia, an evident misprint, perhaps for Jammiguia, i.e. Jamyang Namgyal. He also speaks of the great veneration in which they held their bishop, whom they called Lama. During the first part of the king's life his dbu-bla (religious teacher) was the Saskya-pa head (drun-pa) of the Matho monastery, which was holding this position during the king's disastrous campaign in Baltistan. And this must be the man alluded to by the Portuguese traveler." As far as Jamyang's widow Rgyal Khatoon is concerned, it is said that in spite of marrying in a Buddhist royal family, she remained as a Muslim, till her death. It is obvious that Raja Sher Ali Ghazi Yabgo of Khapulo has tied the matrimonial knot of her daughter Rgyal Khatoon with King Jamyang Namgyal with certain hidden aims. His main intention was to sow the seeds of Islam in royal family in particular and Ladakh in general, but he could not get a major success and almost failed because Yabgo Sher Ali Ghazi's grandson Singgay Namgyal proved himself a true and loyal follower of Buddhism. He with the collaboration of Lama Stagtsang, contributed a lot for the cause of Buddhist welfare and upliftment. His period was perhaps the golden period for Buddhism in Ladakh as he got constructed the monasteries of Hemis, Anlay, Tashi gang and Chemday. Moreover, he sanctioned thousands of kanals of lands and its revenue to the monasteries, and it still continues. The Ladakhies used to say the period, as the combination of lion and tiger. Here "Singgay" means lion and "Stag" means tiger. In spite of many limitations, Rgyal Khatoon, the mother of King Singgay Namgyal contributed a lot for the propagation of Islam in the region. Though the roots of Islam had already spread and strengthened in the Indus belt prior to her arrival in Leh, yet many Balti ulemas, Akhons, masons, poets, artisans, and sportsman, etc. came to Ladakh after her arrival, because of the good, congenial and harmonious family relation between the royal families of Skardo, Khapulo and Leh. Thus, more and more Balties began to enter Leh for trade, business and propagation of Islam. The Balti scholars like Malas and Akhons got a golden opportunity to strengthen their position at grass-roots level. Now with the noble support of Queen Rgyal Khatoon they began to propagate Islam freely and openly. As said earlier, that after her arrival in Leh and becoming the mother queen, she never changed her old faith and continued to practise her own religion. It is said that she used to come from Bazgo to Shay on every Friday to perform Nimaz at the Shah Hamdan Masjid Shay. Later she built a prayer room at the Bazgo palace itself, for her personal prayer. After the death of her husband, King Jamyang Namgyal, she preferred to stay at Hunder Nubra, because Hunder is nearer to her birth place Khapulo, and could contact the relatives easily. At Hunder, she got constructed a small mosque for her personal prayer. Finally, she died at village Hunder and was buried just adjacent to her mosque, as per her wishes. Historian Wazir Hashmatullah has personally seen both the monuments and got repaired the grave through the members of the Jamshed family of Hunder in 1830 AD. But unfortunately, both the monuments got washed away due to the flood in Dok Nalah in 1926 as confirmed by the local elders. She also got constructed a Maney wall at Hunder, so that the departed soul of her husband may rest in peace. As stated earlier, that she got constructed a small mosque in Bazgo palace, where she used to perform Namaz and prayed during her stay at Bazgo palace. Presently, it is called Lakchung or Camchung, a small Chamba has placed inside it and it is in a good condition. It is said that in order to provide accommodation facilities to the Balti travelers, traders, businessman and preachers, she got constructed a sarai called Balkhang which means "Balti house". The main location of the sarai Balkhang was the site, where in the later centuries Moravian missionaries built a sarai named "Baskhang" which means Musafir Khana. This is presently under the occupation of the local Christians. The Imamia Jama Masjid of Tsas Soma, Chutay Rantag and Imambarah and Jama Masjid, Phiyang Chusgo were also constructed during her period with her financial assistance. The early Muslim settlers in Ladakh cannot forget her contributions and support, which she extended to the Muslims during the middle of the 16th century. She boosted the morale of the Balti Muslims.

Singgay Namgyal (1590-1620 AD)

He was the son of King Jamyang Namgyal and queen Rgyal Khatoon. In spite of his Muslim mother, he does not seem to have had any liking for Mohammedanism, but he had inherited the warlike spirit of his grandfather, Yabgo Ali Mir. From the period of his childhood, he was very strong, and clever at wrestling, running, jumping, shooting with bow and arrow as well as matchlock, and riding. During his youth, he invaded Nomads of Guge and other Changthang areas and brought a large number of cattles and valuable articles to Ladakh. Singgay Namgyal sent some troops to invade Chiktan, but again without success; Kaga Tsan-pa, the Ladakhi leader, was taken prisoner with about eighty men. On the other side, the nephew and niece of the chief of Chiktan were detained in Ladakh. Thus in 1625 the chief sent messengers to Stagtsang-Raspa, begging him to intervene; the Kaga and his men were exchanged with the Chiktan family and a truce for one year was concluded. In the following year, Adam Khan of Skardo wrote to Ali Mardan Khan, the new Governor of Kashmir, informing him that Singgay Namgyal the ruler of Great Tibet (Ladakh) had occupied Purig, which is one of the dependencies of little Tibet (Baltistan) an absolute claim going back to Ali Mir), with a large army of horse and foot. As mentioned Khan sent Hussain Beg, a relation of his, with a commando (fauji) of horse and foot. On the 14th Safar 1049 A.H. according to 16th June, 1639, Hussain Beg set forth on his expedition, via the Dacchan-para District (i.e. by the Zojila route). After some time Adam Khan joined him with a contingent of Tibetan soldiers; on 25th Rab'ii (25th August) they met Singgay Namgyal in the neighbourhood of Kharbu. Singgay joined battle, but was defeated, fled and shut himself in the fort of Kharbu. Then he discovered that before he could reach a safe place, he would be killed or captured. Therefore, he very humbly sent a messenger to Hussain Beg and opened negotiations. He promised that, if guarantees of safety and security were held out to him, upon his return to his country, he would send suitable tribute to the imperial court. Then Hussain Beg returned to Kashmir, where he arrived on 22nd Jamidul Aakher (20th September).

The two accounts complement each other. On the other side, the version of the chronicle is totally different: "Adam Khan, the king of Balti, having brought in the army of Padsha Shah Jahan, they fought many battles at Kharbu and, many Hor (Mughuls) being killed, a complete victory was gained over the enemy". But the complete silent of Stagtsang Raspa's biography about the war shows that the account of the chronicle is mere boasting. Singgay Namgyal was well and truly beaten and saved himself only by a promise of tribute, which of course was never kept. Petech says, "After the battle of Kharbu king Singgay Namgyal has promised tributes to the Mughuls; this tribute was never paid and Ladakh remained for all purposes an independent state. But when in 1663, during the reign of Deldan Namgyal the new emperor Aurangzeb made his first and only journey to Kashmir, the Ladakhi King, perhaps feeling uneasy about the presence on the border of a ruler who nursed a rightful grievance against Ladakh and had the means to enforce redress the same, sent him an embassy. The envoys were received by the emperor and repeated to him the kings pledge of loyalty and tribute and promised that a mosque would be built, the Khutba recited and coins struck in the name of the emperor."

The conflict had a serious consequence in the commercial field. As an economic reprisal against the Mughuls, the king prohibited the passage of carvans through Ladakh and even forbade any person from Kashmir to enter his dominions. As a result, traffic from India to central Tibet shifted to Patna-Nepal-Lhasa route, while the trade of Kashmir with central Asia had to take rather devious route via Skardo and Shigar to Kashgar. In 1663, after twenty-four years, the passage was still blocked. The foolish measure must have provoked a real disaster to the economy of Ladakh, which then as always depended above all on the transit trade. It is possible that the noticeable weakening of the strength of the kingdom after the death of Singgay Namgyal was due for the greater part to this severe self-inflicted blow to its economy.

Singgay Namgyal was married to a princess of Rupsho called Skalzang Dolma, and had three sons; Deldan Namgyal, Inda Boti Namgyal and Dechhok Namgyal. The youngest son Dechhok Namgyal was appointed as the Governor of Zanskar and a Kashmiri Muslim Razaq Joo was deputed there to assist him in day to day work, whose offsprings are still there. The second son Inda Boti Namgyal became a disciple of Lama Stagtsang and supervised the construction work of Hemis and Chemday Gonpas, and later became principal Lama of Hemis Gonpa. Finally, he became the Governor of Guge. Singgay Namgyal invited the great lama Stagtsang Raschen to Ladakh, who had visited Udyana and Kashmir, and had seen all the eighty saints face to face. This great Lama, whose name is still remembered, is said to be the author of the well-known book, called *The Journey to Shambala*. And he was probably the introducer of the Maney Walls and Maney Tungchur in Ladakh. Stag means tiger, and Singgay means lion and the period of "tiger lama" and the "lion king" is still remembered by the people of Ladakh as the golden period of Buddhism in Ladakh. It is said that the king as per the instruction of the Lama, governed the country, as per the ten virtues. Singgay Namgyal got copied the religious books in copper, silver, and gold; and that costly offerings of silk, corals, pearls, amber, etc. were sent to the principal monasteries in Lhasa, so as to rest the departed souls of his parents in peace. He did much for the welfare, upliftment and propagation of Buddhism, and was following the "Drukpa" or red sect of Buddhism. That is why the principal monasteries of Drukpa sect in Ladakh like Hemis, Chemday, Anlay and Tashigang were built by him, under the guidance of Lama Stagtsang Raspa and sanctioned thousands of Kanals of land and its revenue to the major Gonpa's which still continues. The Hemis Gonpa was the richest one and has become famous for its beautiful sceneries and annual Mela, which takes place there in the month of June. The best known of his buildings is the Singgay palace which is also called Lehchhen Spalkhar. It is a huge building of nine stories, above the main bazaar, on a top of hill, which was completed in about three years. Singgay palace is still in tact and has not lost its beauty. It is still attracting thousands and thousands of tourists every year and has become a source of income for the people of the region. The Archaeological Survey of India has acquired the palace, a few years back for preservation. Another remarkable building is the Maitreye monastery at Bazgo, above the ruins of the ancient palace. According to an inscription, Singgay Namgyal got constructed several wooden bridges across the Indus, one such bridge was at Alchi.

According to Luciano Petech in his book *The Kingdom of Ladakh* at page 38 writes "That the death of Jamyang Namgyal was followed by an interregnum, during which it seems that the Rgyal Khatoon carried out the government on behalf of her elder son Singgay Namgyal, apparently still a minor. At least this situation which Stagtsang Raspa found during his first visit to Ladakh. On his way back from Uddiyana (Swat) probably late in 1616, he passed through Kashmir to Zangskar and then to Ladakh. At first he settled at Gia in upper Ladakh, as the guest of the local Chief (Cho), who were supporters of the Drugpa sect; one of the family, drun-pa bDe-ba had been a pupil of Padma Karpo. From there he went to Bazgo, where he was honoured by Rgyal Khatoon and Singgay Namgyal. Then he retraced his steps and settled at Gya and Hemis, where he stayed for about three years. In 1620, he left for central Tibet at the head of some twenty disciples. During the same period another holy man reached western Tibet. This was the first Panchhen Lobzang Chhosghi Rgyaltsan, who in the summer of 1618 made a piligrimage to the Kailash and Lake Mansarovar, upon the invitation of the king of Guge. At San-rtse in Guge he received envoys of the king of Man-yul inviting him to come to Ladakh, but he turned down the invitation, although he met several people from the country."

"In 1622, Stagtsang Raspa returned to Ladakh, passing through Guge, where as we are going to see presently, he acted as peacemaker and where the queen Phuntsog had advised him to exert his powers of mediation in the royal family of Ladakh as well. Stagtsang Raspa, during his journey to central Tibet paid a visit to the 5th Drugchen, who advised him to go back to Stod (Western Tibet in general), where the king and his brother were at loggerhands, and remained there for the good of the religion. In 1622, he started his journey with some sixty pupils, intending to perform Kailash-Mansarovar piligrimage. Upon his arrival in that region, he came to know that a war was going on between Guge and Ladakh, and the abbot sMu-rdzin-pa had arranged a truce between the three kings of Guge and Man-yul (i.e. the Jo-bo-bdagpo and the two Ladakhi brothers). sMu-rdzin-pa who was staying in Guge invited Stagtsang Raspa to his residence and apprised him of the situation. Guge and Manyul had concluded a three years truce; now Stagtsang Raspa should try to bring about a permanent settlement. However, the attempt was not even made. Stagtsang Raspa acting on the orders of the Drugchen, suggested that first of all the shrine built by Padma Sambava around the Kailash and on the shore of the Mansarovar should be restored, the work to be under the blessing of the Drugchen. But the Guge ruler Thi-dakpa Tashis, who was a follower of the Gelukpa sect, relied on the earlier forms of prayer (smon-lam) and did not approve of the project. Thus, Stagtsang Raspa stayed at Tsaprang for five days only and then departed for Ladakh. He reached Gya, where he was again received with the utmost respect by the local chief, and went to Bazgo. Once arrived there he came to know that the late King Jamyang Namgyal had undertaken to erect a large statue of Maitreya, but was not able to carry out his purpose "on account of rebellion and troubles". Stagtsang Raspa convinced the royal family to carry out the intention of the dead ruler as a funeral offering (Gon-zogs). The work began on the 19th October, 1622, the queen Rgyal Khatoon supplying for this purpose more than 500 ounces of gold and gems of lesser value; it was inaugurated on 12th June, 1623.

"In the meantime, Stagtsang Raspa had placed at the service of the state his noteworthy abilities as mediator. In a tantalizingly short sentence, we are informed that he arranged peace with Guge and Rutog, with Purig and Zangskar, and with Nan-gon (Skardo). Then he turned to the internal situation."

"The religious life of Ladakh, after the final return of Stagtsang Raspa from Tibet, was dominated by his forceful personality. He achieved the gradual conversion of the royal house to the Ra-lun branch of the Drugpa sect. The final turn came in 1630, in the same year as the conquest of Guge, perhaps at the result of a definite political choice. In that year not only the king donated to Stagtsang Raspa and his sect the estates of Hemis, Matho, Nanchhubab, the Bodthog across the Ronchhu river, Phugtse and Sharnos; but he even expressed the intention of taking away Thiksay from the Gelukpa and handing it over to Drukpa. At the bottom of this generosity there was a personal grudge; during the conflict with his brother, Singgay Namgyal had sought refuge in Thiksay, but the monk shut the gates on his face. To his credit, Stagtsang Raspa persuaded the King to give up his project; he would have none of what amounted to religious persecution."

"Stagtsang Raspa's building activity was also noteworthy. We have already spoken of the foundation of the Dechhen Namgyal monastery at Wam-le (1624). The pet project of Stagtsang Raspa was the construction of the Chhanchub samling convent at Hemis, which became and remained the royal monastery of Ladakh. At first there was a simple hermitage. Then work began in 1630, the main temple Tsuglak-khang was built; in 1638 he was able to consecrate the great assembly hall (Dukang), decorated with paintings. The influence of Stagtsang Raspa on the king must have cost rather dearly to the Ladakhi taxpayers. Apart from the expensive building activity, to which we must add a long series of statues, manuscripts and mani-walls listed in the chronicle. The king on his advice sent frequent mission with expensive presents to the Kargyutpa and other religious establishments in Central Tibet. Each of these missions carried hundred of ounces of gold, many more of silver, besides turquoises and costly shawls. Lastly, we must also take into account the secular buildings, and foremost among them the Lehchhen Spalkhar, i.e. the nine-storyed royal palace towering over Leh. It is peculiar that nothing is known of Singgay Namgyal's Chief Minister. But the only man to bear the full title of Chief Minister (Chhoslon-Chhenpo) was Aagu Garmo, who was an uncle of the queen Skalzang Dolma of Rupsho and he was incharge only during the very last years. One of the foremost noblemen of Singgay Namgya's time was the lord of Sabu, Namka Spalgon of the Minag family, who served four generations of Ladakhi kings. In the pig year (almost certainly 1635) the king entrusted him with the supervision of the copying of several texts Ka-gyur, biography of Padmasambava, life and songs of Stagtsang Raschhen, for which he was duly rewarded. Singgay Namgyal died at Wamley on the first day of the Lahbab festival (22nd) in the 9th month of the water-horse year, i.e. on the 27th November, 1642. (Hashmat 1620) He was less than fifty years old. His body was brought to Leh, where the solemn funeral rites were performed by Stagtsang Raspa. One of the first actions undertaken was the building of a new monastery as a funeral act of merit (dgon-rdzogs) for the late king. The choice of the site was a matter of serious deliberation. After excluding for various reasons Leh, Bazgo and Stagna, the decision fell in favour of Chemray, and in March 1644 Stagtsang Raspa laid the foundation of the main temple (Tsuglag-khang). It was finished on 30th March 1645 or 18th April 1646. Also in other fields Stagtsang Raspa's activity and unrivalled influence continued unabated in spite of advancing age. This was reflected in the continuance of the expensive mission to central Tibet. In 1643, he sent one mission to Dechhen Chhskor. In 1645 a much larger mission was dispatched, headed by Drukpa Dorjay on behalf of the Himis monastery and by Thufstan Lahwang and Aagu Konchhog on behalf of the Ladakhi court. It was this mission which arranged for the funeral rites for Singgay Namgyal to be performed, rather belatedly, at Lhasa during the "Smonlam festival of 1646. Upon the request of the regent queen (Skalzang Dolma) in Febuary 1647 Stagtsang Raspa laid the foundations of the main temple in the Shay palace. He devoted himself to the completion of the Lahchhen Tsuglag-khang Shay. This was carried out with the support of Deldan Namgyal, and was duly inaugurated."

Petech writes (p. 59), "The old queen Skazang Dolma seems to have very active during her last years. In 1649, she sent to central Tibet a mission headed by Thufstan Lahwang, Aaku Bzang dga and Tashi Dorjay on behalf of the court and by Rinchen paljor Saky zla-od on behalf of Hemis monastery. They carried with them the funeral offerings of Aagu Garmo, who had died in 1646. In 1650, the queen undertook a journey to Kailash, against the advice of her revered teacher, and indeed she fell ill at Zangskar and breathed her last at Zangla. Her corpse was brought to Shay, where the funeral rite was performed. In 1650, Stagtsang Raspa sent a final mission, headed by O-lo Nawang Deleks, to the Dalai Lama, the Panchhen Lama, and the Drugchhen and to Dechhen Chhoskor. It settled the details of the annual dispatch of a group of novices to central Tibet, about which a dispute had arisen between the Lhasa government and the Drukpa."

"Stagtsang Raspa was now over 76 and his health was failing fast. He himself gave the necessary instructions for his funerals, and on the 29th of January, 1651, he passed away at Hemis. The death rites were performed on a magnificient scale and five monks were appointed to read holy texts near his relics. In 1655 a grand ceremony of remembrance was held in presence of the king and his brothers. And in June 1663 Stagtsang Raspa's biography, composed by monk Nawang Kungga Lundup Thufstan Gelek on the request of the King Deldan Namgyal, was completed. The death of Stagtsang Raspa left a gape which it was difficult to fill. In due time, his incarnation Nawang Tsoskeys Dorjay was found in the region south of Ladakh, but he never exerted any substantial influence, and his name does not occur at all in the chronicals. The only occasion on which he played a role was at the time of the treaty with Tibet in 1884."

When Singgay Namgyal was a youth, he invaded Guge to reconquer that lost province and carried away ponies, yaks. Goats and sheep and made all Ladakh to be full of these cattles. When he was old, he thought himself; "My uncle Tsewang Namgyal certainly did rule over all the country as far as Ngamring in the east; but during the reign of my father

Jamyang Namgyal all the vassal princess again rose and made themselves independent." So he again went to war and reached at Ngamring area, but at Shrikarmo his army was routed. Later according to an agreement with the Tibetan envoy, it was decided that the boundary should remain as before, and that Singgay Namgyal's dominion should include all the region upto Charta River. On his return journey the popular king of Ladakh died at Anlay, which have been mentioned earlier in detail.

Deldan Namgyal (1620-1640 AD)

He was the elder son of Singgay Namgyal and ascended the throne after the death of his father. His two brothers became vassal kings under him. Inda Boti Namgyal, who became the disciple of Stagtsang Raschen and received religious education from the great Lamas and became a principal Lama of Hemis Gonpa, supervised the construction work of Himis and Chemray Gonpas. And later became the vassal chief of Guge. Similarly prince Dechok Namgyal, the youngest, was made the vassal chief of Zanskar and Spiti and a Kashmiri trader Razaq Joo was deputed there to assist and accompany him. When Deldan ascended the throne, his kingdom was only confined from Purig to the Maryumla, but it was his ambition to restore the lost prestige of Ladakhi kingdom and to bring the rulers of Purig once more under his rule and wanted to avenge his family on Balties. He appointed his Minister, Shakya Giatso, as Field Marshal. In the ox year the Ladakhi army, marched to Purig to re-conquer this lost province. The first territory they invaded was that of the Thi Sultan of Kartse, who was then an independent king in Purig from Kharbu to Drass. Many men and women of Kharbu were made captives and the vassal chiefs of Henasku and Stagtse were brought under subjection. Though Thri Sultan had not yet been attacked, but invaded the territory of other rulers of Purig. The first was the Purig Sultan of shakar-Chiktan, and his strongest castle of Chiktan Razi-Khar was taken. Then the Field Marshal marched against the three strongest castles of Thri Sultan. The first was Sod, and after it had been taken the harvested grains in the vicinity were gathered in. Later the other two castles, Sumtang and Kartse, were taken, and Thri Sultan himself became a prisoner and was shifted to Leh. In the wood-tiger year the Ladakhi army marched against Baltistan and conquered the town of Chorbat and Thursaykhar of Khapulo, and appointed his own Governors there to run the administration. Moreover the rulers of Thursaykhar, Babar and Yaqub, who were the nephews of Raja Shah Murad of Skardo, alongwith their mother was imprisoned at the castle of Bodhkharbu. To take the revenge, the Raja of Skardo Shah Murad with the collaboration of Raja of Shigar, attacked Bodhkharbu and killed many Ladakhi soldiers and a hundred were imprisoned. Finally according to an agreement, both the rulers agreed to release the prisoner of war. Thus, the nephews of Shah Murad, Babar and Yaqub along with their mother were released from the prison and returned back to Khapulo. When the Mughal Emperor Aurangzeb came to know about the activities of King Deldan Namgyal, he sent his envoy to Ladakh, in 1661 AD, to remind the payment of tribute as was promised by Singgay Namgyal to pay the Mughals. Like his father, he promised to pay the tribute and according to the wishes of the Emperor he would build a mosque and circulate coins in the name of the emperor. However, as soon as the emperor's envoy returned to Kashmir, he did nothing, and the tribute was never paid. Again, in 1665 AD, the governor of Kashmir Saif Khan sent an envoy to king of Ladakh. This time the envoy was Muhammad Shafi, who carried the "Farman" enjoining on the Ladakhi king the acceptance of Mughal suzerainty and of Islam and threatening him with an invasion by imperial army in case of refusal. Accordingly, the Khutba was read on a Friday, on behalf of Aurangzeb, in presence of a big gathering. The king and the Mughal envoy Muhammed Shafi selected the site, and foundation of the mosque was laid, King patronized Islam in his kingdom and gave tribute of one thousand gold coins and precious gifts to the envoy. Thereafter he returned to Kashmir with great honour. The Masjid Sharif is the same, which is situated at Lal Chok Leh. As stated earlier, that the foundation of the mosque was laid in 1665 AD by Mughal envoy Muhammed Shafi but it was reconstructed during the reign of king Delek Namgyal in 1680, as per the drawing presented by the Mughals, after the Mongol-Tibetan war. However, the repair, renovation and extension have been made from time to time. As far as the construction during the period of king Deldan is concerned, he built an assembly hall at Leh and the longest Mane-wall in Leh, with the two Chortens at the upper end and the lower end. This was built, so that the departed soul of her mother may rest in peace and for that of his father he erected, three-storey high image of Buddha at Shay palace. Another image of Buddha, two-storey high was erected at the Singgay palace Leh. Moreover he constructed silver Chhorten and an image of Avalokitesvara, of the same height at the assembly hall. He kept one hundred Lamas each at the monasteries of Nubra, Zanskar, Bazgo and Tingmogang, so as to perform the rituals and recite "Om mani padme hung" for the spiritual welfare of his mother. He got constructed the present palace of Shay, below the old ruins. The Archeological Survey of India has made the repair and renovation of the palace, a few years back. Now it presents very beautiful look and scenery. Deldan was not only a wise organizer and popular king, but also an able administrator and ruler, who took keen interest for the upliftment of his subjects and did many welfare activities throughout the country. In 1672, Targais Namgyal, abbot of Thiksay was received by the Tibetan regent, who entrusted him with a letter for king Deldan Namgyal. The short lived improvement in the relations with Lhasa perhaps encouraged the king to undertake an aggressive politics on his western frontier, availing himself of the services of General Shakya Giatso. This introduces into the scene a man destined to play an important role in the following years. He belonged to the Saboo family and was the grandson of Singgay Namgyal's minister Agu Garmo. When the latter died in 1646, he was succeded as Saboo Kalon by his son Chhosnit Dorjay. King Deldan Namgyal coveted his wife and tried to have him killed by an attendant as he was entering the gate of the palace; he escaped at that time, but was murdered by his own steward on his way back to Saboo. While the king was preparing the wedding ceremonies, the widow fled to Igoo and prevented the marriage by shaving her hair and becoming a nun. The clergy intervened and the king had to give up the peoject. This caused a great malcontent and he had to offer images and Mani-walls to atone for the murder of the innocent minister. The son of the victim, Sakya Giatso was appointed to his father's office, although he was very young and lived to become Chief Minister and to hold that charge down to the time of Nima Namgyal. His estate was Igoo and no longer Saboo, which however, remained in the hands of another branch of the family; at a later time we find it owned by Sakya Giatso's nephew Kngga Phuntsog.

Deldan Namgyal is mentioned in several inscriptions but before his official enthronement, the chief minister was Agu Garmo, who had held office under Singgay Namgyal. Deldan Namgyal had three wives. First he married Kunzom. The second queen was Palzes, who in 1696 visited Tashis Lumbu, to ask the Panchhen for tuition. After the submission to the Mughals 1665, the king married Chhuskit Rgyalmo. All the three queens together are mentioned in a colophon. The eldest son of King Deldan Namgyal was Delek Namgyal who was born in 1640 and at the request of his father, was given his name by Stagtsang Raspa himself. About 1678 the king entrusted the affairs of state to his eldest son Delek Namgyal, though remaining the titular ruler. He received a Kharita of Aurangzeb, dated 3rd Jamidul-Aakhir according to 9th January, 1696. Says that, "having been appraised of the death of Raja Aqibat Mahmud Khan grandfather of Raja Nima Namgyal (Delek Namgyal's son and successor), his Majesty is pleased to confer upon the latter a Khilat and a mansab".

Delek Namgyal (1640-1680 AD)

Delek Namgyal was the son of Deldan Namgyal. He ascended the throne, after the death of his father. At that time there was a dispute between the Lamas of red sect and yellow sect in Tibet. Also a quarrel took place between the state of Bhutan and Tibeto-Mongolian monarchy. Since the head Lama of Bhutan was the patron lama of king of Ladakh. The latter sent a letter to Tibet stating that, if the quarrel continues, he is ready to take the side of Bhutan. The Tibetans when heard of this, instead of entering into any negotiation, raised an army at once, and invaded Ladakh. Magic calculations pointed to a

Mongol Lama called Tsang, who was at that time residing at Galdan, as the destined leader. He accordingly turned layman, and heading the Mongol tribe and a powerful army of Tibetans, soon reached Ladakh. The great mistake of Delek was that he did not go to war himself, but contented himself sending his general Gyalsan Tundup of Shay Lonpo. At the beginning a great battle took place at Zhamarting, near the Panggung Lake. The Ladakhies were driven back and very soon the Mongol army arrived at Bazgo. Moreover he did not remain at the strongly fortified castle of Bazgo, where it seems to have had one great advantage, in a continual water supply, but fled to the fortress of Tingmogang. Whereas the great portion of the Ladakhi army found safe shelter at the fortress of Bazgo. There were enough store of grain at both the castles and the Ladakhi army held its own for three years. But they were unable to drive the Tibeto-Mongolian army back again. As a result, the army of the enemy went on raiding expeditions all over the country. When the problems increased, and there seems to have had no solution, the king deputed one of his Minister Shakya Giatso to the Nawab of Kashmir, requesting him to come to his assistance. Ibrahim Khan was the Mughal Governor of Kashmir at that time. He forwarded Delak's letter to King Aurangzeb at Delhi for his consent. After getting the consent from the Mughal emperor Aurangzeb, he agreed to send an army to Ladakh, under the command of his son Fidai Khan for the rescue of the King Delek Namgyal. In this manner the history of Ladakh became connected with the Mughal history. After crossing the Indus River at Khalatsey, 6000 Mughal soldiers, under the command of Fidai Khan and five other Mughal officers advanced to Bazgo. When the Tibeto-Mongolian army heard about this, they left the fortress and arranged themselves in battle order on Chargyal-thang between Bazgo and Nemo. In the battle, the Tibeto-Mongol army was routed. They left behind them a large number of armour, bows arrows and spears, etc. and their rout continued until they reached Spituk. Even at Spituk they did not make a long hold, but continued their flight until they came to Tashigang, where they built a fort around the Gonpa, shut it in with a wall, and surrounded it with water. After the Mughal army rendered this great service to King Delek Namgyal, he left from the castle of Tingmogang and went to meet Mughal Commander Nawab Fidai Khan, to express his very sincere thanks and gratitude. According to Franke, this was not considered sufficient and the Nawab presented a bill to Delek which contained the following items:

1. King Delek was to become a Muslim and to accept the new name of Akibat Mahmood Khan but King Delek's change of religion is very contradictory. While some of the historians including Wazir Hashmatullah speak of it quite affirmative, whereas the Ladakhi historians are silent about it. However, Cunningham is of the opinion, that the least we can accept is that Delek Namgyal was taken to the Nawab's camp, where he was dictated to recite "Kalima"—"That there is no God but Allah and Mohammad (pbuh) is His messanger". According to Wazir Hashmatullah, he found a letter in Archives Leh written by Mughal emperor Aurangzeb in the name of Raja Nima Namgyal in the following words: "I came to know through reliable sources, about the death of your father Raja Aakibat Mahmood Khan. Now you are conferred with 'Khallate Fakhira' Don't allow the Kalmag (Mongol) sect to enter your country. Try to keep your subjects happy and prosperous and keep continue to propagation of Islam in the country." It authenticates the statement of Cunningham, which Delek Namgyal accepted Islam for the time being under the Mughal pressure.
2. To make certain of Delek's change of religion, his son Jigspal Namgyal and wife had to go to Kashmir, to stay there as hostage for three years. (Historians say that they never came back to Ladakh).
3. To make Delek's new name known to the world, a coin called "Jau" was to be struck for Ladakh in Kashmir. This Jau was the first and the last coin of Ladakh. Cunningham, who examined the Jau closely, gave the following reading of its legend; Obverse: Mahmood

Shah; Reverse Butan (Tibet) Zarb (struck) Sanat 878 Hijri. I also observed the same on the coin.

4. Every encouragement was to be given to Mohammedanism in Ladakh and the mosque was erected at Leh, which is the present Jama Masjid of Ahle Sunnat, Leh. The foundation of the mosque was laid down by Mughal envoy called Mohammad Shafi in 1665 AD during the period of Deldan Namgyal. But it was completed as a full-fledged mosque during Delek Namgyal's period after the Tibeto-Mongol war. However, repair, renovation and extension have been made from time to time as per the increase in Muslim population.
5. As far as the pashmina and wool traders are concerned, great encouragement was given to the Kashmiri industry of shawl and carpet weaving. Most of the wool and pashmina for those industries came from Ladakh. Consequently king Delek Namgyal had to agree that the fine wool and pashmina of Ladakh is to be sold to no other country but to Kashmir. At that time the price of seven battis of wool was two rupees only. To carry on the trade four Kashmiris shall reside at Spituk and do the trading with other Kashmiris but the four shall not be allowed to go down to Kashmir, on the other hand no other Kashmiris besides the four residing at Spituk, shall be allowed to go to Changthang area to buy the wool and pashmina from the nomads. (most probably the four Argon families are Gutu, Shangku, Hangloo and Sotay, who are still having their residential houses at Rudok, now in Tibet.)
6. Moreover, an annual tribute, consisting of the following articles was to be sent to Kashmir: 18 piebald ponies, 18 pods of musks and 18 white yak tails, probably for the use of their Hindu subjects in temples, in exchanges the Nawab of Kashmir used to send five hundred bags of rice to Ladakh annually as the income of jagir allowed to him at Nowshehra, at Srinagar. After the Battle of Bazgo, though the Mughal

army returned to Kashmir, yet the influence of Kashmiri traders, travelers and preachers increased. Now they began to trade and propagate Islam freely in Ladakh. Besides the traders and preachers, many skilled and unskilled Kashmiris like the butchers, cobblers, barbars, tailors, bakers, goldsmith and other workers came here. Most of them married the local women and permanently settled here. Till the Tibeto-Mongol war there was the influence of the Balti Muslims in Ladakh, who were mostly Shias but after the Battle of Bazgo the Kashmiri Muslims started pouring in Ladakh and they were mostly Sunnis. Some of the Kashmiri families and Kishtawaries came here to perform the job of Munshis, so as to make the correspondence in Urdu and Persian with the Mughals. and Kashmiris. They are Khoja and Tak families.

How glad was Delek when the Nawab with his large army had left the country! He had just gone, when the Tibeto-Mongolians, who had been waiting at Rudok, came out of their stronghold along with Druk Kushok Mipam Wangpo and dictated to Delek what they wanted him to agree to. It is said, when the Tibetans came to know about the above-mentioned agreement between, king Delek and the Nawab, it was disliked by the Tibetan government since the majority of population and king himself was a follower of Drukpa sect, hence the Tibetan government deputed Kushok Mipam Wangpo, a head Lama of Drukpa sect, to convince the King of Ladakh. The Kushok advised the king Delek, that we belong to the same religion and same culture and language, the outsiders should not be encouraged to interfere in the affairs of Ladakh. It is better to initiate remedial actions and activities for it, and follow the principles of Dharma, otherwise we both will suffer. He further said, "That we assured you, that we will never invade Ladakh in future. Moreover king Delek has to defend the border of Kashmir."

Because of the religious pressure of the great Lama, the king has to surrender all the areas of Ngaris Skorsum, like Guge, Purang, lowo and Rudok provinces. This was the income generated region in the past. The Lhari stream, near the Panggong Lake was identified as the boundary between Tibet and Ladakh. King Delek protested against this sort of policy, but apparently, without any effect. The Lama simply declared it an offering to the religion of Buddha, by saying that the revenue of all those territories was to be utilized to defray the expenses of the sacrificial lamb and the reading of the religious books in Tibet. Though the name was sweet but the loss was bitter, for it meant the renunciation of the large provinces of Ngaris Skorsum.

Regarding the trade with Lhasa, the king of Ladakh shall send once in three years a mission called "Lobchhak" in Tibetan language, conveying presents to the great Lamas of Tibet. As far as the presents to the ordinary Lamas are concerned, the quantity has not been fixed, but to the Dalai Lama's steward should be given thirty grames of gold, ten weights of scent, six pieces of calico, and one piece of soft cotton cloth. The members of the mission shall receive tents at every destination, daily rations and fodder for their animals, free of cost during their sojourn in Tibet. On the other hand, the traders of the government of Tibet shall come every year with 200 loads of brick-tea, and he will submit the following presents to the king of Ladakh:

Chinese tea 22 damo, Chinese silk cloth 7 than, Tibetan woolen cloth 2 than and "khataks" from the great Lamas of Lhasa. The Tibetan mission will also receive the same facilities and convenience during their travel, within the territory of Ladakh.

After signing this agreement, Kushok Mipham Wangpo the Drukchhen returned back, to submit the report to the government of Lhasa. The Lhasa government greatly honored his political services and granted him the revenue of three villages, which, during the later days was under the occupation of the Gonpa of the Drukpa sect, to which he belongs. Consequently, Delek came under the political pressure of two foreign countries, i.e. the Mughal and the Tibetans.

Nima Namgyal (1680-1720 AD)

Nima Namgyal was the son of king Delek Namgyal. He ascended the throne after the death of his father. During Nima's lifetime the quarrel for the succession began. He was the king, who lauded the virtuous and suppressed evil-doers. In pronouncing judgment he never merely followed his own desires, but always consulted his staff officers. He framed the council of elders to assist him in important affairs, for that purpose he nominated the intelligent and wise persons from every village. He laid down the rule that the primary origin of the dispute must be traced before issuing the verdict.

During the reign of Nima Namgyal, the first printing press was established in Ladakh and after the blocks of six religious books had been engraven, he distributed the sacred books, free of cost, among the people. It is said that the art of printing came Ladakh from Tibet and the same had come to Tibet from China. The most famous structure of Nima is a mani-wall at Choglamsar, called Zanag Maney, and the palace of Charasa at Nubra. He was the first king, for a long time, under whom there was no warfare; there was peace and prosperity everywhere, there did not occur strife, robbery, or theft; and the life of the people passed in happiness.

Nima Namgyal was married twice. His first wife died after she had given birth to a son, called Deskyong Namgyal. The song in Ladakh indicates that people took a particular interest in little prince Deskyong, and committed him to the care of his guardian deity. Nima's second wife was Queen Zizi Khatoon of Purig. She had a son Tashi Namgyal and a daughter Shema Tashi Wangmo. According to Petech, "Nima Namgyal occupies a special place among the kings of Ladakh because of his interest in the field of justice. It seems that he carried out a real re-organization of the judiciary. When delivering judgement personally, he always consulted the state officers. On a lower level he appointed elders (rganpo) from each District to decide questions. Legal documents (bka-shog) concerning matters of landed property were not issued on a mere request, direct or through intermediaries, but the request was first referred to a tribunal consisting of the three elder officers of the state, and the contending parts were to take oaths on the three jewels. The roots of the case were carefully inquired into, so that the judgement could also serve as a precedent for the future. Therefore, his legal documents were better than those of all the other Kings. On the whole, this resulted into a sharp decline of crime, such as robbery and theft."

In the cultural field, the king encouraged printing and printing blocks of some devotional works were carved. As usual, he erected many images, many-walls and prayer-wheels. According to chronicles, he was particularly a pious king, "presented to all the monasteries of Tibet, beginning with Lhasa and Sam-yas, gold water and sacrificial lamps. To all the great Lamas without distinction he made presents, whilst the brotherhoods were invited to tea-generals."

On 28th August, 1694, the regent, on behalf of the Dalai Lama, issued to him a most interesting document. It stated that, while Ladakh followed earlier the Drukpa sect, now, after the conquest of Galdan Tsewang its defacto ruler Nima Namgyal showed himself obsequent to the yellow church. Therefore, the Gelugpa convents of Thiksay, Pethub, Lokhil, Diskit, and the monasteries of the other sects, such as Chemday, Anley, Bardan in Zangskar, Matho, Sgang-non, Tagtag, Yundung, Stagna, etc. all of them were under the authority of 'bar-spuns, chief convent of the Gelikpa school. Ang Lobzang Nawang Phuntsog was appointed its representative in Ladakh. As such the prince became the abbot of Thiksay and head of the seven Serpogon Gelukpa monasteries, to which Lhasa issued a set of rules of behaviour (bca-yig). The monasteries of other sects were expected to be subject to this new authority, although this did not actually happen. Also, the college for higher religious studies, which he proposed to set up in Ladakh, never materialized. In the long run, what remained of this ambitious scheme was the succession by incarnation of the Thiksay abbot and their supremacy over the other Gelugpa convents in Ladakh; and even that ceased, when at an unknown date a royal prince became abbot of Pethub and made that monastery independent of Thiksay. On the occasion of his appointment, Lobzang Nawang Phuntsog paid his respects to the Panchhen; then he left for Ladakh. His stay there, however, was not long, because in 1697 he was again in Lhasa, whether this indicated a failure of his mission. Perhaps he found his nephew Nima Namgyal already too strongly established in his position to allow him to play the intended political role. In any case, after 1697 Lobzang Nawang Phuntsog slowly fades out of the picture. Later, he was replaced by another royal prince, this time a younger brother of King Nima Namgyal, who on December 18th, 1697, had an audience with the Dalai Lama. This is almost certainly the Nawang Namgyal of the genealogies.

Petech says, "Relations with the Balti chiefships were more of a problem, although a dynastic tie with the chief of Khapulo came into being when Nima Namgyal married a lady from that family, the Zizi Khatoon, the granddaughter of Hatim Khan and niece of Doulat Khan. This relationship gave him a base of a sort on that turbulent frontier, but it also exposed Khapulo to the enmity of the other chiefs and compelled Ladakh to shoulder a heavy military responsibility. At some time before 1715 some military transactions, about which the text is reticent, involved Baba Hatim Khan of Khapulo. Trouble broke out again in 1716, when Hatim Khan's son-in-law Daulat Khan revolted. Forces from Shigar and Skardo came to his support and seized the castle of Saling. Hatim Khan asked for help, and Sodnam Lhundup was sent out again, with Tsultim Dorjay at his second in command. At first the Ladakhis suffered a reverse near Risna of Surmo-brog, notwithstanding the sturdy defence of some officers. Eventually Sodnam Lhundup defeated the Shigar and Skardo forces and attacked Saling with gunfire. Doulat Khan escaped with his life, the rest of his followes surrendered, and the matter was brought to a quick end. These military events help us to place in proper focus the foremost leaders of Nima Namgyal's reign; the most evident feature was the increase in the hereditary character of the highest offices of the state. There was first of all the branch of the Saboo family that had shifted to Igoo and for which about this time the name Bankapa was coming into use. Its head was the old minister Sakya Gyatso; he was still in office in 1697, when he acted as promoter of document. But he seems to have retired or died soon after, without leaving male issue. His succession was taken up by his two nephews Kungga Phuntsog and Phuntsog Namgyal. But by far the more influent of the two was Kungga Phuntsog. As we shall see later, he remained in office also during the following reigns, for a total of about fifty years.

The other outstanding family was that of the chiefs of Gya, the only autonomous feudatory in Ladakh proper. The family entered government service, ascending at once to the highest rank, with Sonam Lundup. He first appears as Nono (not yet as chhoslon) in the unpublished Gya inscription of King Deldan Namgyal and prince Delek Namgyal. In 1697, he was Kalon of Stog, and had received at least some of the estates confiscated by Deldan Namgyal and Delek Namgyal to the heirs of the murdered Chhosnit Dorjay. In 1698, he (Nono Sonam) visited the 6th Dalai Lama. Then he took charge as Chief Minister. In 1726, he went again to central Tibet to visit both Dalai Lama and Panchhen Lama. Petech says, "His tenure of office seems to have covered the whole of the reign of Nima Namgyal. He exploited his position for increasing the estates of his family and was even suspected of aiming at the throne."

When King Nima became old, he appointed his elder son Deskyong as king of Ladakh. But his stepmother, Zizi Khatoon wanted to get a part of the kingdom for her own son Tashi Namgyal. Since she had always been kind to Deskyong, she persuaded him easily to give all Purig to Tashi Namgyal. This was against the wishes of the state officials, who did not like to have a divided empire. They entered a petition that either Tashi should be made a Lama or live quietly at Tingmogang. When the quarrel became acute, old king Nima seized the reins of the government once more and ruled for several years. Finally on the request of the Ladakhi rulers, the Dalai Lama deputed Lama Katog Rigzin Tsewang Nurboo to Ladakh to settle the dispute; he was a Ningmapa incarnate from Kham. The Katog arrived at Wamley on 18th September 1752. He convened both the rulers and dignatories there and the dynastic quarrel was settled by a simple recognition of the existing situation, on 1st December 1752. "Whatever the number of sons born at the castle of Ladakh may be, the eldest only shall reign. The younger ones shall become Lamas at Pethob Thiksay, etc., but there shall not be two kings. The king of Zangskar, having his dominion at the Indian frontier, shall remain king as before. The Hanasku ruler, obviously being of royal decent and his kingdom of little importance shall also remain. With these two exceptions, it shall not be permitted that in one kingdom exist two kings." King Tashi Namgyal should remain ruler of Purig as long as he lives; afterwards it should be reunited with Ladakh. During his last days Nima Namgyal joined Tashi Namgyal at Mulbe and died there.

Deskyong Namgyal (1720-1740 AD)

He ascended the throne after his father Nima Namgyal, but he was an insignificant ruler. He married with a princess of Lowo, Nilza Wangmo, but could not live in peace, because of differences and separated. Soon after a son, Saskyong Namgyal was born. Subsequently he married another princess Thi Gyalmo, and a son, Phuntsog Namgyal was born. He was an utterly insignificant ruler. The reign of the government was in the hand of his stepmother queen Zizi Khatoon. With the help of his queen mother, Tashi Namgyal captured Purig and made Mulbe his capital, where he got constructed a palace Mendok Khar on the top of the hill. The ruins of the old palace are still there. But the Gonpa is in a good condition.

The daughter of Zizi Khatoon Shema Tashi Wangmo was got married with the Raja of Kishtawar, though the ministers and other officers of the Ladakhi government were not happy with this marriage, with the outsiders, who was non-Buddhist. The queen did not agree with them. She said that the parents have more rights over their daughters, than anybody else. Later, when the news came in Ladakh, that Tashi Wangmo is being teased and tortured by the members of the royal family of Kishtawar and was not allowed seeing the light of the day. Now the queen was very anxious and she decided to depute a group of Ladakhies to Kishtawar, to bring her back by fair means or foul. When they reached Kishtawar, the Raja who was very fond of the queen expressed his desire to go to Ladakh along with his wife. When Queen Zizi came to know, that her son in law is also coming to Ladakh, she thought that he would certainly create problems in the administration of her son Tashi Namgyal in Purig. Therefore, without the knowledge of the authorities of Ladakh, she gave secret orders to this effect. A loyal servant of the queen went on this mission, and at a bridge on the frontier, between Kishtawar and Paldar, the servant, approaching the raja in the manner to assist him to cross the bridge, threw him into the water of the stream and got killed. Later, Shema Tashi Wangmo was got remarried with the Raja of Khapulo.

Phuntsog Namgyal (1740-1760 AD)

Saskyong Namgyal, being the elder brother, was the legal heir of the throne, after his father Deskyong but Phuntsog Namgyal, who was the second son, seized the government through the treachery of his mother. His elder brother Saskyong Namgyal was sent to Himis Gonpa to become a Lama. And he himself began to rule over Ladakh. But much against his own will Phuntsog's realm was very small, as Purig was still in the hands of his uncle Tashi Namgyal. Tashi brought the whole kingdom into great danger of a war with Kashmir, as he tyrannized not only over his Ladakhi subjects but also the Kashmiri traders. As such a war not only endangered Ladakh but central Tibet as well. A report in this regard was sent to Dalai Lama in Tibet. Hence, the Dalai Lama deputed, his envoy, the great Lama Rigzin Tsewang Nurboo to resolve the differences in Ladakh and maintain peace. The Lama convened a great council at Anlay monastery, where all the princess and ministers of Ladakh were invited. All decided to agree the decisions and obligations imposed upon them by the great Lama. After discussion and consultation, he declared the result. Whatever the number of princess born at Leh palace may be, the eldest son only shall reign. Moreover, the younger ones shall become Lamas at Thiksay, Pethub and other monasteries, but there shall not be two kings. The kingdom should not be divided between two brothers. The Raja of Zanskar was to remain as before, so as to protect the frontier against Himachal and

Kishtawar. Those members of the royal family who had received the castles of Zangla and Henasku with sixty or eighty peasants attached to them were also to remain as before, because their kingdoms were of little importance. And Uncle Tashi Namgyal was to remain by all means, probably because of his old age. Thus, he ruled over Purig, throughout his life. It is said that Tashi Namgyal had no children. When he died in Purig in 1758 and his kingdom has been annexed to Ladakh. His widow Stanzin Chuskit remained in Mulbe, under the protection of his brother, the former minister Wangyal, who had been appointed fortress commander of Hembabs. He acquitted himself well, for which he thanked both the lady and the king. Then he accompanied her, who by now had become a nun, in her pilgrimage to Lhasa, where in the second half of 1768, they paid their respect to the Dalai Lama. At that time Tsewang Namgyal had already chosen him as his new Prime Minister. According to the decision of the council, Phuntsog Namgyal has to surrender the kingdom and his elder brother Saskyong Namgyal, who was a Lama at Himis Gonpa, was convened at Leh palace and was made the king. It is said that the deposed king Phuntsog Namgyal and his mother equally divided the property in the Leh palace and both shifted at the castle of Sakti.

Tsewang Namgyal II (1760-1780 AD)

Tsewang Namgyal was the elder son of Saskyong Namgyal, with his first wife Gyalmo Norzin Wangmo of Lowo. And according to the Anlay agreement, he ascended the throne after his father. Saskyong's second wife was Gyalmo Kunzom; she was at Himis, when he was in exile. During that period a son was born to her at Himis. He was made Lama and his name was Gyalhras Mipham Tsewang Thinles, but he is known as Mipham Tsephel Thustop Dorjay, as a respectable Lama of Himis Gonpa. He did remarkable job for the upliftment of the Himis Gonpa. His younger brother became a famous medical practitioner, and served the people in the field of medicine and the sister was married in Lhasa.

Though the public, the ministers, the noblemen, the council of elders, and the merchants all were very happy and contented with the new settlement but the new king Tsewang did not quite justify the amount of trouble, the great Lama Rigzin had taken about his election. As soon as the great Lama has left, Tsewang became troublesome, or, as the chronicles say, "the evil one entered his mind". His father expired, when he was young, because of this, he was indulged in bad habits. His engagement was made with the princes of Zangla (Zanskar) but before her arrival at Leh, Tsewang married with Mashoqa Bibi, a low caste woman of Tsangra Kartsey, who was very famous in the region for her beauty. She came to Leh along with her brothers Nasib Ali and Rahim Ali. According to the historians, A.G. Sheikh and S.S. Gergon, Bibi was a crazy and arrogant lady. She used to throw the newly prepared silky garments, after using it for only once, with the intention that the nobles and elites would take them away to their home for the use of their ladies and whenever they assemble in the functions, wearing these garments, she used to pass on comments, to humiliate them. Beside this, she used to cut siky garments into pieces and throw them downwards to all side from the roof of the Singgay palace, so that the common people stick the pieces on their cap as a decoration piece. Such was the rude behaviour of the Mashoqa Bibi and due to egoism she wanted to show her superiority among the people. When the princes of Zangla, came to know about this affairs, she returned at once to her home at Zangla, and later married with the Raja of Zanskar. According to Hashmat & Francke "The Ladakhies were not happy with their low caste queen, they were even less pleased with Tsewang's further activities, viz. that he had one groom only for each 500 horses, and a lamp in grandest style at night (may be for security purposes). Moreover Tsewang made the taxes payable three times in a year, so as to overcome the expenses. He fell in the bad company of Mirza Malik, a horse trader and assassinated Kalon Kunkyap and Tongspon Tundup, and imposed heavy fines and punishment to the nobles and officials. The low caste people were encouraged and appointed on high posts. Hence a revolution took place. In the eyes of the Ladakhies the source of all the offences was the low caste queen. She was expelled from the palace, and according to some historians, she was hanged at Chhagon, Leh, as per the decision of the council of elders. Her father Nasib Ali and Kalon Wangyal of Stok were also expelled from the country and Kalon Wangyal went to Lhasa in exile and never returned to Ladakh. Later Tsewang Namgyal was married with a princess of Sodh, called Begum Wangmo, who is known in Ladakh as Gyalmo Kunzom, she had two sons and three daughters. The elder son was Migur Tsettan Namgyal and the younger was Migur Tundup Namgyal. Gyalpo Tsewang Namgyal was also having another wife from Purig, called Gyalmo Khatoon Tsering, who gave birth to Prince Jigsmat Namgyal, who later became a Lama at Thiksay Gonpa." According to Lama Lobzang Chhoklang of Thiksay, he has seen a grave below the Gonpa on the right side of the road called "Abi Zizi Spurkang". Probably, Khatoon must have died at Thiksay under the care of her son Jigsmat Namgyal and burried there as per Muslim rituals. Gyalras Jigsmat Namgyal had been the head Lama and 5th Khanpo of Thiksay Gonpa.

When the administrative affairs of the country went from bad to worst, the Kushok Gyalhras of Himis Gonpa and Chhagzot Tashi, with the support of the public, deposed the king Tsewang Namgyal and advised him to become a Lama and live at Chemday Gonpa. His elder son Tsettan Namgyal was made the king at the age of ten years and ascended the throne. Moreover, the deposed king was strictly advised, not to interfere in any kind of administrative affairs and he was given land and pasture separately at Stok and Saboo for his personal expenses.

Looking at the kings of this period, the thought cannot be avoided that the dynasty was on the decline not one of the king of this chapter was great as a warior, or as a politician, or administrator; and women became occasionally the ruler of the state.

According to Luciano Petech in his book *The Kingdom of Ladakh* at pages 116-17 "His friends were mostly Muslims, and he gradually became estranged to Buddhism, ceased to follow the local customs and leaned heavily toward Islam; the entreaties of his officials were of no avail. Worse than that, he fell under the spell of a Muslim girl of the lowest class, usually called the Bibi. She came to Leh with her brothers Nasib Ali and Rahim Ali from Kartse in Purig (Hashmat refer Nasib Ali as her father). The king fell deeply in love with her and pandered to her smallest whim his first wife quitted him and returned to Zangla, her home, whereupon he married the Bibi: the people called her, half in derision, the Bhemo Rgyalmo. The officials tried to oppose the marriage and asked for an explanation, whereupon the king, on the advice of his new wife, undertook to crush the opposition by terror; the Minister Kunskyab and the village headman Tongspon of Tingmogang were put to death, several nobles were clapped into prison with iron on their feet. To increase his income, the king made taxes payable three times in the year. Conditions became nearly unbearable, the country was exploited and sucked dry by and for the family of the Bibi; Nasib Ali was even appointed acting Prime Minister. This lasted for some time. At last the nobles and the people, driven to desperation, rose in arms and stormed the palace of Leh. The king was not bodily harmed; but the Bibi was nailed to the gate of the Bazar and flogged to death. After the tragic end of the Bibi, the king married Begum Wangmo of Sod in Purig. Once more a Muslim, she bore him two sons; Tsettan Namgyal and Tundup Namgyal; they were mere boys when their father abdicated. His secondary wife Khatoon Tsering bore one son, called Jigsmat Namgyal. During the last period of his reign the king, perhaps under the influence of his third wife, inclined more and more to the Shia form of Islam, revived the old title "Aaqibat Mahmood Khan and for three years abstained from maintaining the customary ceremonial lamps in Leh, devoting the equivalent to the upkeep of his horses. His craze for horses increased, if possible, and this cost to the state great sums. A large portion of them was embezzled by minister Wangyal, who laid the fault at the door of the innocent beasts."

"It was perhaps in order to obtain the cash needed to cover these great expenses that the king resumed (or rather started) the Ladakhi coinage of Muslim type. This had been agreed to but never actually carried out by Singgay Namgyal and Delek

Namgyal. In 1781, a Muslim goldsmith of Leh was hired to strike the new Ladakhi coins (Jau)."

"This disastrous reign, which apparently taxed severely the economic strength of the country, ended with another revolution (1782). The rebels occupied Leh and the king and the minister took refuge at Hemis under the protection of the Mipham. There the king, despairing of ever recovering his throne, abdicated on a promise of safety for him and for Wangyal, whom the people wanted to kill. The king received as usual the estates of Sakti and Saboo for his maintenance, plus some meadows at Matho for the upkeep of his beloved horses. He died at Matho at an unknown date." Here I want to mention briefly about the historian Luciani petech. He was the first Europian, who did research on "Ladakh chronicals" in 1935-36 from Rome University and got doctorate degree on the said topic. In this connection, he visited Ladakh several times. He was familiar with the classical Bhoti language. He published his book namely *Kingdom of Ladakh* in 1977 from Italy, Rome, which is considered most authentic book from historical point of view.

Tsettan Namgyal (1780-1790 AD)

Tsettan Namgyal was the elder son of Tsewang Namgyal. Thereby, he ascended the throne at the age of ten as per the resolution of the council of Anlay, and his younger brother Tundup Namgyal had to enter the Himis monastery to become a Lama. As per the consultation between the nobles and the Head Lama of Himis Gonpa, he was got married with princes of Pashkum.

People thought that the dynasty was making a new start, because Testtan Namgyal was a man of character, than that of many kings before him. He was diligent, and obtained proficiency in Tibetan grammar and mathematics. He was familiar with the Persian and Kashmiri language and other such languages. He also knew well how to govern. He was devout, and knew the duties of a king. He was fearless before the enemy. He did many welfare activities for the upliftment of his subjects. He was very gentle and humble.

According to the Luciano Petech at page 123, "Tsettan Namgyal was still a boy, being probably born about 1779. Till at least 1794, he did not bear the royal title. But was styled "Lha-sras" a few years later Tsettan Namgyal assumed the royal title." According to the chronicals, "after the death of Tsewang Namgyal the Himis Skyabgon Gyalras Mipham and the nobles had a conference. They requested Prince Tsettan Namgyal to take a wife from Pashkyum in Purig and invested him with the sovereignty." His brother Tsepal Namgyal became a monk at Himis and their half-brother Jigsmat Namgyal took holy order at Thiksay. Of his three half sisters, one was given in marriage to the chief of Pashkyum, another to No-no Tsewang Tundup and third retired to a cell and died there.

The young king had a careful education; he became proficient in the martial arts as well as in literature and above all in calligraphy. He lighted the tax burden on the people and was much beloved. Official relation with Lhasa was continued, although the central Tibetan texts are very sparing in information about it. Thus in 1784 a mission of about twenty persons, led by the Naris Gopa Samphel was received in the Tibetan capital. Much more important was the invitation tendered to the 8th Drukchen Kun-gzigs chosgi-snanba (1768-1822). Eventually he set out on his journey in the 5th month of 1801, visiting the Kailash en rout. There he was met by the Hemis treasurer Chhagzot Tashi and the royal official No-no Phuntsog Rafstan. On 10th October 1801, he was at Hemis, where he was received by the king and the Kalon and from where he proceeded to Leh. The reception he found in Ladakh was lavish, and both the king and nobility vied in bestowing upon him precious gifts, of which the chronicals gives a list. But at that very time a smallpox epidemy broke out, to which the young king fell a victim. The Drugchen performed the funeral rites in a grand style, in the 1st and 2nd month of 1802, and left for Tibet soon after.

In memory of his late father he built the Mane Ringmo, the second largest mane-wall in the country, with chortens at either end, so as to rest the departed soul in peace. Tsettan was very fond of games and was a great polo player. In a Ladakhi song it has been mentioned that he used to play polo, at the polo ground of Murtse garden. It is also said, that once his horse got shy, ran away with him, and threw him off. In this accident, he is said to have lost one eye. When Tsettan Namgyal was 24 years old, an epidemic of smallpox broke out in the town and unfortunately the king died at Karzoo Bagh Leh, in his prime youth, without leaving any children, but the queen was pregnant at that time. Drukpa Thamschat Khenpa, was the head Lama of Himis Gonpa, who once received handsome presents from the king, performed the last funeral rites of the deceased king in a grand style.

Tsepal Tundup Namgyal (1790-1841 AD)

When Tsettan Namgyal died without any issue, his younger brother Tsepal Tundup Namgyal, who was a Lama at Himis Gonpa was called back to become the king. He inherited from his brother not only the kingdom but also his wife the lady of Pashkyum, who is called Zizi Khatoon in the chronicals. She bore him a daughter, and then (about 1810) a son called Tsewang Rabstan Namgyal. Though he was a Lama but he had always been considered second husband to the queen, as per the polyandry system in the past. Later he married with another lady called Spalzes Wangmo. King Tsepal was opposite to his brother Tsettan. He loved an easy life, and was lazy in every respect. He never went to battle, although he had plenty of opportunity to do so. He was doing favour and partiality while giving judgment between rich and poor. Besides, he seems to have inherited the taint of madness from his father, for many strange things are told about him. The private servants in the palace had to promise daily not to sleep at night. The king also did not sleep at night. He rose when the sun grew hot. In the morning, when washing his hands, he required twelve basins full of cold and hot water. He used to travel in the provinces during the night carrying torches in the hands. He imprisoned the Raja of Zanskar and Kalon of Purig and kept them at Leh. He did not like and agree the officials of the old regime and expelled them and got appointed his own loyal, lazy and inefficient men on the high posts in and outside the palace, and took counsel with them. Kalon Tsewang Tundup was an efficient and powerful minister and he brought the kingdom to prosperity and merit. He also assumed concurrently the office of treasurer, which gave him the economic control of the country. An independent source confirms that about 1812 the Kalon was perfect master of the supreme authority and the Raja took no part in the affairs of State. He was the brother-in-law of the king but the king Tsepal took away the privy seal from the minister to his own palace. Thus, Kalon Tsewang Tundup seems to have been offended and humiliated, for he disappears from the page of history. According to Petech, "Tsewang Tundup kept political powers in his hands, but after 1806 ceased to command the army in the field. That task was normally entrusted to Sonam Stanzin, usually called Nono Stanzin, who was an able negotiator than a successful general. As it appears from the document concerning him, he was the Nangso of Nubra; he is called Kharpon Stanzin in an inscription from Hunder in Nubra, and the Kaga Stanzin of Nubra mentioned in Tsepstan account of Dogra war. He was a prominent official, but he never became minister."

During the reign of this king Moorcroft visited Ladakh, 1820-22 AD. This event is described in the chronicles in this manner; the Bara Sahib and Chota Sahib came to Leh, via Kullu and Lahol, with great wealth. They gave all sorts of rich presents to the nobles of Ladakh. "We must see the king". They said, and all that was said in reply was, "What evil there is in Indian one cannot know!" An audience for consultation was refused for several months, but at last they saw the king. They presented a variety of things, but the best were a penknife, scissors, and a gun. They said, "we have come to see the way in which your ministers and people behave, and your majesty's wisdom; and there is a likelihood of this country being conquered, if we built a tower here it will prove useful to the king." The king and his ministers, in considering the case said, "If they built a fort, no one knows what means of doing harm it may be!" and did not allow them to build it. Then they gave the king a letter in a box and said, "Accept this; it may cure the king's mind!" They stayed throughout both summer and winter, and departed. These were the first European Sahibs who visited Ladakh.

How much Tsepal must have regretted, about twelve years after, that he had considered worthless the friendship of the English! How useful it would have been to support him against all kinds of external enemies! When it was too late this visit of the sahibs was remembered, and the assistance of the English solicited, as the course of events will show. The principal reason why Tsepal did not accept that assistance of the British was hardly his mistrust, but his extreme laziness, and his desire to remain undisturbed. His carelessness became most evident when the people of Kullu and Lahol, who had once been the subjects of the Ladakhi emperors, came on raiding expeditions to his own country. The army of Kullu invaded Spiti, and after having destroyed the village, and carried away all the property, they returned home. The Ladakhies petitioned Tsepal that he should wage a war of revenge, but he said: "You have not tried your best!" and punished them.

Later on the people of Kullu and Lahol conspired against Zangskar. They stole ponies, yaks and other animals and whatever there was of value, and again returned home. But now under the command of a general of Paldar, an army was raised, and attacked the enemy. All the Lahol villages from Spadum to Aring were destroyed and later on peace was made. At this time king Tsepal said, "You Zangskaries have not yet tried your best." And punished them.

One year later, an army of Mande and Waran from Kishtawar attacked upper Zangskar, upto Dung ring. They burnt the villages with fire, whatever of wealth and cattle they got they carried back with them. From all these notes it looks as if the Ladakhi kingdom of those days had got quite a name its neighbours for being an easy prey to conquerors. And in course of time its fame may have traveled as far as Jammu.

Thus, the king never bothered about the welfare of his subjects and he never asked whether his subjects fared well or ill, he took interest only in what concerned his own pocket. There was abundance of wealth in the royal treasury and the king decided to use the wealth for building purposes. The first work he undertook was the new palace of Stok. The other palace built by Tsepal Tundup Namgyal is the palace of the crown prince at Leh. Tsepal's eldest son was to be married to a princess of Lhagyari Tibet but due to some misfortune in Tibet, the princess could not come here in Leh. Tsepal erected a number of idols, mostly made of silver; a Vajrapani, a figure of the Guru Padma Odbar, a white Tara, who since the days of Rgyal Khatoon was supposed to be incarnated in the Ladakhi queens. He also built a Chorten of silver, with ornaments in gold, copper, and precious stones. The Dogras probably carried most of these silver images away.

The elder son of Tsepal Tundup Namgyal was Tsewang Rabstan alias Chhogsprul, about him a great Lama of Tibet, Yangzin Eshay Dulba issued a letter declaring him to be an incarnation of the Himis Sku-zabs Lama Bhulwa Dorjay. Consequently, the boy was kept at Himis and Chemray Gonpa for close observation. Having thus becomes so important personage; he became crazier and found it difficult to obey the father and mother. But there was still one person whose word he heeded; this was the queen's own steward, Chhagzot Sonam Wangchuk. The queen mother was very proud of her son. Whenever the king was on tour to Purig or Nubra, the queen and Chhogsprul used to go there with him, and they passed their time, both day and night, with dancing and singing for the amusement of the prince. Who was interested in dine and dance.

When the prince was about 16 years old, the king and his ministers tried to motivate and convince him to marry, for the sake of the dynasty, but he refused continuously. He replied, "I have to be at Himis Gonpa as a Lama." Since there was no other son, the king, his ministers, nobles, council of elders and stewards, etc. once again approached and pressurized him, so as to preserve the dynasty. This time he consented and married with Skalzang Dolma, the younger daughter of Kalon Tsewang Tundup. Having once tasted the sweetness of matrimony, he married yet another lady, Sonam Palkit of Kalon Pangkhapa, and yet he married a third lady named Zahra Khatoon, the daughter of the Raja of Pashkyum. It was happened in a horse year (1834 AD) that he took these three wives, and it was in the same horse year that Zorawar Singh, with the Dogra army, arrived at Kartse.

According to A.H. Fancke, who says, "that the chronicles have not told us much to enlist our admiration, still in the memory of the people. Tsepal Tundup Namgyal lives as the ideal patriarchal king of Ladakh? As he was the last independent king, all the virtues of his predecessors were believed to have been united in him. From this point of view, we can understand the description of the state of the country before the outbreak of the Dogra war, as it is given by the Tsebstan of Khalates: "At the time of the father king, the following were his subjects: the people who dwelt between the Zojila, Ladr, Sahedulla, and Polong dandra, they all were his subjects. Besides the father king, no one was allowed to say anything here. To say "Salaam" to the king there came from Kashmir a man called Malik annually, and together with him about one hundred pony men. In reply to this the Ladakhi king sent with a man from Khalatse, called Dragshos Tundup, various products of Ladakh as a present; for instance, a horse, a yak, a sheep, a goat, a dog, and also more valuable things. The head steward of the king's household was the Lonpo Phuntsog Rabstan of Nemo; the royal cook was a man of the house 'cook' at Wanla. The royal butcher was Stobdan of the house butcher of Alchi, and another man in Rubchu. All the grain for the royal household had to be brought from Nubra, and a nobleman, called Kaga Stanzin, had the care of it. The needful butter had to be provided by a man from Zangskar. Besides this the peasants had no taxes to pay, and there was no unpaid forced labour.

When the king's marchant "Lobchhak" went to Lhasa after every three years, as per the treaty of Tingmogang, every village had to send one man for the carvan. This man received two Jaus from every peasant in the village, as wages for his journey. For the same carvan every village had to give two hides, but the larger villages three. They were used to wrap up the goods.

Toll had to be paid by the Kashmiris, Yarkendis, and the Lahoul traders on entering Ladakh; but it was not asked of the people of Purig, Baltistan, and Tibet.

"Several villages were in debt to the king, and all their fields had been given to the king as security. On the day when the king's son (probably Chhogsprul) was made assistant king to his father, all the debts were remitted. That act of king was very much liked and appreciated by the people."

Dogra's Invasion of Ladakh (1833, 1834, 1839 and 1842)

3

Dogra Colonel, Basti Ram, on the request of Sir Alexander Cunningam, has recorded the history of the Dogra's invasion of Ladakh in 1846. He published in his book *Ladakh*, the events which seem to be perhaps the most correct.

As the Dogras could not march through Kashmir, which then was the territory of the Sikhs, hence, Maharaja Gulab Singh sent his General Zorawar Singh, with about 10,000 soldiers through Kishtawar. The following were the Military Officers in the Zorawar's camp—1. Mian Rai Singh, 2. Mehta Basti Ram Kishtawaria, 3. Mirza Rasool Beg Odpan puria Doda, 4. Rana Jalim Singh Arnoda, 5. Sangay Mankotia, 6. Mian Tota, 7. Sardar Utam Singh Padhyar, 8. Wazir Khoja Bhunja Kishtawaria, 9. Imam Mali Mudwa, 10. Syed Madin Shah, and Sardar Samad Khan. Zorawar alongwith a huge army, arrived in Suru-Kartse, via Botokol and Kalon Mulbe Tsewang Namgyal, was the Governor of Ladakhi king in Suru-Kartse. Tashi Wangchuk of Saboo was the Kharpon. He immediately informed the king at Leh about the activities of the Dogras, since there was no tradition of keeping regular army in Ladakh. Hence a Ladakhi force of about 5000, which had been mobilized in haste, and placed under the command of Stokpa Kalon Dorjay Namgyal, who was a youth of just 18 years. At Sangku, the Ladakhies had entrenched themselves on a hill, and defended it with much vigour for a full day.

Unfortunately, they could not do much harm to the Dogras. Only six or seven Dogras were killed, while the Ladakhi losses are given by Basti Ram as thirty killed and as many wounded.

After the battle of Sangku the Ladakhis marched during the night across the Russila to Shargol, where they halted for eight days. Thus the most important fortress of the district, Kartse, the seat of the Thi Sultan, remained in the hands of the Dogras and they further improved their hold on the country by building a fort at Suru. Taxes were levied on the peasants of all the villages which had been taken possession of. Every peasant had to pay four rupees.

Leaving thirty-five men in the castle of Suru, the Dogra army moved down the Suru river. First of all Langkartse was taken, and by and by, fighting occasionally, but never with the whole Ladakhi army, the Dogra army arrived in the plains of Pashkyum. But this time the Ladakhies were in expectation of reinforcements. The old king Tundup Namgyal had sent his ministers, Mourup Stanzin and Kalon Bangkapa, to mobilize all those districts which had not yet sent any warriors, and now a force of about 4000 men was advancing towards Pashkyum, Apparently, before the arrival of this army, the young minister or general Stokpa Kalon Dorjay Namgyal attacked the Dogras, and the fortune of the day was almost on the side of the Ladakhies, when their brave young general was suddenly struck by a musket ball and died. This was for the Ladakhies, superstitious as they are, the signal for a general flight. They fled in all directions, but most of them across the Pashkyum Bridge, towards Mulbe and Shargol. After having passed the bridge they had sense enough left to break it down. But the Dogras knew another method of crossing the river; they did so, on inflated skins, and in pursuit killed many Ladakhies and made many more prisoners. Then the Dogras directed their attention to the Pashkyum castle, but found it empty, as the chief had fled to the castle of Sod. After ten days firing Basti Ram seized the castle and few hundred of soldiers were made captives. The fugitive Ladakhi army had arrived meanwhile before the two new leaders, and told them terror inspired stories of the greatness and armament of the Dogra army.

But winter began to make itself felt in the Dogra camp, in spite of his successes, Zorawar would very much have liked to end the campaign and march back to Kishtawar, at any rate to spend the winter there. But he knew very well that he could not come before his sovereign, Gulab Singh, without a present of a considerable sum of money, and until now he had got nothing except the tax amount collected at Kartse. So he levied taxes on the peasants of the Pashkyum district, and then sent an envoy to open negotiations with the Ladakhies. He offered to go back, if a sum of ₹ 15,000 was paid to him promptly. That was exactly what the Ladakhi generals wished to hear, and a messanger on horse back was at once sent with a letter to king Tsepal Tundup Namgyal. The king as well as the council of noblemen, was pleased with the offer and the sum would have been paid at once if the queen, as the chronicles tell, had not interfered, and prohibited the payment of the sum, which, in her eyes, was thrown away. Thus, the messenger when he arrived back in the Ladakhi camp, brought nothing but a letter in which the two generals received orders to bring Zorawar's head and hands to Leh, otherwise they would lose their own heads.

When the Dogra envoys returned to the Ladakhi camp, to receive ₹ 15,000 as per the promise, they were, as Basti Ram tells, treacherously seized and thrown from the Darkyed Bridge into the stream. Not only that, but Kalon Bangkapa, by a circuitous route, attacked the Dogras in the rear, made some prisoners, who were at once bound and thrown into the river, and compelled the Dogras to go back to Langkartse near Kartse. Now would have been the time for powerful attacks on the Dogras instead the foolish Ladakhies left the enemy unmolested for about four months.

During his time they seem to have tried to increase their army by further mobilization. The Ladakhi Empire never had a standing army. Since the introduction of the fire-arm, which had taken place during the reign of Singgay Namgyal, under whom fire-arm are mentioned for the first time, every household was furnished with a matchlock. This old weapon and certain supply of gunpowder had to be kept in readiness for time of war. When the call to arm was sent round the country, one man with the matchlock had to come from every house, carrying on his back provision to last him for a whole month and blanket for the night. This load was so heavy, Artillery there was none. Cavalry it would have been easy to rise, but it was not of much use in the mountainous country. The whole army may have amounted to 15,000 men.

Now that the winter was almost over, the Ladakhies decided in a long consultant to make use of the heavy snowfall, to which the Dogras certainly were not accustomed, as they thought, and to attack them at Langkartse. If there was anything that impeded the Dogras, it was not the heavy snow of the late spring but the extreme cold of mid winter, which deprived them of the use of their fingers and thus also of their superior arms. When the Ladakhi army arrived before Langkartse nobody knew what he has to do, as there was no agreement between the leaders. The Dogras watched the endless consultation, which apparently led to no result, and saw the whole army after all settling down to prepare the evening meal. The Dogras knew by this time that they had nothing to fear from this sort of an enemy. They attacked the Ladakhies, and, as these did not receive any clear orders from their officers, they hurried away from their teapots and fled. During their flight, however, they made use of their arms, and the Dogras lost, according to their own statement, three leaders and twenty men killed, and about 60 persons wounded. Similarly, a party of 400 fleeing Ladakhies broke through a snow bridge over the river and were drowned. Two hundred, as the Dogras say, were made prisoners, among them Mourup Stanzin, the general without any initiative.

The Ladakhi army retreated as far as Mulbe and the Dogras moved down to Pashkyum for the second time. When the Ladakhies heard of this movement, they retired still further towards Leh. Thus both armies were moving in the same direction, the Ladakhies being generally two days in front of the Dogras. Those Purig Chiefs who had been kept in prison by Tsepal some time before, served as guides to the Dogras. Why the Ladakhies did not break down all the bridges during their retreat is difficult to understand.

When the Dogras arrived at Kharbu, the people of Lamayuru felt much fear, and, to save their property, they sent a pony and some money as a present to Zorawar, who was well pleased, and sent a soldier to Lamayuru as a safeguard. When the Dogra army arrived at that place the people of Tia and Tingmogang became frightened. They sent two horses with some money, and also received a safeguard. When the Dogras had got as far as Nyurla they were met by representatives from the villages of Saspola, Alchi, Nemo and Likir, who all brought presents and did homage to Zorawar Singh, and he promised to protect them.

At Basgo, the first meeting of Zorawar with king Tsepal Tundup Namgyal took place, and it appears as if the peace negotiation had been practically finished at Basgo and that Zorawar went up to Leh only, as he said "to see the capital". When the Wazir came to Leh he had only a very small detachment of soldiers with him as a guard; but he had given secret orders that more soldiers, always in twos, should come up after him; and shortly a considered number were assembled in Leh. But Basti Ram gives a different explanation of practically the whole Dogra army being at Leh. He tells that Zorawar made present of 100 rupees in a bag to the crown prince, Chhogsprul, who was about 17 years old, which he swung round the young man's head. The young prince mistook this act of goodwill for an attack, and drew his swords. Then also the by-standing Dogras drew their swords. King Tundup Namgyal was frightened and bowed down on his knees hand folded and requested Zorawar, not to take the action of the youngsters as seriously, and hurriedly removed the crown prince from the scene. Consequently, the next morning, all the Dogra army reached at Leh.

The second part of the peace negotiation took place in the Karzoo Bagh, where Zorawar had his tent. Zorawar's first act was to restore the whole kingdom to Tsepal Tundup Namgyal, which the later accepted with much pleasure. However, the kingdom was henceforth to be considered a vassal state of the

Dogra kingdom of Jammu. King Tundup Namgyal was asked to pay an annual tribute of ₹ 20,000. Besides, he was ordered to pay on the spot ₹ 50,000 towards the expenses of the war. As so much money could not possibly be procured in Leh, it was arranged that only ₹ 37,000 were to be paid at once, in cash and jewels, ₹ 6000 after one month, and ₹ 7000 after four months.

After a stay of four months, Zorawar left Leh, and marched back to Lamayuru. The war would perhaps have been at an end now. But at the instigation of Mihan Singh, the Sikh Governor of Kashmir, the Ladakhies revolted again and again against their powerful masters. The first Ladakhi who listened to the promises of Mihan Singh was the chief of Sod. His castle had been bombarded. When Zorawar was in Leh, the chief of Sod marched against the Dogra fort at Suru, captured it, and put the small garrison to death. Zorawar heard about this event at Lamayuru. He marched at once to Suru, where he surprised the Ladakhies and seized thirteen, who were hanged. However his thirst for revenge was not yet quenched, he declared a reward of rupees fifty per head, who help to trace for any others of the chief of Sod's force. The peasants of Suru-Kartsey, who were anxious to get the reward of rupees fifty, soon accused 200 men of having partaken in this chief's insurrection. They were all beheaded without trial.

Then Wazir Zorawar Singh marched towards Zangskar and reached there in 10 days. The king of Zangskar promised to pay a tax of 3½ rupees for each house. After doing all this arrangement he was intending to go to Jammu, to tell the story of his successes to his master Maharaja Gulab Singh, but he received a secret letter from Munshi Daya Ram regarding the negative attitude of the Ladakhies.

During the winter of 1835-36, King Tsepal Tundup Namgyal listened to the suggestions of Mihan Singh, the Governor of Kashmir, and began to organise a revolution against the Dogra rule. He closed the roads to the trade, and imprisoned and tortured the Dogra representative, Munshi Daya Ram, who was stationed at Leh. At that time Zorawar was campaigning in Zangskar, when he obtained the submission of the country. Upon hearing of the revolt, Wazir marched from Padum, the capital of Zangskar and via Kharnak and Sang, he along with his army reached at Miroo on the 10th day. When the Ladakhies, beyond their expectation, came to know about this event, became very anxious. Raja Tundup Namgyal at that time was at village Shay, celebrating the "Shubla" (Harvest festival) along with the members of the royal family. Out of fear, he along with his courtiers and nobles reached at Chushot to greet the Wazir. In the meantime Chhogsphurul, who was the instigator of these crises, left Shay along with his two queens Sonam Palkit and Zahra Khatoon via Gyamtsa to Hunder Dok. His 1st queen Skalzang Dolma was pregnant, so she stayed at the royal palace of Shay. The mother queen ran away towards Tangtsey. Chhogsphurul reached at Tangtsey, via Nubra. Since Sonam Palkit was pregnant, hence she stayed at Tangtsey. Chhogsphurul, his mother and one of the queens Zahra Khatoon went to Anlay, where from they marched to Spiti. It is said, that from Spiti, Chhogsphurul went to Shimla, and both the mother and son complained before the Nawab Governor General Bahadur Hind, against the Maharaja Jammu for capturing his country, and requested for the help. He replied that the king of Lahore is a friend of British Government. We can't provide help against him, the time will come, and that Ladakh will also be a part of British Government. At that time, we will return your country to you. At the moment, wait and see. You will be provided with all facilities. But because of unfavourable acclimatization, Chhogsphurul died very soon. Later his mother also died. When Zahra Khatoon was alone, she returned back to Ladakh along with the ashes of her husband. Here at Matho, Queen Sonam Palkit has possessed 50 per cent of the estate. The rest 50 per cent was given to her. She occupied the estate for a long time. Later she married and finally migrated to Pashkyum and died there.

When Raja Tundup Namgyal reached before the Wazir, he humbly bowed hand folded before Zorawar and expressed his sorrow for what had happened. The Wazir said: "you failed to fulfill the promise. Although we conquered your country with only 10,000 men, we did not place a single man of our own over your country; and never interfered in your sovereignty; and this is the way you show your gratitude!" The Raja was much ashamed, and requested, that I would be truly faithful and obedient in future. The next day, the Dogra army accompanied by the Raja reached at Leh, where the balance of ₹ 13,000 for the expenses of the war was demanded, and the additional expenses of the second expedition was also demanded. Raja did not possess any cash now. It was paid by taking the property of the royal families. But there were the additional expenses of the new war and to meet them Steward Gonbo offered all sort of things, like the utensils of gold and silver, tea and wool, etc., which were accepted by the Wazir, as nothing better could be got out of the country. After the crises, the Wazir had to arrange matters on a new principle. Tundup Namgyal could not be trusted with the government any longer; he was deposed and the village of Stok was granted as estate for his personal maintenance, and the Stok palace for his residence. Under these circumstances, the Namgyal kingdom of Ladakh was ended in 1834 AD. Then arose the question, who will take the place of Tundup Namgyal as Raja. There was no person in the royal family. Chhogsphurul was the rightful successor to the throne, but he fled away. His elder son was just few days old at that time. Leh Lonpo Mourup Stanzin was a relative of the deposed Raja, and before becoming the prisoner of war, he was a minister and trusted noble of the Raja. He had performed good services to the Dogras during the first expedition. As a prisoner, he was ill treated by the deposed Raja. Wazir nominated him to rule over Ladakh, and Bazgo Kalon Tsewang Stobdan was appointed his prime minister. Eighteen thousand rupees was fixed as annual tribute. He got constructed a fort at Skara on the bank of Nalah Sangto, and 300 soldiers were deployed there under the command of Dalil Singh Thanedar. Then he went to Jammu, taking along with him Mourup Stanzin's son and several other people as hostages.

When the plot of revolt was hatched in Ladakh, the idea was also transmitted to Purig. The people of Purig were assured that a huge army from Lhasa is moving towards Ladakh for military assistance. It will be difficult for the Wazir to counter them. The good hearted rulers and nobles of Purig never waited, to reach the Tibetan army in Ladakh; instead they revolted against the Dogras, as soon as the Wazir along with the Dogra army departed from Suru towards Zangskar. The Raja of Sod recaptured the fort of Pasri-Khar, and the Dogra soldiers posted there were assassinated. Beside, Choki Chhubar Khan was besieged. The people of Suru-Kartse also got killed the Dogra soldiers and besieged the fort. Wazir came to know about these events at Lama-Yuru. He hurriedly arrived at Pashkyum. The estates and administrative powers of all the Rajas of Purig were ceased. Thereby, Rahim Khan Raja Tikche, Azam Khan Raja Wakha, Kalon Mulbe, Mohammad Ali Khan Raja Pashkyum, Salam Khan Raja Sod and Chhagdor Namgyal Raja Tambis were deposed, and Rahim Khan brother of Mohammad Ali Khan was appointed as Kalon of the whole region from Fotola to Daras and Suru. This Rahim Khan performed his best services, during the 1st Ladakh expedition of Wazir and not participated in the revolt later. For this very reason he was honored. After making the administrative arrangements up to Suru, Wazir went back to Jammu via Zangskar and Padar. In the meantime, Padar was already conquered by Wazir Lakhpat. On the way, he made the suitable arrangement of Padar and reached Jammu.

On his arrival at Jammu, Raja Gulab Singh gave a good respect and encouraged him. Deputed his "Dewan" (Prime Minister) to receive him. When he arrived in the court, he was hugged and honored. He ordered that Wazir should be treated like the members of the royal family and the royal salute "Jai Deva" should be used for him. It is true, that because of his victorious services, he was due for such honors. Wazir remained in Jammu for five years and later he again came to Ladakh, which is revealed in the next chapter.

Wazir Zorawar Singh's Expedition No. 3: Annexation of Ladakh and Purig, and Conquest of Baltistan

After the return of Wazir Zorawar Singh from Ladakh, Raja Mourup Stanzin did well for sometime, later he got indulged in luxurious activities. He got married to the princess of Pashkyum, and got constructed a beautiful palace at Murtse to accommodate her. There, he did the arrangement for polo and other entertainments. Thereby he took much interest in his new queen, and song and dance and paid less attention towards the administration of the country. Consequently, the power came in the hands of his ministers, like Kalon Tsewang Stobdan, Pangkhapa and Gyapacho Tsewang and they misruled the country. In the meantime, Col. Man Singh, who was the Subedar of Kashmir deputed by the Lahore government, plotted against the Dogras in connivance with the prominent people of Purig. He deputed one of his employees Fateh Singh Jogi, along with some other persons to Kargil, and motivated the people of Purig to revolt against the Dogras. Kalon Rahim Khan easily became the prey of the Sikhs, he revolted against the Dogras with the hope that the Sikh promised to afford all sort of military assistance to him. He took Raja Mourup Stanzin and some of his Ministers into confidence and asked them to request the government of Lhasa for military assistance. He managed the assistance from Skardo too. In short, he did the efforts to mobilize all the regions of Purig and Ladakh to revolt against the Dogras and get the assistance from Kashmir, Lhasa and Baltistan. In Purig the revolt took the practical shape, as Nidhan Singh Kardar of Drass and Kargil and some Dogra soldiers were assassinated at Karket. Beside the payment of tribute and taxes from Purig and Ladakh were ceased. In Ladakh the Dogra Thanedar appointed by the Wazir was humiliated. When Wazir Zorawar Singh came to know in Jammu about the new circumstances, he prepared himself for the 3rd expedition in the summer of 1896 Bikrami according to the 1839 AD. There was a chaos and crisis in Padar also, since the people of Chamba killed and imprisoned the Dogra soldiers and recaptured Padar. Hence Wazir marched towards Ladakh, along with 5000 Dogra soldiers. As soon as he reached Kishtawar, he went to Padar. He plundered the area and recaptured Chhatargarh and renamed it as Gulabgarh. He built a fort and deployed Dogra soldiers there. Later he came back to Kishtawar and via Darun and Suru went to Ladakh.

Mohammad Shah the son of Raja Ahmad Shah of Skardo came to the Wazir, during his first expedition, probably he was in Zangskar and complained that his father declined him as successor and made Mohammad Ali Khan, the son of the second wife as crown prince and mentally tortured him. Since, as per the local tradition, it was the right of the elder son to succeed. Hence, he requested for military assistance. At that time Wazir was busy in Ladakh. So he didn't want to indulge himself in other problems. Moreover he didn't want to miss the chance of capturing Baltistan. He assured Mohammad Shah, that "you have come forward to help the Jammu kingdom; hence "you will be provided full support." He made the arrangement of his accommodation at Suru. He stayed for one or two years in Suru and then he was sent to Ladakh, where he stayed with ease. But later when Raja Mourup Stanzin and his ministers were fed up with the Jammu kingdom, they revolted against the Dogras, and wanted to make friendship with Ahmad Shah to grind their own axe. Instead of supporting Mohammad Shah, they sent a message to Ahmad Shah to depute his men to arrest the fugitive son. Ahmad Shah did the same he got arrested his fugitive son from Ladakh and imprisoned in Skardo, where he was tortured. When Wazir Zorawar Singh came to know about this event, he made the determination to teach a lesson to all these mischiefs. First of all he wrote a letter to Raja Ahmad Shah, revealing that his son came for the help of Jammu government and interfered and invaded Ladakh. "If you fail to release and send him back immediately to our camp, the Dogra soldiers will forcibly enter your capital and release him from your prison." But Raja Ahmad Shah didn't respond to it.

On arriving Suru, Wazir decided to precede Ladakh via Zangskar. He had to wait few days in Suru and Zangskar for a favourable climate. When the Ladakhies came to know that the Wazir has reached Zangskar with the intention to come to Leh. The plans of the mischievous failed. Leaving the idea of revolt aside, they began to think for self defense. Out of fear, Raja Mourup Stanzin along with a group of people marched towards Zangskar and Spiti. He was of the opinion that if he could have a compromise with the Wazir, then he will attend the Wazir's camp and will express that he has come to receive him here otherwise if he found the situation unfavourable then he would fled to Spiti. Really, the situation was unfavourable, so instead of proceeding to Zangskar, he fled to Spiti. But because of his bad luck, Wazir came to know this well in time, he was followed by the Dogras and before crossing the border of Spiti he was overpowered. When, he found no chance of fleeing, he made the last struggle before surrender and some people were killed from both sides. Finally he was arrested at Taboo. Then he was locked up in Leh prison along with his companions. In the summer of 1897 Bikrami, according to 1840 AD, Wazir entered Ladakh for the 3rd time and punished all those people who participated in the disturbance. Mourup Stanzin was dethroned and imprisoned in Leh fort, his property was ceased to pay the dues of tribute. Similarly, fines were imposed to Kalon Bazgo and Gyapacho, etc.

Now the time had come to annex Ladakh properly with the Jammu kingdom. Hence, he appointed Mian Magna as Thanedar and made him the administrator of the country. Onpo Rigzin, who is later known as Gobind Ram was appointed as Kalon for his assistance. Raja Tundup Namgyal was reinstated as nominal king, so as to keep continue the royal linage and the royal palaces and the seat of the Raja was handed over to him. As soon as he did the arrangements properly in Ladakh, he left for Kargil and Skardo. In the meantime, the Rajas of Kargil made efforts to get the military assistance from Kashmir but neither did they receive help from Kashmir nor from Ladakh. So all Kargilies became silent and Kalon Rahim Khan fled to Skardo.

Annexation of Purig and Conquest of Baltistan

During the short period the Ladakhies proved that they are not the men to rest in peace under the Jammu government. Therefore Zorawar hatched the plan to exploit the Ladakhies against the Baltis so as to keep Ladakh free from any form of revolt against the Dogra rulers. Therefore Zorawar decided to do an expedition against Baltistan, pretending to come for the rescue of Mohammad Shah son of Raja Skardo. There is a contradictory statement about the number of soldiers, but it is considered that it was not more than seven or eight thousand, including the porters and warriors. The old Ladakhi General Kalon Pankhapa was appointed as the Commander, and the old Raja Tundup Namgyal was also deployed with him. In short Wazir marched from Ladakh to Skardo including the Ladakhi soldiers, along with his own army when they reached at Hanu, Wazir kept the Ladakhi army under the Dogra commanders Mohiuddin Shah and Shahji, and deputed them via Hanula, Chhorbat and Khapulo. And he himself went to Garkono, along with the Dogra army. During those days the route from Leh to Skardo was via Garkono, Morol, and Kharmang. The present Olding route was not in existence at that time. At Garkono Wazir crossed the Indus River and reached at Pasri-Khar Sot. Here he punished the people of Purig, who revolted against the Dogras. He annexed all the regions of Purig and appointed Dogra Thanedars at Kargil, Daras and Suru. He also deployed a required number of soldiers with them. After making the administrative arrangements of Purig, Wazir mobilized army and porters from the region. Then Wazir crossed the mountains from Pasri-Khar and got down at Chey Chey-Thang and was ready to move towards Skardo. When the news of Wazir's invasion came to Skardo, Raja Ahmad Shah deputed his army at Morol and Chhorbat, to stop the way of the enemy. He deployed the soldiers from Keres and Khapulo at Chhorbat under the command of Yostrang Karim. The soldiers from the village of Rongdo to Kharmang were placed under the command of two brothers Botopa Wazir Ghulam Hassan and Wazir Ghulam Hussain and deployed at Morol, at the border of Baltistan to counter Wazir Zorawar Singh. It is difficult to reveal the correct number of the soldiers, but it is expected that it was about twenty thousand, including the warriors and the porters. The Balti army stationed themselves near Morol on a high plateau, before Wazir Zorawar reached at Chey Chey-Thang. The route of Chey Chey-Thang is just adjacent to this plateau after crossing the Indus on its right side, as its left side is closed because of the merger of Suru River. So the Balti army stationed at such a place where no other passage is possible. This field is now known as "Thamo Khoni Thang", i.e. battle field. On the top of this field the Balti army of Skardo built Morchas for ambush, and they stopped the route which leads to the Wangko pass, which made the advancement of Zorawar impossible. Zorawar had to face two problems; first the river and second the enemy. Though it was the winter season but the whole river was not frozen, so as to cross the river on the surface of ice. Moreover, it was too difficult to construct a bridge under the threat of bullet from the enemy. Because of these problems Wazir had to stay at Chey Chey-Thang for two weeks, and had to face the shortage of ration and other provisions. It was awfully cold, hence the army was discouraged. But because of the courageous and good strategy of Wazir, he was able to overcome all these problems. One night Wazir deputed Mehta Basti Ram along with some soldiers to look for a possible way to cross the river. But the water of the river was not frozen at any place. In the meantime, the Dard of Village Garkono suggested that the part of the river which has not frozen can be made frozen to ice by adopting a local method and it would be possible to cross the river through the artificial ice. Therefore in front of Nalah Chethang, just below the Wangko pass where Wazir Ghulam Hussain was stationed along with his army to stop the advancement of Wazir, the water was frozen from both sides of the bank of river Indus and a very small portion of the river was open. They joined both the ends with some logs. It is said that Raja Ali Sher Khan of Kartak Shah made the correspondence secretly with the Wazir at Chey Chey-Thang. Though he had deputed his soldiers with the Balti army to counter Wazir at Thamo Khoni Thang and secretly he helped Wazir, so whoever may win the battle, he would not be in loss, and he also contributed in preparing the frozen artificial bridge. The time and the venue of the bridge was decided in collaboration between the people from Chey Chey-Thang and the people of Raja Ali Sher Khan from Morol. The pieces of ice which floats in the river during the winters got blocked and froze on the logs. The pieces of ice were joined together with one another and due to awfully cold of the winter; it became a sheet of ice, over the open space within some hours. Now it was possible to pass on over the frozen surface of the river. Wazir and his soldiers became very happy on this success. Before dawn, a group of Dogra soldiers under the command of Mehta Basti Ram passed through the newly created ice bridge and attacked the Balti soldiers of Wazir Ghulam Hussain. It is said that the creation of the bridge and crossing the river was made with a good strategy that the Balti soldiers could not know about it, unless Mehta Basti Ram reached at Wangko pass. At that time, the Balties were sleeping, when suddenly the Dogra soldiers appeared, and Wazir Ghulam Hussain himself was busy in ablution. He hurriedly arranged the army. It was a sudden attack by the Dogras and the bunkers became useless for the Balties. They fought hand to hand bravely and almost killed all the Dogra soldiers. Wazir was watching the scene from Chey Chey-Thang. He deputed reinforcement; Wazir Ghulam Hussain was killed in this battle. Because of his death and arrival of reinforcement, the Balties were discouraged and fled away and joined the soldiers of "Thamo Khon". Now the Dogras captured the Wangko pass, and they were free to cross the river without any hindrance. Wazir Zorawar Singh attacked the Balti soldiers of "Thamo Khon" along with all his soldiers. Since the Balties were on the top inside the "Morchas", they fired heavily on the Dogras, but Wazir Zorawar Singh deployed a group of Dogra soldiers on the top of the hill, through a narrow route. They destroyed the posts of the Balties and they were compelled to come out of their bunkers. They could not counter the Dogras in hand to hand fight. Finally, when many Balties got killed in the battle they fled away and the Dogras captured the battle field.

The exact number of casualty couldn't be ascertained but it is believed that almost one thousand Balties got killed in this battle including Commander Wazir Ghulam Hussain and many prominent Balti officers. Wazir Ghulam Hussain and Wazir Sultan Beg were fleeing from the battlefield of Rongdo but before arriving at Morol they also got killed. The grave of Wazir Ghulam Hussain still exists at Thamo Khon and that of his brother Wazir Hussain at Morol. About Raja Ali Sher Khan, it is believed that his men who were on the side of Balti soldiers were secretly instructed by him not to fight with the

Dogras but to keep themselves away from fighting. Therefore they acted according to this instruction. As Zorawar Singh entered Morol beating the drums of his victory of Thamo Khon and chasing the fleeing army reached Hamza Gund. This event happened around first of Phagun 1896 Bikrami. This battle was a deciding factor in the conquest of Baltistan. Though the Balties fought another war near Hamzagon but it was meek and ineffective.

Just after Morol the route passes through "Sanjak", which means soft sand dune, this dune is formed over a period of time, when the river gets stagnant at a plain on its course and takes the shape of a big lake, all the sands carried off by the river gets deposited here thus forming this dune. This dune is formed right from below Skardo, where the river got blocked because of the falling of a huge mountain, till Ladakh. The route again goes down to the bank of river. After this route passes through a tough terrain on which a footbridge is being built with wooden logs. This was destroyed by the Baltis. And they built their post in the Nullah right after this bridge and stayed there. The next day when Zorawar reached there he found that the route was closed due to the broken bridge. Visibly it was a huge bottleneck for him but after the victory of Thamo Khon the situation for him had changed and the inhabitants of Kharmang region were happily ready to serve the Wazir. People of Hamzagon suggested the Wazir to abandon the usual route and should cross over the hill from the area where the bridge is broken. Therefore the Wazir along with his army marched on top of the hill and descended right there where Baltis had set up their bunkers. Because of the fact that the Wazir came from the top of the hill, the Baltis failed to counter him and ran away. Thereafter, he had to face no obstruction in the way, till he reached Skardo. During the 1st Ladakh expedition of Wazir Zorawar Singh, relation developed between him and Raja Ali Sher Khan, which has already been mentioned. After returning from Ladakh, he again became the ruler like that of the past, but due to the invasion of Raja Ahmad Shah, he could not recover the humiliation and loss of property. To take the revenge, he never minded to sacrifice his own freedom. Probably, he wouldn't have done this, but there was no chance of compromise with Ahmad Shah. Nor the entire force of Baltistan had the strength to stop the invasion of Zorawar Singh. He made no mistake and took the advantage of the situation, as far as possible. He deputed his soldiers along with Balti army under the command of Trangfa Abdul Ali to fight against Wazir Zorawar Singh, and was in the good book of Raja Ahmad Shah. On the other hand, he made secret correspondence with Wazir Zorawar Singh at Chey Chey-Thang and helped him secretly in the battle field to cross the river, and was able to win the confidence of Wazir Zorawar Singh. Hashmatullah says "I came to know in Skardo, that with the consultation of Wazir Zorawar Singh, the inhabitants of Kharmang were wearing a distinguished badge, and it had been decided that the Dogras would not harm the inhabitants with such batches." Therefore, neither these people attacked the Dogras nor the Dogras harassed them. Because of this strategy the soldiers of Kharmang came out of the battle field without any injury or loss. Besides, Raja Ali Sher Khan himself came at Hamza Gund to greet the Wazir and assured to extend all sort of cooperation to him. In recognition to his services the Wazir assured them that he would not interfere in the affairs of Kartak Shah. This promise is almost still continuing. Raja Ali Sher Khan reached at Kharmang along with Wazir Zorawar Singh and performed properly. Raja Ali Sher Khan, Raja Ahmad Khan Tolti along with Wazir Parkuta came to see Zorawar to express their loyalty. After four days of his departure from Kharmang, Wazir reached at Gol. The Ladakhi army who had proceeded from Hanu, via Chhorbat and Khapulo also reached at Gol and joined the Wazir's army. The travel via Hanula was also full of difficulties because of heavy snowfall and awful cold. But the Ladakhies are habitual of it. No other race of the world could show such courage. All the soldiers crossed the Hanula successfully. Though Raja Ahmad Shah had made full preparation to stop the army from crossing, his most confident person Yustrong Karim along with the soldiers of Keres, Khapolu and a few from Skardo were ready to fight. But the luck favoured Wazir Zorawar Singh and the nature helped him. Though Raja Mehdi Ali Khan of Khapulo had been imprisoned by Raja Ahmad Shah but the real heir of the throne Raja Doulat Ali Khan was at Nubra. When Wazir Zorawar Singh conquered Ladakh, the mode of administration changed. On the one hand, he deputed his cousin brother Haider Khan to mobilize the people of Khapulo in his favour; on the other hand, he did efforts to develop the relation with Wazir Zorawar Singh. When Wazir's army marched towards Hanu, in the meantime, Doulat Ali Khan made the strategy and mobilized the people, through Haider Khan. When the Ladakhi army arrived near Poyon, Raja Doulat Ali Khan also marched from Nubra towards Poyon. Yustrong Karim stationed all the soldiers on a terrain between Kostang and Poyon, to counter the Wazir's army. When the Dogra army under the command of Mohiuddin Shah reached at Poyon, they stationed in the fort. In the meantime, Raja Doulat Ali Khan left Siksa and met the Dogra officers at Poyon. His confident man Haider Khan deceived Yustrong Karim, by telling that he knew about the topography of the area very well, and that he would go forward along with the half army and after crossing the river. Thus, it would be very difficult for the Wazir's army to counter the Baltis from both sides and they would be easily captured. Yustrong Karim could not understand this plot hatched by Haider Khan. He divided his army in two groups and Haider along with a huge army of Khapulo region arrived at Poyon fort. And after greeting Doulat Ali Khan and Dogra officers he assured them to be loyal and faithful. This changed the whole situation and Doulat Ali Khan, who had been in house arrest for last 13 years, got a ray of hope to be a ruler again. When Yustrong Karim reached at Poyon, he got the message of Haider Khan, that "we are loyal to Raja Doulat Ali Khan and he has accepted the authority of the Dogras, and we do not want to keep any relation with you." Yustrong Karim gunned down the messenger and after doing so, he returned back to Khapulo along with the soldiers of Skardo. The soldiers of Khapulo had been mobilized to counter the Wazir's army, but he joined with Raja Doulat Ali Khan and the Ladakhi army along with the army of Khapulo entered Khapulo. Since all the inhabitants of Khapulo had confidence in Doulat Ali Khan.

Hence, Mehmood Shah Alias Mehdi Ali Khan had to step down as ruler. Raja Doulat Ali Khan captured the fort and once again became the ruler. Yustrong Karim marched from Poyon and positioned at Keres. The Ladakhi army took rest at Khapulo for some days and became the guest of Raja Doulat Ali Khan and moved forward. Raja Doulat Ali Khan performed his best services to the Dogras. Yustrong Karim positioned at Keres and fought with the Ladakhi army for two days but he came to know about the arrival of Wazir at Parkuta, he left the fort silently, crossed the river and accompanied the Ladakhi army. They crossed the river and attended before Wazir Zorawar Singh and assured him their full support and loyalty. In short Wazir Zorawar Singh entered Skardo without any resistance from Ladakhi and Dogra joint army. All the rulers of the area where from his army passed were with him, and the Wazir of Doghonipa Bono Raja Mohammad Shah, who was at Ladakh during his arrest also accompanied him along with his supporters.

When the Wazir reached Skardo, he found Raja Ahmad Shah fortified in the Kharpochhey fort. On the north of Skardo town, there is a high mountain on the bank of Indus River. The mountain is formed in such a way, that nobody could climb the mountain from all sides. But on the east, there is a small plateau, where the fort had been built. The wall of the fort had been built with big boulders. There were two passages to the fort, one in the east for communication and second towards north for domestic use and fetching water from the spring or river. A zigzag route on the rock leads to the fort for the common use and the entire passage was under the visible range of the fort. Except these there was no other route to reach the fort. The domestic route towards north leads to the spring and river was covered and could not be seen from outside. Beside it was not possible to reach at this route from the Skardo town or river. Above the fort on the top of the rock, is a small plateau. It has two routes to reach there. One is from inside the fort and another from the west, where the New Rangga village is situated. A tower was erected there to stop the route for enemy. This tower had been built at such a place wherefrom few people can create hindrance to proceed further, and there is no other route to climb the rock except it. Moreover the fort cannot be captured except from the said plateau. This fort was considered unbeatable in those days. Wazir surrounded the fort and it was very limited because both the routes of communication from east and west got blocked. Though the attack on the fort was continued but it was useless. Within fifteen days, they were not able to capture and besiege; hence efforts were made to act according to a new strategy, through Raja Ali Sher Khan. A Muslim officer Syed Mohiuddin Shah of Zorawar's army also joined Raja Ali Sher Khan in the plan. It is said that Raja Ali Sher Khan took the vow before Raja Ahmad Shah that nothing would happen with him. Raja Ahmad Shah came out of the fort, to meet Wazir with confidence but was arrested. Thus, Wazir captured Skardo deceptively without any resistance. Wazir Zorawar Singh had the victory at the battle field of Thamo Khon, which made the conquest of Little Tibet, i.e. Baltistan very easy. Now the vassal kings of Kartak Shah, Tolti, Khapolu, and Keres, etc. became obedient to the Wazir and were with him and the Baltis were fully discouraged after the conquest of Kharpochhey, i.e. Skardo. Therefore, Raja Haider Khan of Shigar and prominent personalities of Chhorbat also came to the Wazir to express their obedience and loyalty. But Raja Ali Khan of Rongdo and Raja Jabbar Khan of Astore did not come to the Wazir. However before attending them Wazir thought it important to reduce the influence of deposed Raja Ahmad Shah and strengthen the government of his son Mohammad Shah. Therefore Wazir Hussain Golwala and other courtiers of Raja Ahmad Shah were imprisoned and took all the movable properties of the deposed Raja as tribute and deposited in the government treasury, the total amount was approximately two lac rupees, consisting of cash and other valuable articles like gold, silver and ornaments, etc. Thus after taking Ahmad Shah in confidence and consolidating his rule, he invaded Rongyul, i.e. Rongdo. Wazir deputed one thousand Dogra soldiers under the command of Mirza Rasool Beg and Mohammad Khan via Kachura, and the Balti soldiers under the command of Dogra officers and Raja of Kharmang via Baghardo Chhary. When the Dogra soldiers reached at the fort of Rongdo, i.e. Mehendi, they found that Raja Ali Khan had fled away, leaving his fort and country. Hence, the fort was captured without any interruption. Later they received fifteen thousand rupees as war penalty and reinstated him as ruler of Rongdo. In the meantime, Kalon Rahim Khan had fled from Pashkyum to Skardo. Later when he came to know about Wazir's Skardo invasion, he left for Rongdo, wherefrom he was trying to proceed towards Gilgit, but he was arrested and brought before the Wazir. This man had been the instigator of revolt in the Purig area. Wazir inquired him about his misdeeds in the presence of the nobles of Ladakh and Baltistan, and finally he had been severely punished. Wazir ordered the executioner to cut off the limbs of the body and to dip the stump at once into the boiling oil, and then the executioner had also to cut off his nose, ears, and tongue to be left in the field to die. Similarly, other persons of Purig who were involved in the revolt were severely punished. Rahim Khan could not save his life and while crying, he died after three days. His family members went back to Kargil, it is believed his offsprings are still there.

After the conquest of Rongdo, Wazir deputed Mohiuddin Shah to invade Astore, along with five hundred Dogra soldiers and a good number of local soldiers. This army moved via Shakarthang. On knowing about the invasion Raja Jabbar Khan of Astore became fortified. Mohiuddin Shah besieged the fort and the battle continued for 20 days. There was no permanent arrangement of water. To bring water the external passage was blocked by the Dogras. Jabbar Khan was compelled to come out of the fort. Then he was arrested by Mohiuddin Shah. After the conquest of Astore, Mohiuddin Shah came to the Wazir along with Jabbar Khan. Wazir kept Jabbar Khan as a prisoner for a short period because the Sikh ruler of Kashmir raised objection, that Astore is a territory of Sikh regime and Zorawar Singh has no right to interfere in their territories. Hence, Jabbar Khan was released who went out from Skardo. Therefore, Zorawar Singh could not have a political gain from this invasion. However, after few years, the Sikh ruler invaded Gilgit and captured Astore too. Finally,

Astore and Gilgit came under the Dogra Ruler of Jammu including Kashmir and the desire of Zorawar Singh was fulfilled.

In the beginning Zorawar Singh stayed in the Matam Sara of Kharidong and the soldiers in the camps. In the meantime, he got constructed government quarters known as Ranbir garh and a temporary fort on a top in the north of Khanqah Syed Mehmood. Later, he stayed there along with the Dogra army. He got built a very strong fort on the bank of Nallah Satpar on the top of a hill. One portion of the fort had been completed under his supervision. He deployed about one hundred Dogra soldiers there, under the command of Bhagwan Singh Kishtawari, who had been appointed as Thanedar and Bhupat and Mukhtar Khan as his Munshi. When Wazir consolidated the administration of Baltistan, he left for Leh via Khapolu in the summer of 1797 Bikrami according to 1840 AD. Along with the Dogra and Ladakhi army, the deposed Raja Ahmad Shah, his Wazirs and nobles, and some people of Shigar, were in the prison.

Since the Wazir decided to invade Lhasa, during his stay in Baltistan, therefore, he mobilized the soldiers of Baltistan and kept them under the command of the representatives of their concerned Rajas. At Khapolu Raja Ali Sher Khan also joined along with the soldiers of Kharmang and Tolti and deployed his brother Haider Khan and Ghulam Ali in the service of Wazir. The Raja Khapulo, Doulat Ali Khan agreed to proceed along with the Wazir. In the meantime, the epidemic disease smallpox spread in Khapulo, because of that many soldiers had died. However, Raja Tundup Namgyal had seen many revolutions in his life; he had suffered more than his constitution could stand. Moreover, the long journey had been unbearable for him. Among the nobles first of all Pangkhapa died with smallpox and then Raja Tundup Namgyal met with the same fate, and within a few days he died. His steward Acho Gonbo was very faithful. Knowing the fact that smallpox is an epidemic disease, he, according to the local tradition, fastened the legs and arms jointly and put the body in a big pot, i.e. "Deeg" and put salt and other local medicines, so as to protect the body from decomposing and stinking. Then the corpse was carried to Stok palace, via Nubra, through his servants, where after performing the rituals and prayer, the body was cremated.

The Wazir along with the whole army reached Ladakh, via Khapulo, Chhorbat, and Nubra. The first task, which he did in Leh, was the nomination of the successor of Raja Tundup Namgyal. Actually Chhogsphurul was the heir to the throne but he fled to Shimla via Spiti and died there. Before his departure to Spiti, the first queen Skalzang Dolma gave birth to a son. His name was Jigsmet Chhosgi Singgay or in short Jigsmet Namgyal. He was putting up at Shay palace along with his mother. Though the child was a minor, but he was the heir of the throne after Chhogsphurul and Wazir convened him at Leh along with his mother. He made the arrangement to perform the traditional rituals of succession at the royal palace of Leh. A court was arranged in a room of the palace called "Thagchhen Kongma". All the prominent persons and nobles of Ladakh and Baltistan participated in the function. Wazir got Jigsmet Namgyal ascended the throne with great regards and pomp and show. Though, the dignity of the throne was only by name. The Wazir put the turban on the head of Jigsmet Namgyal with his own hand and wore the gown and offered the shield and sword and said that his grandfather had died in the service of the Jammu kingdom. "I feel sorry for that and you are being made the vassal king in his place and placed on the throne. We would be responsible for your convenience and to look after you in future." Later Raja Doulat Ali Khan of Khapulo, who had relation with the old regime, offered shield and sword. Similarly the elites and nobles of Ladakh offered traditional "Khataks" and congratulated him. Now Wazir began to prepare for his Tibet expedition, after performing the rituals. It is not out of place to mention here about Chhogsphurul, who died before his father at Shimla. After Chhogsphurul, the Ladakhi royal family was devided in two clans Stok family and Matho family. The offsprings of his first wife Skalzang Dolma settled at Stok palace, whereas the offsprings of the second wife Sonam Palkit settled at Matho palace and the third wife Zahra Khatoon migrated to her home town Pashkyum. Skalzang Dolma gave birth to Prince Jigsmet Namgyal. He was ascended on the throne as a vassal king, after the death of his grandfather by Wazir Zorawar Singh. At that time, he was a small boy. He was succeded by his son Raja Sonam Namgyal, whose son is Jigsmet Dadul Namgyal. He had two sons. The elder son Raja Kunzang Namgyal served in the Indian army as Lieutenant. He died few decades back and was cremated at Stok with full royal honour. The younger son became a Lama in the Hemis Gonpa. Raja Kunzang Namgyal married with Rani Parvati Devi who was the daughter of Abbay Thakur, a member of the royal family of Lahol Spiti, she is called Shema Diskit Wangmo in Ladakh. Col. Prithi Chand who is considered the saviour of Ladakh during the war of Pakistani infiltrators in Ladakh in 1948-49 is from this very family. Once she came in politics and fought the parliament election winning the seat with good margin and served the people of Ladakh for full five years. Raja Kunzang Namgyal had two sons and two daughters. The elder son prince Jigsmet Wangchuk Namgyal married a lady of Nubra Kalon called Shemchug Spalzes Wangmo and had children. He is looking after the royal estates and running a Leh based family trust namely NIRLAC (Namgyal Institute for Research on Ladakh Art & Culture). His younger brother is Prince Skarma Namgyal, who is looking after the royal properties at Kulu in Himachal Pradesh. The elder sister princes Sarla Angmo has married with a prominent local leader Thufstan Tsewang Lonpo of Shay, who had been Member of Parliament and Chairman & Chief Executive Councillor, LAHDC Leh. Princes Sarla Angmo is presently President Mahila Mandal Leh. The younger sister has married with the son of a noble Buddhist family of Leh called Shangara, whose ancestors in the past used to precede Tibet for Lobchhak trade to pay homage to the Dalai Lama as representative of the King. As far as Matho royal family is concerned, Sonam Palkit, the second wife of Chhogsphurul, gave birth to Phuntsog Stanshong Namgyal, whose son is Tashi Lhawang Namgyal followed by Nangwa Thayas, who is the father of Kushok Bakula. Thus, the Matho royal family has given two great Lamas, viz. Kushok Bakula and Galdan-Thi-Rinpochhe Shash Kushok to the Buddhist community of Ladakh. This is memorable. About the expedition of Baltistan, Hashmatullah writes, "I got a copy of a note written by an eye-witness, which he has narrated in a very beautiful way, and some events have been revealed in detail, which I could not discard. Earlier, while explaining the events I did not include the notes with the reason, that it is bifurcated in parts, its beauty losts." He had written the notes in Hindi, which is translated as under."

"I Ganga Ram Nakashi submit the application in the court of Shri Maharaja Gulab Singh Sahib, that there is no genius person like that of Wazir Zorawar Singh. I shall praise him till my death. He prayed at the temple of Satila Devi and promised, if he wins the battle, he would reconstruct it very strong. Since the Devi came in dream and gave blessings for his triumphs. However keep in mind the regards and respect of Maharaja Gulab Singh and Sochit Singh, and would be successful in every respect." The Wazir promised that he would build a temple of the Devi in Baltistan. He stationed at Chey Chey, and gheraoed the Baltis at Tental Watery. First he deputed the Maliks of Murwa under the command of Imam Malik. Zamindar Zafar Lone got prepared the posts. He had been an old and faithful servant of the Jammu government. He has kept himself and his property for the service of the Jammu region. Mukhtar and Mohammad Khan both are real brothers. They went on the other side, along with the Maliks of Murwa. Both the brothers are very loyal. Maizban Khan and other soldiers were deployed with them along with the goods. It was very difficult because of heavy snow fall. They made the arrangement to cross the river. Rahim Khan was the leader of the Bhotis. He was not in a position to attack the Dogras, but because of fear he went across the river, otherwise he would lose his nose and ears. Mehta Basti Ram was convened by the Wazir, and ordered to cross the river to see the possibilities of placing the logs over the river for preparing ice bridge. The people of Nagsen and Padar were deputed with him. He ordered that the ice bridge should be get ready during the night. A man came to Wazir Zorawar Singh and said that it was difficult to place the logs and prepare the ice bridge there. He asked for two men who knew to swim, so as to cross the river during the night. Therefore Wazir asked Kamanda resident of Johdpur to cross the river with the help of cow skin bag and promised to pay ₹ 50 as reward, if he succeeds. Many other people were deployed with him. Mehta Basti Ram was able to cross the river through the logs.

The first battle with the swords took place at Tatri. Mirza Rasool Beg was a brave and good administrator. He was a Jamadar in the army. He invaded the enemy just after crossing the river. He encouraged the soldiers to climb the hill and asked to be loyal to the regime. Rana Jalim Singh of Arnoda, Samad Khan Jamadar of Pathan soldiers all fought bravely with the enemy. Zorawar's servants Kalu Negi, Sokia Kumhar and Gopi Shah, etc. followed them. These all people climbed the hill from the opposite side of the river. The Balti soldiers surrounded them. About 3000 Balti soldiers were gathered there but the Baltis had to face lot of human losses. Mian Mutssadi of Raina Rama fought with the sword bravely, and many Baltis got killed. Bhupat Mahan Singh of Kastigarh also killed many Balti soldiers. The cook of the Wazir Damodar was so stupid, but he too killed many Baltis like a soldier and enlightened the name of Brahmans. Ten to twenty portars were told to proceed on the other side. They fought with sword at Tatri, two or three persons were killed in this battle. Dhana Sardar was shot in the belly and died. Bhaikam was his brother. The Zamindar of Rajgarh Narban was killed. He was unmarried. Rahim Khan Jamadar was convened and deployed in the battle field. He along with Rana Bhagwan Singh of Badharwah fought bravely with sword and the enemies ran away from the battle field. Rana Dilip Singh of Galhyanwala was a dull person but when he had the sword in the hand, he used it bravely. Mian Mubarik Thanedar Sakta Kishtwar was a young man, he was a very good fighter. Azim Khan Jamadar of Moryan and his brother Saadullah Khan and their army were well prepared with weapon. They fought very bravely during the night along with another army. Mian Mubarik and the two brothers Mahan Singh and Manggal Singh fought courageously. Phinu and Chadta, both were very good fighters. Hundred rupees were given to them as a reward. Wazir Laaba, who was along with the Dachhni soldiers against the soldiers of Skardo confiscated the weapons like guns and swords, etc. at village Katni. Kamon Kotwal and Mukhdam Bhago got the news that ten soldiers were killed and nine injured. The loyal soldiers fought with sword bravely. Wazir Zorawar Singh observed the war on telescope, and found that each soldier had killed at least two enemies. The man on telescope only knows, whether it is true or false. The Balti soldiers with their commanders ran away from the battle field. Many soldiers and zamindars were got killed. Later, the Dogras also attacked on Morol village. Many soldiers of the enemy were got killed.

Raja Ali Sher Khan was conferred with rope of honor. The said Raja invited the Wazir to come at Hamza Gund, so as to have a rest there with ease, since it was the land of Jammu region and safe. The Raja offered a sword and a gun as good will, and Wazir conferred rope of honor to Haider Khan, in whose village he stayed the night; both the Rajas accompanied the wazir. They were given "Kanggan and Kantha", i.e. ornament for the wrist and the pearl-necklace as reward and granted estates. From Hamza Gund the army proceeded for Kharmang. All the soldiers stationed in the village and Wazir stayed in the fort of Raja Ali Sher Khan. All the soldiers went to see the fort. It was lunar eclipse on that day, hence parties were arranged. They marched from Kharmang and stayed at Mayurdo, the next day traveled on a hilly route. There were two different routes for the foot soldiers and riders. It was a very dangerous route that people used to call "Ram Ram". From Mayurdo they reached at Parkuta and from Parkuta arrived at Gol and stayed there. Ali Sher Khan was there to guide them. Some soldiers were deployed to destroy the tower.

When Raja Ahmad Shah of Skardo came to know about the Dogras invasion, he became fortified along with his subjects and nobles. Gradually the army reached at Skardo, and Ahmad Shah became fearful to see the Dogra army. The army stationed at Thurgo, and the tower which is between Thurgo and Skardo, was ambushed. The guards at the tower fled away due to fear.

Ahmad Shah also fled away. Both the armies on foot and riders attacked and burnt his house to ashes. The army besieged the fort. They shot the missiles like Jamburay and Jazail, and fear was created in the mind of the people. The ambush ended after five days. Ahmad Shah was discouraged and came to the Wazir and surrendered. His elder son Mohammad Shah was made the ruler, and Wazir Bono was made his Wazir. The people used to call "Juju" (Instead of salam it is used in Ladakhi language). Ahmad Shah regretted but Mohammad Shah was conferred with rope of honor. Mehta Basti Ram was deployed in the fort who brought out all the valuable things from the fort. All the belongings were got collected. The people of the fort were weeping. Mohiuddin Shah fled away, Wazir Abtara followed him. Though Mehta Basti Ram was an officer but was keeping no authority. The writer Ganga Ram Nakashi has written: "Wazir is an incarnation, an authority and superman. He reinstated the government of Khapolu and Chhorbat to their concerned Rajas, to rule as per their wishes. Ten thousand people along with the women and the children were gathered in the fort. The next day the men and the women were looted (raped). Wazir sahib also came there and Holi was played. The Baltis felt it very much, as hard like bullets. The Rahim Khan of Pashkyum, who was Kalon and collector of the area was arrested by Mohammad Jan, and the Wazir did the justice of Nosherwan with him. He issued order, anyone who kills the cow and bull would be given life punishment. It was ensured, that the subjects are safeguarded. My pen is helpless to admire the rule of Wazir sahib." Ganga Ram Nakashi has not made any exaggeration in writing the notes. "Ahmad Shah showed some haughtiness, so Wazir Zorawar Singh got him arrested and handed him over to the army, who got written an agreement, that he will pay ₹ 10,000, within a month, otherwise he would be got killed. The Ladakhi Raja died in the way because of smallpox. Later Wazir sahib went to Shigar, along with 300 soldiers and stayed there for 5 days. Shigar is so beautiful that one didn't like to return from that place. I can't resist myself from praising Shigar."

Wazir Zorawar Singh's Tibet Expedition: Conquest of Purang and Destruction of Dogra Army

4

As soon as Jigsmet Namgyal ascended the throne and the traditions were fulfilled, Wazir Zorawar Singh prepared for the expedition of Lhasa. At that time he was having more than three thousand Dogra soldiers, and to assist them, he mobilized 4-5 thousand local soldiers from Baltistan, Purig and Ladakh, besides a huge number of porters.

The Balti soldiers were under the command of their concerned rulers. The soldiers of Purig were also distributed under the command of prominent persons of their concerned region. The name of the deposed Raja Mourup Stanzin was proposed to command the Ladakhi army, who was in the prison at that time. But he didn't accept this honor, because of the religious attachment with Lhasa. Therefore his younger brother, Nono Sonam, Ghulam Khan former Raja Chushot and Tsewang Stobdan former Kalon of Bazgo, who had been released from the prison, were made commanders of Ladakhi army. All the local soldiers were distributed under the command of Dogra officers in different platoons. Later, the total army was divided into two groups. The first had been put under the command of Mian Rai Singh and deputed via Rupsho and Anley, and the second was under the command of Wazir himself, and marched via Changla and Tangtse. It happened on May, 1841. Both the army met at Rudok. The Tibetan army was fortified which was not more than three hundred.

Mehta Basti Ram was deployed to conquer the fort, he invaded the fort and after a short battle the commander of the Tibetan army was killed and his army discouraged. On their request a compromise got settled between both the army and the battle was ended. The next day the "Zongspon" Rudok came to the Wazir along with his officers and Lamas and surrendered. Wazir captured the fort and the Tibetan army who were the inhabitants of the neighbouring villages was allowed to proceed to their home. Instead, he deployed his own army in the fort, and Alchi Lonpo Dawa Tundup was kept there to assist the Dogra officer.

There were two routes to proceed to Gar from Rudok: one via Tashigang, along the Indus and the second via Lubra, directly to Gar. Wazir proceeded along with the army via Lubra whereas Mehta Basti Ram along with a small group of army went via Tashigang, to make the arrangements for surrender in case there were any inhabitants so as to ensure no interference of the enemy on the Ladakh route. Here a minor battle took place, and Mehta Basti Ram was able to overcome it easily. He got them surrendered and after getting the promise of loyalty from the Lamas and the public he proceeded towards Gar. At Gar the two armies met again. Here the people surrendered without any interference. There was scarcity of fuel in this area, there was no wood. Though this place was colder than Ladakh, the people did not build houses, instead they lived in tents, made of Yak wool which were warmer than a mud house. In Gar, there was an ordinary house for the Tibetan officers, Wazir got it repaired and made it the store and kept some soldiers to guard it.

After his departure from Gar, Wazir reached at Mansar without any interference and the people surrendered. Hereafter, at a distane the route follows via three streams. All these three streams flow along the Kailash and fall in river Sutluj. It is called "Tokpo Ralsum". The middle stream is called "Shar-Tokpo". Wazir stationed at the bank of this stream, but during the night the Tibetan army stationed at Purang suddenly ambushed Wazir's camp. There was a chaos and crisis among the Wazir's army, but he managed to overcome the situation and attacked the Tibetans. The battle continued for about three to four hours. Many soldiers got killed from both the parties. Mahan Singh's son also got killed in this battle. Finally, the Tibetan army was defeated. Wazir proceeded further, along with the Dogra army and reached "Tsomo-Mapham" called Mansarowar Lake. This is a sacred place for Hindus. Different historians have revealed differently about the length of this lake. Actually it is not so far. A man on foot can take a complete round of the lake within three days. The Kailash Mountain, which is just ahead of the lake, is not so long as considered in old books. A man can have a round of Kailash easily in a day. According to the old text no Raja could have approached Kailash, except Raja Man Data till this time. But it was Wazir Zorawar Singh, who with the blessings of the Jammu kingdom captured Kailash Mansarowar and the surrounding areas and conquered Purang.

After the defeat at Tokpo-Ralsum the Tibetan army fled to Takla-Khar, and consolidated their position. They prepared themselves to counter the enemy. When Wazir marched from Mansarovar Lake, he reached Kartong fort on the Lhasa route, but found it empty. He captured the fort and deployed a group of Dogra army under the command of Wazir Atbara. He did the arrangement at Kartong and marched towards Tagla-Khar, which was the capital of the Purang area. Here the Tibetan army fought bravely, but was ultimately defeated. The Wazir conquered the fort and the Tibetants left the fort and fled away. The Tibetan General Darpon Shata also ran away towards Lhasa. Tagla-Khar is one of the best places of Purang as far the climatic condition is concerned. Wazir made it his capital, and opposite to the Tagla-Khar, on the left bank of River Karnali (Ghakra) near the route, built a grand fort on the top of a hill and deployed Mehta Basti Ram there along with the Dogra army. At that time the province of Naris Korsum comprising of Rudok, Kugay, and Purang and Spiti was under the control of Wazir, and to defend the areas, he deployed

Ladakhi and Dogra army at all the places. Mehta Basti Ram and Wazir Atara were at Purang. Rahim Khan Raja Tikchey along with his son in law Ghulam Khan was deployed at Spiti. Similarly, he deployed some soldiers at Tarthapuri. After this conquest the territories of Jammu kingdom got extended up to the boundaries of Nepal and Kumaon district of Allahabad province of British Government. The distance of Nepal's border and Kumaon district is about 15-20 miles from Tagla-Khar. Since the border of Jammu touched with Nepal, after the conquest of Purang, the King of Nepal deputed his representative along with 120 soldiers, to the Wazir expressing that there had been peaceful relations between the two kingdoms but suddenly it turned into neighbours. Hence, the two governments have to keep in mind the unity and integrity of each other in future. But Wazir thought it unwise to develop relation with Nepal, unless he would have an agreement with the British Government in India. He hosted the representatives of Nepal for few days and sent back by ensuring a better relation in future. In the meantime another event took place. Cunningham sahib requested the Wazir to depute one of his officers at the border of the British Government, so as to develop the relations, friendship, unity and integrity between the two countries. Therefore Wazir deputed Mehta Basti Ram and Kalu Jamadar to discuss. After the agreement of friendship was signed, Cunningham advised the Dogras, that the climate was unfavourable and cold. "The enemy is waiting for such an opportunity. You are far away from the capital Ladakh and it is very difficult to arrange transportations and ration. If you are willing to conquer Tibet, it is better to wait for the spring to come."

Mehta Basti Ram returned and revealed it to Wazir, what Cunningham has suggested him. Wazir appreciated the suggestions. Alas! The mistake done by Mirza Haider Gorgan regarding the Tibet expedition was repeated by Wazir Zorawar Singh. He learned no lesson from it. He proceeded from Ladakh at such a time, that he arrived at Purang in winter. Neither was it a suitable time for invasion, nor to proceed further. History repeats itself; the result was very destructive, like that of Mirza Haider. Since Mirza had to return back from there during the winter, because of the bad relation with his own government, from where Lhasa was only eight days away. Because of unavailability of transportation and ration, his army got ruined on the way. However, he was able to save the lives of most of his army men. But the inhabitants of a warm country like the Dogras, could not face the extreme cold of Purang, against the Tibetan army, and almost all the Dogra soldiers including their General became the prey of the cold and high altitude. However, the shortcoming of these brave invaders was fulfilled by Col. Young Husband in August 1904, where he unfurled the British flag on the potala palace of Gyalwa Rinpochhey.

In short, keeping in view the unfavourable climatic condition Wazir stopped the advance and leaving Mehta Basti Ram in the Tagla-Khar fort, he himself went to the pilgrimage of Gonpa Khoshaq. This Gonpa is considered a sacred place and is situated on the left bank of River Ghagra, just ahead of one halting place from the newly constructed fort of Wazir at Tagla-Khar. Wazir halted there for few days and returned to Purang. Thereafter, Wazir deputed some soldiers at the Nepal border to observe the tower of the actual line of control. They came back with positive report and that a big boulder had placed on the old border. On the one side of the boulder are written Sanskrit words and on the other side Tibetan. This indicates the old border and it is in tact. When he was satisfied with the report, he began to consolidate his own army. Shortage of ration was there, it was not possible to transport it, except from Ladakh. But the distance was very long and the route was very difficult. So this problem remained.

Wazir thought that the winter season had started and he had no intention to proceed further. There was no chance of attack from the enemy, and he thought it not necessary to stay in the battle field. Hence, he marched from Tagla-Khar to Mansarovar Lake, with the intention to reach Leh. The Wazir expanded the territories of Jammu regime from the sources of Indus and Sutluj to the upper reach of Ghagra valley and the border of Jammu touched with Nepal. The sacred places like the Mansarovar Lake and Kailash mountain were also under his control. The Maryumla was the border between Lhasa and Jammu. It had been the border between Ladakh and Lhasa in the past too, during the reign of some able Ladakhi kings. Thereby, the source of River Brahmaputra was also under his control. In short the Wazir extended the kingdom of Jammu upto the famous places, wherefrom the following four popular rivers of India flow:

1. Singgay Khabab (Lion mouth) Indus
2. Langchhen Khabab (Elephant mouth) Sutluj
3. Mupja Khabab (Peacock beak) Ghagra
4. Stachhok Khabab (Horse mouth) Brahmaputra.

Since the luck of the victorious brave General had been reached at its climax, but as said there is down fall after every success; he had to face the defeat. This courageous and brave person unfurled the victorious flag of Dogra's from Suru to Ladakh, Ladakh to Skardo and from Skardo to Purang. And with the same spirit he sacrificed himself on the flag of government of Jammu. Though the European writers took special interest in Asian conquerors, they charged many crimes towards this brave man, but the Buddhists of Great Tibet and Muslims of Little Tibet still praise him, saying that the Wazir neither harmed any innocent people, nor destroyed any religious structure during his invasion, for which he would be remembered for a long time in future.

When the Tibetan people in Lhasa came to know about the interference of Wazir, they had been preparing for the counter attack. After performing the pilgrimage of Mansarovar Lake and Kailash, Wazir had preceeded about two halting places towards Ladakh, when he came to know about the advancement of the Tibetan army, on 7th November 1841 AD, he became so furious and emotional, that he never cared for his own security, and in order to stop the advancing party, he deployed 300 soldiers under the command of Nono Sonam to assist Atbara Thanedar at the Kartong fort. He sent back his family members to Ladakh escorted by some soldiers, and he himself was busy in arranging the army to encounter the

Tibetans. He got the news that the soldiers stationed at Kartong fort including the reinforcement headed by Nono Sonam were killed by the enemies. Now Wazir deputed 600 strong soldiers under the command of Nono Sonam, Ghulam Khan, Mahan Singh, Bhupa Kotwal, and Mian Sanggara, on 19th Nivember 1841 to stop the advance of the Tibetan army, and he himself followed them along with all the Dogra soldiers towards the battle field. Even his army could not meet the advancing party, when he came to know that all the soldiers were got killed by the enemy, and the rest were arrested. Their commanders Nono Sonam and Ghulam Khan were made prisoner. The number of Tibetan army was much larger, consisting of 10,000 soldiers, than that of Wazir. There was awfully cold in the region and it was at its climax. Transportation was not good. In spite of these hardships, Wazir considered them weak and jumped in the battle field like a lion. A fierce battle took place on 10th December 1841 at Toyu, situated between Kartong and Tagla-Khar. Gun battle started by both the parties and it continued for three days.

But luck did not favour him, a bullet of the enemy was struck on the right thigh of Wazir. He fell down in the battle field from his horse. On seeing this enemy ambushed him from all sides. But in this awkward position he never left his sword and attacked the enemy soldiers, whosoever came in front of him. When the enemy observed that it was difficult to catch the injured lion alive, they deployed a person on the back side of Wazir to throw a spear on him, locally it is called "Dung". Its both ends are sharp like a spear, and a rope is fastened in the centre. It is being revolved over the head, with one end of the rope in the hand, and thrown on the target. The "Dung" struck on the back of Wazir and the sharp edge damaged his chest. Because of this injury, Wazir died in the battle field on 12th December 1841, according to 27th Maghar 1898, Bikrami.

During Zorawar Singh's departure to Tibet expedition, he locked the window of the gate of Leh fort, and the word "Talaq" was inscribed on a sheet of iron connected with the lock. It is said, unless Tibet was conquered, the lock of the window would not be opened. The order is still followed, but the political condition has changed now and it seems to be very difficult to fulfill his desires. However, Wazir Zorawar Singh's memory still exists on the gate of the fort, and it will remain in tact in the future too.

After the death of Wazir, the Dogra army discouraged, and the condition of the battle changed. The Dogras became helpless, and the soldiers ran away every side. The Tibetans followed them and the maximum were got killed. It is said that the total army of about 6,000 including the porters, hardly about two thousand came back alive. Out of this about one thousand soldiers were imprisoned by the enemy. Among them the Dogra soldiers were not more than one hundred. Those Dogra officers who remained alive were also got arrested. Wazir Zorawar Singh's army fought this battle in a very difficult situation. The battle field was more than 15,000 feet high from the sea level, and the climatic condition was not good. It was awfully cold, even during the day the temperature remained minus, and during the night it was so cold, that only those who were habitual of such climatic condition could face the situation. They also kept the leather coats and full dresses. But the Dogras were not having these types of clothes, and during the awfully cold they spent many nights in the open fields. Moreover the rain and heavy snowfall made their journey unbearable. It is said that the toes and fingers of some soldiers were frostbite and almost the hands and feet of all the soldiers were got affected with cold. There was no wood in the area, so as to bask before a fire and save the life. Here still people use bush as a fuel. As long as it burns, it has the warmth, but after burning, nothing is left except the ashes. It was so cold that some soldiers burnt the butt of their rifle to save the life. Above all, there was shortage of ration and during the last few days they could have nothing to eat.

The Dogra's were discouraged, when their commander was killed. They had no option but to run away from the battle field. These are the causes for the destruction of the army. The Tibetans did not follow the absconders; hence most of the people came to Ladakh, along with the Ladakhies, and some arrived at Tagla-Khar, with the sad news of destruction. The soldiers of the Tagla fort thought it better to save their life, so all the soldiers along with Mehta Basti Ram went towards Almoda, via Changlao Chheyla. Though there was no danger on this route, but due to heavy snowfall and awfully cold half of the soldiers died in the way and hands and feet of rest of the soldiers became the prey of frostbite. In short among his army, the life of only those few people, who reached Almoda or were able to reach Ladakh fort, were saved. When the Dogra's in Leh came to know about the Tibetan invasion, they deputed reinforcement from Leh to help Zorawar, under the command of Pehalwan Singh Kamidan, Munshi Gorandata, and Subedar Teg Singh. Probably, the Wazir must have ordered them to do so. These soldiers were far away from the battle field, when they came to know about the battle of Toyu, and destruction of Dogra army. Hearing this sad news, they returned back to Ladakh and were busy in the consolidation of the fort. The conquests of Wazir Zorawar Singh had terrorized the mind of the Tibetan people. He was considered a very special man. It is said that after his death his blood and flesh were distributed by the Tibetans among themselves, they took his head to Lhasa and built a "Chhorten" to keep it, which still exists. A piece of his body has been kept in Tashigang Gonpa. On the appointed days, prayers are performed according to the Buddhist tradition, so that the spirit of the late Wazir may not enter in the body of a person to destroy Tibet once again. About the cause of the erection of the "Chhorten" it is said, that in the process of reincarnation, the spirit of the General may not invade Tibet again. The memory of Wazir Zorawar Singh still exists in Purang. The following Dogra officers were made prisoner of war at the battle of Toyu by the Tibetans:

1. Mian Rai, 2nd in command
2. Tsewang Stobdan Kalon Bazgo
3. Nono Sonam, brother of Kalon Bazgo
4. Ghulam Khan Raja Chushot.
5. Mourup Stanzin
6. Acho Gonbo

7. Raja Ahmad Shah, deposed Raja of Skardo.

All the prisoners were sent to Lhasa and the Tibetan army captured Naris Korsum, Gar, and Rudok during winter. The effect of Wazir Zorawar Singh's defeat in the Tibet invasion was far lasting. Not only the conquered areas of Tibet were recaptured by the Tibetans, but they also consolidated position of the previously conquered areas. To set the things on the right path two more expeditions were sent to Ladakh and Baltistan.

Tibet's Invasion on Ladakh and their Defeat

5

Revolt of Ladakh, Purig and Baltistan: Dogra's Ladakh invasion No. 4, commanded by Dewan Hari Chand and Wazir Ratnu: Compromise with Government of Tibet

The Tibetan army thought that none of the Dogra soldiers could save their life in the battle field of Toyu and the Ladakhies were not their enemy. They never followed the fugitives, and spent rest of the winter with ease in the surroundings of Naris Korsum, Gar, and Rudok, besides they consolidated their rule in these regions. Those soldiers, who were deployed by Wazir Zorawar Singh in the fort of Gar and Rudok were captured by the Tibetans after the battle of Toyu. Most of them were killed and the fugitives, who were able to save their life, arrived in Leh fort in a deplorable condition. About one hundred soldiers, who came from the Purang side, including the soldiers of these border forts were able to reach Leh. Because of the destruction of the Dogras, the Ladakhies and Balties wished to be independent again, but due to their laziness and mutual bickering and disturbances, it helped to some extent to the Dogra rulers. Though the number of the Dogra soldiers at the Leh fort was very small, however, without the assistance of the neighbouring states, the Ladakhies were not having the courage of revolt. Although, the whole winter season expired in discussion to obtain the cooperation of Purig and Baltistan and to acquire military assistance from Tibet, hence they could not take any action before the summer started. When the plot against the Dogras was finalized, the process of deployment of the soldiers started. Acho Gonbo who had been Lobchhak (Head of the annual trade mission) used to go to Tibet and had a good relation with the nobles and prominent persons of Tibet. He approached the Tibetan General P.C. Shata and decided to eradicate the Dogra soldiers from Ladakh and restore the rule of Ladakhi Raja, again. In the beginning of the year of 1842, according to 1898-99 Bikrami, the said general proceeded towards Ladakh along with 3000 Tibetan army from the surroundings of the Gar area. Onpo Tsewang Rafstan was deployed to Sham area (Lower Ladakh) to mobilize the army. The army from upper Ladakh was mobilized by Acho Gonbo himself and reached at Leh along with the Tibetant army. In the mean time the army from Sham also reached at Leh. The whole army entered the Leh palace during the night. Jigsmet Namgyal the grandson of Tundup Namgyal, who had been appointed as nominal Raja by Wazir Zorawar Singh in place of his grandfather, was declared as independent Raja. The weapons stored in the Tingmogang and Leh palace were distributed among the soldiers. Those who could not get the weapons were given wooden spears. However, when the arrangement was made, the government of Raja Jigsmet Namgyal was declared. There were two groups of Dogras in Leh. One was under the command of Maghna Thanedar at the Leh fort and the second was under the command of Kamidan Pehalwan Singh at Karzoo Bagh. It was not a safe place. When Kamidan observed that the soldiers were gathering at the Leh palace, and the situation not normal, he left Karzoo Bagh and shifted to a place just adjacent to the Leh fort, which was stable for Ladakhi kingdom since there was shortage of accommodation inside the fort. He got repaired the structure as far as possible, and the required arrangements were made. The rebels also came in action; they in collaboration of Tibetan army surrounded the cantonment, fort and the stable. But they were not able to stop their internal communications. The irritation continued for a long time. Finally, the rebels decided to attack the fort and the cantonment, during the night. But to their ill-luck, they spent most of the time in discussion and arrangements and attacked at the dawn. The Dogra army countered the cantonment and inside the fort. The battle continued till morning. In the morning, Kamedan Pehalwan Singh from the cantonment and Maghna Thanedar from the fort came out with the army and attacked the rebels. They fought hand to hand and many Ladakhis were killed. Finally, the Ladakhis were defeated and began to run away. The Dogras followed them up to the town. It is said that thousands of Ladakhi and Tibetan soldiers were killed in this battle. Not only the Ladakhis but the Tibetan army was also discouraged after this defeat. They could not mobilize them for a long time and even could not besiege the Dogras any longer.

Wazir Zorawar Singh had built a temple in Leh town. During this period, the Ladakhis and Tibetan Buddhists were not contented with the military activities but indulged in the religious activities who destroyed the Hindu temple called "Devi"at Leh. Besides, the religious goods which were kept inside the temple were also destroyed carelessly.

This made the Dogras irritated and angry, who till then honored the Buddhist religious places. Later, during the invasions they took revenge and looted the valuable goods of Buddhist Gonpas. Though on this occasion, they only looted valuable goods but not damaged the sacred religious monuments. These events were happening in Ladakh. Purig was also facing the same situation. Since the revolt took place in all the Border States at a time with the mutual conspiracy. Kalon Mulbe arrested the Dogra soldiers of Mulbe fort and thrown them away in Nallah Wakha from the Darket bridge. The Raja also got killed the Dogra soldiers of Pasri-Khar along with the soldiers of Chhubar-Khar and Chokyat-Beroi. Similar activities were done in Suru-Kartsey. Raja Pashkyum also imprisoned the Dogra soldiers but took least interest in the revolt. That is why he was called at the capital Leh and he was allowed to go back with the strict warning, but unfortunately he could not reach back Pashkyum. In spite of all these efforts of the revolters, there was peace in Daras. Revolt was at its peak in Baltistan too. The events are revealed as follows.

When Raja Ahmad Shah was released from the prison of Wazir Zorawar Singh, he was again arrested by the Tibetans at the battle of Purang. Being like minded he became their friend and plotted to fight against the Dogras. He deputed his representative Yustrong Karim to Skardo to mobilize the Baltis through his trusted Haider Khan Shigar, and Kazim Beg Skardo. So all the three prominent persons made efforts to create hardness and problems against the Dogras and gradually, came in agreement with other dignitaries, like Ali Khan Raja Rongdo, Doulat Ali Khan Raja Khapolu, Khorram Khan Raja Keres, and other nobles of Baltistan. Later they arrested the Dogra Thanedar of Skardo Bhaghwandas and his soldiers and they destroyed the Dogra fort and the store room. Haider Khan deputed these prisoners to Nihali, and full arrangement of their security was made there. Then Suleman Khan Raja Shigar was arrested and he ruled over his kingdom. Since Mohammad Shah Raja Askardo did not participate in the revolt, hence he was arrested and imprisoned at Khanqah Kawardo, and capturing Kharpochhey fort and Haider Khan, he ruled over Skardo. Thus, he left no sign of the Dogras in Baltistan. Haider Khan arranged the reinforcement wherefrom Wazir Shuja reached Skardo along with 140 warriors and remained there to support and assist Haider Khan. Therefore, after the death of Wazir Zorawar Singh, his conquered areas were confiscated by the ex-rulers. In Phagun 1898 Bikrami when Maharaja Gulab Singh was proceeding to Peshawar via Kashmir to make the arrangements and receive General Palak, he got the sad news of Zorawar's assassination at Barah-kot of Hazara region. Therefore, he immediately made the arrangement to depute second expedition to Ladakh. At that time Dewan Hari Chand, who along with Painda Khan were busy on the bank of River Indus at Palyan as a representative of government of Khalsa was called back. He was deployed from that very place by appointing the Commander-in-Chief of Ladakh expedition. Dewan marched from Hassan Abdal and reached at Haripur Jammu within a day and night by crossing the distance of 150 "kos", wherefrom he went to Jammu along with Raja Dhayan Singh. Later he reached at Mirpur after making the arrangements of ration and weapons. There he stayed for fifteen days and mobilized the soldiers. When he arranged the requirements, he left along with 6000 soldiers via Uri and reached Kashmir, where Sheikh Ghulam Mohiuddin, who was the Subedar of Kashmir, appointed by government of Khalsa Lahore, did all sort of arrangements for them. This army has to stay for fifteen days in Kashmir, where from he deployed 500 soldiers each day towards Ladakh. Wazir Ratnu was 2nd in command of this expedition. He marched one day earlier of Dewan, the next day Dewan himself marched towards Ladakh and staying at various destination reached at Daras. All the route from Sonamarg to Daras was covered with snow, and because of its shining with sun rays the soldiers had to face eye sore, but they recovered very soon. He had to stay three days in Daras. Suchita Thanedar Daras reported in detail, the obstructions they faced at various places, from Daras to Kargil. "That the enemy has erected posts right from terrain of Kharul to Nallah Kargil and has stationed soldiers with weapons. And it was difficult to pass through the route." But Dewan never cared for it and marched forward. At Kharul the forward army had to face the enemy and return back to Chhani-Gund. Dewan deputed some soldiers via Chhani-Gund Nallah to climb the hill, so as to attack the enemy from the top of the hill. But the hill was covered with snow, therefore the plan failed, and the army returned back. Finally, Dewan waited till the snow was melted. After one month he deputed 3000 soldiers with a gun via Nallah Chhani-Gund to climb the top of the hill, under the command of Ram Singh Jamadar. Under the hill on the plateau of Tiktikmo were the positions of the enemy and Dewan himself along with Wazir Ratnu and rest of the soldiers marched from the main route and reached Kharul, where the soldiers of the enemy were ready to counter the Dogras under the command of Bahadur Khan Kargili. Dewan stayed at Kharul and was waiting for Ram Singh to reach on the top of the hill. When Ram Singh's army arrived on the top of the hill, then Dewan fired the gun heavily on the positions of the enemy. The enemy was under the fire of the Dogras from both the sides, hence there was no alternative for them but to run away. After the Tiktikmo, the Kargilies positioned at Lankore village but the gun of the Dogras was on the top, therefore it was difficult for them to continue there, hence they ran away from there too. Now there was no alternative for the fugitive soldiers of Purig but to break the bridge over River Suru, after they crossed it. But unfortunately their own senior people blocked the passage of the bridge with stone and wood, so that they could not dare to run away. Dogra soldiers were following them and the firing continued from the hill. In such a situation, it was difficult to open the passage of the bridge. Hence, the people out of fear jumped into the river. In the meantime, the Dogra soldiers also reached at the bank of the River. Those who were still on the bank were killed with sword and those, who were swimming in the river, were killed with bullets. Those who were not expert in swimming became the prey of the wave of the River Suru.

In short, among the huge army of Purig, only those soldiers could save their lives, who were able to swim and reached on the other bank of the river. Their number was very low. The triumphant Dogra army stayed for the night at Kargil. Instead of Choki Chhubar-Khar, Dewan arranged to build a strong fort, opposite to it on the left bank of River Suru. One Dogra officer was deputed to Sot, so as to destroy "Pasri-Khar" with fire. Thereafter, he marched from Kargil and reached at Pashkyum. Raja Pashkyum Mohammad Ali Khan was at Leh, his fort was destroyed with fire, and those who were instigators of the revolt were severely punished. Later they proceeded ahead of Pashkyum. Dewan marched towards Ladakh after making the political arrangements of the villages on the road side. On the way, he burnt Malduk-Khar palace of Mulbe. The valuable goods of the destroyed fort, like planks and logs, were sent to Kargil to re-use those in the newly built fort of Kargil. Those people, who were found responsible for the revolt, were handed over to Thanedar Kargil, so as to put them in prison.

When the army reached ahead of Bodh-Kharbu, they met Mohammad Ali Khan Raja Pashkyum, who was coming back from Ladakh.The place where the Henasku Bridge over Nalah Kanji is situated, on its right Pashkyum's army took position on a rock and attacked the Dogra army on the other side of the river. The Dogra army never imagined to face such a situation. Because of this sudden attack some Dogra soldiers were killed. The Dogra army prepared themselves to attack the enemy, but the army was beneath on the bank of the river, and the Raja's soldiers were on the hill behind a rock, so it was very difficult to counter them, so they were in a fix. Then suddenly, one of the representatives of the Raja who was a former Dogra soldier, shouted loudly, that the gun men are not more than thirty, and attack on them was possible. After performing this service, he sacrificed himself for the sake of the country. Thus, the Dogra soldiers advanced further and got killed all of them. Though some Dogra soldiers were killed, but among the Raja's soldiers only one person reached at Chiktan to tell the sad story to them. The people came from the village, they took away the dead body of the Raja and buried at Chiktan. Thus the Dogra soldiers cleared the obstructions and proceeded further.

Raja Mohammad Ali Khan remembered the punishment, which was given to his brother Kalon Rahim Khan by Zorawar Singh at Skardo, who abstained himself by involving in such crises again. But it was the Raja of Ladakh who misled him from the right track, and took the promise from him that he would stop the Dogra army at Kargil. It is said, that he was in a fix, what to do and what not, but he was afraid, that the Ladakhi Raja would invade him, therefore in order to keep them away he broke down the planks of the Khalsi Bridge into the river. That is why, when the Dogra army reached at this place they had to face the problems to cross the river. They got repaired the bridge in a day and crossed the river to reach Khalsey. There are two routes ahead of Khalsey. One upper route goes from Tingmogang and comes down at Bazgo, another lower route goes from the river bank via Nurla and Saspol and reaches at Bazgo. Ahead of Bazgo this route leads from a narrow gorge, wherefrom it is impossible to pass, if the enemy creates obstructions. Hence for convenience and to capture the Tingmogang fort, which was considered one of the strongest forts of Ladakh, he devided the army in two groups. He deputed Wazir Ratnu from the river bank route to Bazgo, and Dewan himself from the hilly route proceeded towards Tingmogang. Dewan destroyed the fort of Tingmogang and surrounded the Nallah Kesar, so that the army of Wazir Ratnu can climb the Nallah safely. Later both the army reached at Bazgo. There was a strong fort at Bazgo called Rafstan Lartsey Khar; the army had destroyed it partially. Later on they marched towards Leh, Ladakh.

Kamidan Pehalwan Singh taught a good lesson to the Ladakhi and Tibetan joint army. Hence, they could not unite them again. However, after this defeat they made efforts to mobilize them again, but before planning some practical activities, they heard the news of arrival of the Dewan's army in Ladakh. This made them frustrated and discouraged. The number of the Ladakhi army gradually decreased. When Dewan's army reached near Leh, the Tibetan army came out of Leh palace and instead of fighting with the Dogras, they marched towards the border of Lhasa. Besides, Raja Jigsmet Namgyal, along with his mother, who ruled over the rebels for about six weeks, left the palace and fled away towards Lhasa. Thus the palace of Ladakh was the centre of the rebels which became empty completely.

When the Dewan reached at Leh-Ladakh along with his huge army, he unfurled the flag on the building adjacent to the Leh fort, and praised the bravery of Kamidan Pehalwan Singh's army. He rested at Leh for few days. Later he deputed a group of soldiers to Zangskar under the command of Mian Jawahare Singh to crash the rebels, and some soldiers were sent to Nubra under the command of Mian Naraina. Those porters, who came from Kashmir along with his army, were given the wages and rewards. Among the nobles of Ladakh, Onpo Rigzin, Tsewang Stobdan and Acho Gonbo were honored and rewarded. In the meantime, the valuable goods like the Chhorten of silver and gold, furniture from the Leh palace were removed. Moreover in response to the destruction of the temple, the valuable goods of the Gonpas were shifted to the fort, so as to transfer Jammu but he neither disregarded the sacred things, nor damaged the religious articles and statues. He also did justice with the rebels.

In the meantime, the General of the Tibetan army Darpon Pishi Shata, who fled from Ladakh to Rudok, made the efforts to get the detail information about Ladakh through Raja Jigsmet Namgyal. When he came to know that a major portion of the Dogra army had proceeded to Zagskar and Nubra, and the Kashmiri porters had gone back, he determined to invade the Dogras once again. He deputed about one thousand Tibetan soldiers to invade the Dogras under the command of his younger brother Chhagchhung and Kalon Raga Shah's brother Karan Shah. After crossing the pass of "Changla" the army arrived at Chemrey. Onpo Rigzin and Acho Gonbo informed the Dewan about the latest developments. Hence, Dewan immediately deputed a platoon to counter them. Under the command of Kamidan Sardol Singh and Lala Ramji Mal Munshi, a battle took place at lower Chemrey between the two armies. The enemy fought bravely but was finally defeated at Chemrey Gonpa. When Dewan came to know about this situation, he kept a required number of soldiers at Leh to defend the capital. He himself marched towards Chemrey along with rest of the soldiers to fight the Tibetans. On first day, he stayed at Chushot. The next day he reached at Chemrey and besieged the Gonpa. A canon was fixed on the top of a hill just opposite to the Gonpa. The cannon-ball reached inside the Gonpa. The Gonpa is situated on the top of a hill, but had to fetch water from the canal or spring. Dewan surrounded the Gonpa from all sides and stopped their way of supply and finally the enemy was compelled to surrender. Dewan deployed Bakhshi Nihal Singh inside the Gonpa to sign the agreement of forgiveness. He did the needful. Dewan sent Chhagchung and Karan Shah along with their companions to Leh, Ladakh guarded by Wazir Ratnu, and he himself stayed few days at Chemrey to make essential arrangements. He appointed Sardol Singh Kamidan and Ramji Mal Munshi as incharge officers at Chemrey and left for Leh Ladakh. It is not out of place to mention here that the Chemrey Gonpa is under the Hemis monastery and it is the greatest and most famous Gonpa in Ladakh. The Lamas are popular for their far sightedness and good strategy. When the Tibetan army arrived at Chemrey, the "Chhagzot" of Hemis provided all sort of arrangements for them; similarly when the Dogra soldiers of Dewan reached at Chemrey to counter them, the "Chhagzot" of Hemis Gonpa remained ready and alert to serve them apart from providing transportation and other requirements. Thereby he maintained an equal balance between the two groups. Both the parties were happy with him. In response to the services rendered by the Steward of Gonpa Hemis, Dewan neither seized the valuable goods of Gonpa, nor did he damage the sacred monuments.

In the meantime, after nine days in the prison, an event happened. One night the prisoners attacked the guards, killed some persons with stones and some were injured. When Dewan came to know about this event, he followed the fugitives and surrounded them few miles away from Leh, Ladakh. The Tibetan took fugitives position on a slope of a hill and began to throw stones over the Dogra army. The Dogra soldiers fired from the foothill and killed about 100 Tibetans. About 400 were re-arrested. A group of these fugitives ran away from another route but they were also arrested and sent to Kashmir escorted by 200 riders. Those who were able to run away from Ladakh, told the sad story to Darpon Pishi Shata, Kalon Ragasha Commander-in-Chief and Kalon Zoorkhang. Thereafter, 6000 Tibetan soldiers along with cannon which they had seized from the Dogras in the battle of Toyu, marched towards Ladakh with the intention of attack. They reached at Tangtse and built a strong cantonment at Lung-Yogma.

This information was also brought to the notice of Dewan by Sardol Singh Kamidan and Ramji Mal Munshi. He ordered Sardol Singh to take position on the hill under which the enemy had built their cantonment. He himself marched along with all the soldiers leaving only one hundred soldiers at the Leh fort to guard it. Within two days he met with the army of Sardol Singh. They stayed for the night at Durbuk. Even the soldiers had not cleared the dust of their weapons, when the guards informed that the enemy wanted to ambush during the night. Hence, the soldiers never took rest and were ready throughout the night. The enemy as expected came forward at night with the intention of ambush, but the Dogras were ready to welcome them. The enemy soldiers were seen clearly in the moonlight. The Dogras shot the cannon balls and fired guns over them. Beside, the swords did their own job. Finally, Tibetan officer Daspon Aggyam was injured, he turned his horse back. On seeing this Tibetan army ran away. The Dogras followed them up to the cantonment. When they entered inside the cantonment, the Dogras besieged it. The battle continued for eight days. The cantonment was so strong that the Dogras failed to capture it. On the eighth day they invaded the cantonment once again but in vain. Because of the fire by the enemy about 300 soldiers of Damjad Singh Kamidan were got killed, and many were injured. The loss of lives of the Tibetan army was less; however one of their officers Chhagzot Mikmar was dead because of gun firing, however, they failed to capture the cantonment.

The Dogra soldiers were morally discouraged because of this failure. However, Dewan made efforts to boost their morale tactfully. Finally, the luck favoured them after four days.

A person namely Thangpa Joldan of village Nurla was one among the Dogra soldiers. He had been officer in charge of the stable in the past during the Ladakhi kingdom. The horses of the Raja used to graze there at Lung Yogma and whenever there was lack of grass in the field; the land was being irrigated through the water of the Nallah. He told the Dewan, that if the water from the Nallah was brought and put in the field, the cantonment would be filled with water and it would compel the enemy to come out. Dewan examined the spot and the proposal was found very genuine and easy to execute. He acted immediately and diverted the whole water of the Nallah in the field. Thus, the water of the Nallah came out continuously for three days and the cantonment was filled with water. The enemy tried to save themselves from this man-made calamity but found no way to get rid from this misfortune. Their belongings and weapons, etc. drowned into the water. The fort was surrounded by the Dogras from the outside. Neither had they a dry place to sit upon, nor the passage to come out. It compelled them to surrender. They requested the Dewan for forgiveness. Dewan showed generosity towards the enemy and deployed two Dogra officers Qazi Nadir Ali and Wazir Mutasaddi to console and comfort them. All the Tibetan Officers came to the Wazir without weapon. Dewan was kind enough to deal with them. All the weapons and other goods of the enemy were confiscated. He gave a way to the soldiers to come out of the cantonment. Beside, all the articles which they got in the battle field of Purang from Wazir Zorawar Singh, were taken back. Jawala Brahman, who was in their prison also came before Dewan. The rebels like Mourup Stanzin, Acho Gonbo and the deposed Raja of Skardo Ahmad Shah, who were accompanying the Tibetans, were arrested. The cantonment was totally destroyed. In short Dewan got a victory over the Tibetans.

Now, the Dewan got an opportunity to fulfill the desires of Wazir Zorawar Singh, but he never took solid efforts to get back the region conquered by the late Wazir. Instead, due to tiredness Dewan returned to Leh to enjoy the great victory and left Wazir Ratnu behind so as to escort the Tibetan officers and other prisoners to Leh. When Dewan left for Leh, the mind of the Tibetan officers changed and they refused to proceed to Leh, along with Wazir. In this struggle Kalon Ragashah was got killed at Aamtat hill near Shachukul. Only Pishi Shata, Tsepchhot and Zurkhang arrived at Leh. When Maharaja Gulab Singh came to know about the fresh invasion of the Tibetans, he deployed 4000 soldiers from Kashmir for reinforcement of Dewan. After the victory over the Tibetans, he was not in need of any reinforcement. Dewan asked them to go back. The government of Lhasa, through Garpon Jorgais prayed for compromise. Garpon came to Leh in the court of Dewan. The government of Lhasa appointed Pishi Shata and Kalon Zurkhang to participate in the talks, which were held in prison at Leh, and the government of Jammu empowered Dewan Hari Chand, Commander-in-Chief for Ladakh expedition and Wazir Ratnu 2nd in command to make the compromise. They, on behalf of the government of Jammu and Lhasa, signed the agreement. When they signed the agreement, Dewan proceeded to Jammu along with two Tibetan representatives, their officers and prisoners of war. The Tibetants officers were conferred with rope of honor. Raja Ahmad Shah along with his attendants, was presented in the court as prisoners. He was kept in prison for some years at Gomut Darwaza. One of his sons Mohammad Ali Khan fled to India and died at Ludhiana. Later, he was shifted to Kishtawar and kept in house arrest till his death. After his death, his offsprings were granted estates in Kashmir. They settled at Taral.

Wazir Ratnu stayed few days in Ladakh; he handed over administration of Ladakh to Maghna Thanedar and went back to Jammu. Onpo Rigzin was appointed his Assistant. According to the agreement the borders of Ladakh remained the same, as were during the reign of Raja Tundup Namgyal. When for the first time Zorawar Singh conquered Ladakh and those regions which he conquered later, like Rudok, Ghar, Kugay and Purang, etc. are now known as Kangri region that remained with Tibet. Beside the relations of Tibet which were with the Rajas of Ladakh during the Namgyal dynasty kept continued by both the governments of Lhasa and Jammu, and the prisoners of wars were exchanged. In recognition to his services, the government of Lhasa conferred the status of "Kalon" to Darpon Pishi Shata, and after some years, he was elevated to a higher post of the government of Lhasa. As far as Kalon Zurkhang is concerned, it is said that he died earlier. Dewan took the following rebels along with himself to Jammu; they were: 1. Deposed king Mourup Stanzin, 2. His son Gurmet, 3. Eshay Tundup, 4. Tsering Tobgais Ladokh and 5. Acho Gonbo. Among them only two persons Gurmet and Eshay Tundup returned to Ladakh after few years and the rest were died at Jammu. Similarly, Dewan also took with him to Jammu, some Rajas and Nobles of Kargil; among them Salam Khan Raja of Sot died at Jammu and the rest returned to their home. After few years Raja Jigsmet Namgyal, his mother and his companions, were sent back to Ladakh by the Tibetan officers, escorted by soldiers. It is because of Dewan Hari Chand's generosity that he restored to him all the estates of his grandfather situated at Stok. Chhogsphurul's second son

Phuntsog Stanshong Yurgyal had already got 50 per cent estate of village Matho, which continuously remained in his possession. Since then the two brothers Jigsmet and Phuntsog, the Stok family and Matho family stayed separately at their own estates. Thus, their offsprings still occupy the concerned estates.

After the death of Jigsmet Namgyal his son Sonam Namgyal was made nominal Raja, and the total estate of Jigsmet Namgyal remained in his name. The government sanctioned an honorarium in his favour. He was the nominal Raja of Ladakh till 1914. After becoming a Lama in the Gonpa, his son Jigsmet Dadul Namgyal became the nominal Raja and got the estates at Stok and some property been allotted in his name at Nubra. When Chhogsphurul's second son Shongh Yurgyal had died, his son Lahwang Namgyal became the patron of Matho, and after his death his second son Nangwa Thayas Namgyal was looking after his estates. His elder brother Thustobs was a Lama at Gonpa Hemis. The head Lama of Pethub Gonpa Kushok Rgyalrhas Bakula was the son of Nangwa Thayas and he served the people of Ladakh spiritually, politically and economically, for which he was remembered by the Ladakhis. After this Dogra expedition there was continuous peace in Ladakh, and never required to send a fresh expedition to Ladakh. The region is progressing day by day because of good governance. Hashmatullah said, "Now the Ladakhies have learned English and Urdu education and got government jobs. Its foundation was laid by me, and I am proud of it."

In this connection the efforts of the priests of Moravian Mission in Ladakh is praiseworthy.

Removal of Disturbances in Baltistan, Purig and Zangskar

Dogra's Expedition No 5. Commanded by Wazir Lakhpat Kishtwaria

Wazir Hashmatullah says, "Though, according to the sequence, this expedition should be narrated in the events of Baltistan, but the revolt of Baltistan is related with the revolt in Ladakh. Hence, in order to keep the events intact and to mention all the expeditions of the Dogra's at one place, I have narrated this expedition with the events of Ladakh, so that all the expeditions of Dogra's concerning this region could be seen at a same place. I have already explained earlier about the revolt of Baltistan. There Suleman Khan Raja Shighar and Mohammad Shah Raja Skardo were in the prison and Kacho Haider Khan was ruling over Skardo and Shighar. The Dogra officers and soldiers deployed at Skardo were in prison at village Nyali and surrounding areas, thus the Dogra's rule in Baltistan came to an end. Therefore, to remove the chaos and crises in the region and to punish the rebellions, Maharaja Gulab Singh deputed his confident Wazir Lakhpat Kishtawaria to Baltistan."

Wazir Lakhpat, along with 3000 Dogra warriors marched from Kishtawar and reached at Suru, via Nallah Chilung, so as to check the rebellions, because the people of Suru also revolted. Therefore, he had to face the rebels everywhere in the way. But he crashed them and arrived at Kargil. Before he arrived at Kargil Dewan Hari Chand and Wazir Ratnu had left for Ladakh after defeating the rebels of Sot at Tiktikmo. Wazir Lakhpat first did the internal arrangement for the region and then with the consultation of Raja Ali Sher Khan of Kartaksha (Kharmang) prepared for the travel of Baltistan. Wazir crossed the Daras River at the Karket Bridge, wherefrom he reached at Shingho Shighar. Here the rulers of Skardo had built a tower, where he had kept some soldiers to guard. They fought with Wazir's army, but their number was very few, all of them were got arrested. Hereafter Wazir's army arrived at the Devsai desert, wherefrom the army descended in the Nallah of Kafchun. Wazir travelled with good strategy and quickly, that nobody came to know unless they reached at Kafchun village. When Kacho Haider Khan was informed about the arrival of this army at Kafchun, instead of fighting he fortified himself in the Kharpochhey fort. When Wazir Lakhpat arrived at Skardo, he surrounded the fort. The fort's location was naturally very strong, as mentioned earlier, it was considered un-beatable. The fight continued for few days, but Wazir was helpless to capture the fort. Therefore, he with the support of Raja Ali

Sher Khan and Raja Mohammad Shah bribed Wazir Mohammad Ali Chheykhatpa, who was the officer in charge of the main gate of the fort. He agreed that the gate would be opened during the night. There was a tower on the hill; towards New-Rangga, wherefrom the upper route of the fort was being guarded. The soldiers deployed at the tower were also under the command of Wazir Mohammad Ali. He assured on behalf of the soldiers that they would not disturb any more. Therefore, according to the agreement Wazir deputed a group of soldiers at night on the top of the hill from the New-Rangga side, and he himself along with rest of the army attacked the main gate of the fort. Since the gate was open, the Dogra soldiers entered the fort and a fierce battle took place. The besieged fled away because of horror. Some crossed the river by swimming and some ran away from the land. Many people drowned in the river. In short the people inside the fort had to face a great destruction. In the morning, the Dogra's unfurled the flag on this hill.

When Kacho Haider Khan observed, that luck was not favouring him, and it was useless to counter the Dogra's, therefore in order to save his life he along with his companion ran away to Shighar during the night. There he planned to proceed to Yarkend along with his companions via Nallah Thaley and Saltro. But luck did not favour him, when Raja Doulat Ali Khan came to know about it well in time. He as a loyal subordinate of government of Jammu deployed his men and got arrested him along with eighty companions. He was brought at Khapulo where these persons were placed before Wazir Lakhpat. The sincere effort of Doulat Ali Khan Raja Khapulo was highly appreciated by Wazir Lakhpat and Haider Khan. Later Wazir took him to Jammu along with himself. Since Kharpochhey was the centre of the mischiefs, hence Wazir set fire to the fort and destroyed it. But he spared the beautiful mosque inside the fort, and rest of the buildings were destroyed, so as to keep it unfit for re-use. That was a great loss of the old monument.

The mosque is still in a good condition. Later the fort was repaired and renovated. Newly built small rooms are now under the possession of the army. Though Wazir Zorawar Singh had laid the foundation of the new fort towards the right bank of Nallah Satpar on the top of a hill, and the construction was in progress during his time but it was Wazir Lakhpat who during his stay at Skardo got completed the fort. Bhagwan Singh, who was released from the prison of Nayali was appointed Qilladar. There were deployed about 300 Dogra soldiers. He made the villagers of Skardo region responsible for their own rations. Every village had to pay annually, two to four mds of agricultural seeds, 22 mds Barley, and 1 md Butter, 10 md Salt, 2 mds Grass, 4 mds Wood, besides the traditional taxes. Except this nothing was imposed on the villagers of Skardo. The Raja of Skardo was made responsible to collect the above-mentioned goods and had to hand over it to the Qilladar. Mohammad Shah was made the ruler of Skardo who never interfered in administration. Doulat Khan of Khapulo and Khorram Khan of Keres were reinstated Raja's as usual and their estates were restored. Raja Ali Sher Khan of Kartaksha improved the relations with the Dogra's because of his sincere services to them. He remained the "Jagirdar" of Kartaksha as usual and never interfered in his area. The Raja of Tolti Ahmad Khan was also reinstated. After making these arrangements Wazir Lakhpat went to Shighar. Here the real heir of the estate, Suleman Khan had died, hence his son Imam Quli Khan was made the Raja, and his estate and powers were restored to him. Moreover some soldiers were kept there to guard the area. Wazir proceeded to Rongdo to check the crises, after making needful arrangements at Shighar. While crossing the forest of Bhishu, the army attacked Rongdo, and the battle was won easily. But the Wazir of Raja Mohammad Shah Doghonipa Bono was killed in the battle, who was a faithful servant of Raja Mohammad Shah and a guide to Wazir Lakhpat. Here Ali Khan was the Raja at that time and Wazir also restored his estate. But his son Hussain Khan was taken with himself as a hostage. Some soldiers were kept to guard at Astaq fort. Jabbar Khan was the Raja of Astore at that time. He was also responsible for creating disturbance in the area. Wazir Lakhpat invaded Astore via Harpola.

Jabbar Khan fortified himself, but Wazir besieged the fort. Due to shortage of food inside the fort, the Raja came out and surrendered. Wazir punished him and went back to Skardo. When Wazir reached back to Skardo, the construction of the fort was completed, and the army was stationed inside the fort comfortably. There was peace and prosperity everywhere in the region. Thereafter Wazir went back to Jammu via Kishtawar, along with the prisoners of Baltistan. When he reached at Purig, he took the Rajas of Purig with himself to Jammu as prisoners, who were Hussain Khan Raja Pashkyum, Salam Khan Raja Sot, Rahim Khan Raja Tikchey, Tsewang Namgyal Kalon Mulbe, Chhaghdor Namgyal Raja Tambis, and his brother Kunga Namgyal, Wazir Quddus Beg of Sot and some other dignitaries. Who were responsible for the disturbance and had participated in the revolt. A number of people who participated practically in the revolt, or assassinated the Dogras in Baltistan and Purig were given capital punishment. Their heads were put on display at prominent places so as to terrorize others. He deployed forces at the forts of Kargil. Daras and Suru for the defense of Purig. This arrangement was continued till the recent past. Over a period of time this fort system started to decline. Similar arrangements of the forts of Shighar and Stagh in Baltistan also ended. Now the regular armies are stationed only at Skardo and Leh forts.

In short, the Baltistan expedition of Wazir Lakhpat had been highly successful in every respect. Whatever arrangements he made in Baltistan and Purig, exist like a foundation stone even now. As soon as Wazir Lakhpat did the arrangement of Purig, he turned towards Zangskar because these people had also revolted. The Thanedar Jamadar Dheenu appointed by Wazir Zorawar Singh and the Dogra soldiers under him were got killed. Thus, the Raja of Chemur ended the Dogra rule and crown prince Balchu was deputed to Ladakh to convey this good news. When Wazir Lakhpat reached Zanskar the public surrendered without showing any form of resistance, and even the Wazir didn't bother the populace, although he made Raja Chemur hostage and took him along to Jammu and confiscated all his property. Balchu was not present there at that time therefore, he escaped before being made a prisoner, later he died in Kashmir due to smallpox. This way the entire family was finished.

Wazir Lakhpat appointed Mehta Basti Ram as Thanedar of Zanskar and deployed few soldiers with him. He abandoned the fort built by Wazir Zorawar Singh and constructed a new fort which still exists. During this time he also imposed tax on the population. After setting the military and civil administration on right track he left for Jammu.

The Dogra Rulers of Ladakh

6

The following ten personalities were the Dogra administrators, who ruled over Ladakh after the annexation of Ladakh with Jammu by Wazir Zorawar Singh:

1. Magna Thanedar
2. Mehta Basti Ram Thanedar
3. Mehta Manggal Thanedar
4. Wazir Shibsaran Thanedar
5. Syed Akbar Ali Shah Wazir
6. Mr. Doru Wazir
7. Mr. Johnson Wazir
8. Pandit Radha Krishen Koul Wazir
9. Khan Bahadur Sardar Mohammad Akbar Khan Wazir
10. Choudry Khoshi Mohammad Mohtamim Bondabast Wazir.

1. Magna Thanedar (1898-1902)

During the Dogra's rule, he was the first ruler of Ladakh. He was appointed by Wazir Zorawar Singh. The old fort of Ladakh was got repaired and renovated under his supervision. In the heart of the Leh town he built a beautiful house, which is still known as Magna Haveli. Previously the veterinary hospital and Kotwali had been accommodated in it. Now the Tehsildar's bunglow and co-operative shops have been constructed there. He planted trees on Leh-Kashmir road below the agricultural land in Leh, which is situated opposite to tourist reception centre Leh and is known as Mangla Bagh.

2. Mehta Basti Ram Thanedar (1903-1916)

The polyandry system of marriage was prevalent among the Buddhist of Ladakh. Consequently, a large number of women were un-married. Some of the women entered the Gonpas as nun, they are called "Chomos". Some are wanderer and vagabond and have illegal children as often. They remain homeless. Mehta Basti Ram renamed them as "Ghulam Zadah" and prepared a list of such children. He sanctioned rations for them and made the arrangement for their education. He established a handicraft centre, where durets, etc. were being made. An officer was the incharge of the centre. This continued till the period of Mr. Johnson. During the reign of the Ladakhi Raja's it was a custom to keep sheep and goats owned by the government. There are still some tribes in Tangtsey and Rupsho, who look after the sheep and goats of others on contract basis, on two conditions—the first condition was that the man has to return equal number of animals at any rate which he received at the time of contract. Secondly, he has to give in detail, the correct quantity of the increase and decrease of the animals. In both the conditions, he had to pay annually, one seer butter per goat, one seer pashmina, one seer wool per sheep to the owner. Mehta Basti Ram started to keep the sheep and goats of the government, which became a source of income. This system continued for a long time but now it has discontinued because of ill-administration. He got constructed a beautiful house in Leh town, called Basti Haveli, which still exists. The drawing room of the building has been converted into ration store and the quarters are being used by the Tehsildar and other officers. The construction of the present Bazaar of Leh had been started by him. On one side of the Bazaar was built the court and treasury building and the quarters for the employees. These buildings have been annexed with the Chokhang Vihara now and its one part is being used as office of the LBA youth. Mehta Basti Ram was an able and good administrator. His sympathetic rule is still remembered by the people.

3. Mehta Manggal Thanedar (1917-1922)

Mehta Manggal was an able administrator. He made the revenue settlement of whole Ladakh for the first time, and reformed the tax system. The second great work of the officer is the demarcation of the border between Tibet and Ladakh. The fort built by Magna Thanedar was small, therefore he extended the area of the fort by constructing buildings attached to it, and got constructed the wall and ditch around the old and new fort. There are many new colonies founded by him. The following colonies are very famous: Ranbirpur, Rampur Chushot, Partapur, Manggal Chak (Martselang).

He got constructed the Khuls for the above-mentioned villages and settled the homeless people there. Residential houses were constructed for them, they were provided with plough—ox and seeds. Imposed tax on subsidized rates was exempted to benefit them. In short, he provided all sort of support to them, so as to develop and improve agriculture, which was need of the hour at that time. As far as Ranbirpur is concerned, the Dogra administrator established the village under a systematic way and proper town planning. Probably they must have done so in other places. There was a Bazaar in the middle of the village. Small huts were got constructed on the both sides of the Bazaar. It is said that the old people used to play polo and other games there. There was a beautiful "L" shaped sarai building consisting of two storeys which was called "Kothi" by the local people. It was meant to facilitate the army and other government officials during their to and fro journey. A local resident Tundup Tashi was the chokidar and was looking after the sarai for few generations. Few years back the kothi was converted into a community hall by the local people. Proper walling has been made around the village. The left over portion of land has been utilized for plantation purpose that is why during the pre-independence period Ranbirpur Bagh was very famous for its greenery and density in whole Ladakh. But after independence cutting of trees started to use as fuel in government offices and within a short time the greenery was converted into a desert. Illegal occupation of land started. It is said that the Dogras also brought some Kashmiris to settle there and provided them with housing and agriculture facilities but due to unfavourable climatic condition and agricultural system, they could not adjust themselves there and went back. The ruins of the huts are still there which remind us the Dogra's period but most of the households have shifted to new places. They built new houses and plantation have been made at the old site by dismantalling the huts. The Dogra's wanted to make Ranbirpur a model village and made efforts in this regard. The sarai at the halting places on Leh-Kashmir, Tibet and Kullu route and in the Nubra region, still exists which are the contributions of Mehta Manggal. He planted trees all over Ladakh and white lead trees on the route side. In Leh town just adjacent to the court building, he planted trees after levelling the land called "Gulab Mandi Bagh". It is because of his wisdom, that he introduced the "Race" system at the halting places for the convenience of the travellers and government officials. Since, in a region like Ladakh where there is less population and the inhabitants are scattered, this system is highly appreciable. Earlier there was no postal system and at the time of emergencies special messengers were deployed. He appointed postmen and made the postal system regular. As far as education is concerned, he established a Pathshala in Leh town for Sanskrit language and the students were paid scholarships, so as to motivate them. The "Ghulam Zadah" illegal children were also admitted in this Pathshala to seek education. He made the arrangement to export and sell the Ladakhi salt at Kashmir and improved the trade. The construction of Leh Bazaar, which was started earlier, was completed by him. In the hilly towns of Himalayan regions, this Bazaar is very beautiful in every respect. He introduced "Hakim" system of treatment for the convenience of the government employees. The medicine were supplied to the "Hakim" by the government who had to treat the employees free of cost. Mehta Manggal was very favourite ruler. All the Ladakhies still remember him with great respect especially in the case of land settlement.

4. Wazir Shibsaran Thanedar (1922-1923)

He developed a garden in Leh, which is called Wazir Bagh. Within the garden, the Yarkendi Sarai, Charas Godown, Church, and Morvian Mission Charity Hospital have been constructed. The trees are no longer seen now. Today some of the portion of the Wazir Bagh is used as Police Station and the sarai has been converted into taxi stand and parking.

5. Syed Akbar Ali Shah Wazir (1923-1926)

During his period the status of Thanedar had been redesignated as Wazir. The Wazir introduced the law of Jammu kingdom here and introduced the coin "Jao" in Ladakh in the name of Maharaja Jammu. It is he, who introduced "Chadar" instead of "perak" among the Muslim women. He encouraged physical cleanliness and made the people habitual of cleanliness. Once, some Muslims reached in his court as witness in connection with a case. He asked them to recite "Kalima", but none of them could recite. He was annoyed and called the local Molvi and instructed him to establish a Maktab and give basic religious education to the Muslims, so that they could recite Kalima and know the basic things. He made efforts to eradicate some social evils prevailing in the society but failed.

6. Mr. Doru Wazir (1927-1928)

He introduced the "Jarib" of Punjab and Jammu and Kashmir into Ladakh. He took interest in agricultural improvement. He granted concessions to the homeless persons and outsiders in respect of construction of houses, exemption of taxes, and exemption from government duties, etc. But he did not get a sufficient time to improve this system. He made reforms in the local administration. He was a scholar and wrote a good book on the geography and geology of Jammu and Kashmir state. This book is a first detail geography of this state which scholarly discusses the political and historical aspects also. Ganga Singh was his assistant, who established the "Behesht Bagh" which is just behind the Kigutak and is presently used as Muslim burial ground in Leh.

7. Mr. Johnson Wazir (1928-1939)

He was in the service of Government of India in the tourism department and visited Ladakh. Later he joined the service of the state. He built a very beautiful bungalow, for himself in Gulab Mandi. This was the first European type of bungalow in Ladakh, which later converted into government offices. He constructed official residence complex for the government officers, but presently it has been converted into taxi stand. He got constructed a canal from the Indus to irrigate the desert of Gopuk just adjacent to village Spituk, but the water could not flow in the canal and the plan failed. Later he constructed another canal just below the said canal and settled the population there. He planted trees in a vast garden and constructed a bungalow inside it, which still exists. Beside, he constructed a canal for the barren land of Ule-tokpo to inhabitate the people there. He inhabitated the people at other places and planted more trees in the gardens. He got constructed a grand fort at Chushot, it does not exist now, however a damaged old Sarai is there. He repaired and renovated a Sarai, just adjacent to the Bazaar, called Balti Sarai for the people of Baltistan who used to come to Ladakh for the trade of dry fruits and butter and to purchase wool, pashmina, salt, and tea, etc. from here. He raised the store of grain. Because of his good strategy and policy, he brought about reforms in the administration. He made amendments in the land settlement system of Mehta Manggal. He made reforms in the contract of goats and sheep and in the process of receiving the amount of profit from the government traders. This increased the revenue of the government. He was a man of merriments who loved sports, dance and music. In spite of this, his system of administration was very admirable. His court was open for everybody. Chhang and tea were used to serve in the court as per the local system. A number of settlements of the cases and disputes promptly attended to verbally. There was no system of maintaining files. Usually the decision was recorded on the backside of the application, and handed over to the applicant. People still remember him and admire the system.

8. Pandit Radha Kishen Koul Wazir, (1939-1943)

His great contribution was the land settlement of Ladakh. The people didn't accept the newly imposed revenue tax and complained against the system. Finally, some modification was made in the proposal of Mr. Johnson and the public was satisfied with it, as a result the land settlement had not come in force. He made reforms in the system of forced labour. During his rule postal service was properly established in Ladakh. Beside, he improved the plantation system in the region.

9. Khan Bahadur Sardar Mohammad Akbar Khan Wazir, (1955-1957)

Khan Bahadur Sardar Mohammad Akbar Khan ruled over Ladakh for three years. He made reforms in the previous system of administration and found a great corruption in the treasury because of misappropriation of funds. He also found some corruption in the import system of "soda", etc. He made the inquiry and rectified it, and recovered the losses of the government. He punished the defaulters. He improved the trade system of Lhasa.

10. Choudry Khoshi Mohammad Mohtamim Bondabast and Wazir, (1963-1966)

After Khan Bahadur some more Wazirs came but they had not been so popular as per their efficiency and performance. Finally, Choudry Khoshi Mohammad Mohtamim Bondabast and Wazir, made the legal land settlement of Zangskar and Ladakh under the supervision of Commissioner of Settlement Mr. Talbot and the imposition of heavy tax was removed. He made reforms in the forced labour system and provided basic amenities at the halting places.

Sources of Revenue

Ladakh has witnessed various sources of revenue prevalent in the region from time to time in the process of development. They are:

1. The period of Buddhist dynasty, 2. The administration of Wazir Zorawar Singh, 3. The basic observation of revenue by Magna Thanedar and Wazir Ratnu, 4. The modification

and reform of Mehta Basti Ram, 5. More modification of Mehta Manggal, 6. The improvements made by Mr. Johnson, 7. Land Revenue of Pandit Radha Kishen, 8. Administration of Mr. Kalark, 9. The legal land revenue of Mr. Talbot and Choudry Khoshi Mohammad.

1. The Period of Buddhist Kingdom: There was no land revenue during the Buddhist rule. However, the peasants were responsible to make the arrangements of the domestic requirements of the king, and they were themselves responsible for the administration and defence of the country. Some details are as follows:

- **Grain:** Twenty-four villages of Nubra region were responsible to arrange the grain for six months, and the villages of Lamayuru, Skurbu-chan, Tingmogang, Saspol, Bazgo, Shay and Thiksay were arranging the grain for the rest of six months. Moreover, the cultivation of the king's land had to be made by forced labour through the peasants, and all the production had to be deposited in the state godown.
- **Meat:** The areas of Rupsho, Tangtsey and some villages of Rong were responsible to supply the requirements of meat, for the whole year.
- **Butter:** Zangskar region was responsible for the supply of butter and a small quantity of butter was procured from Rupsho, Tangtsey and Rong.
- **Wood for Fuel:** The villages in the Nallah's like Chiling-Sumdo, Khardong, and Hunder-Dok, etc. were responsible to arrange 3000 mds. of wood for the Raja for the purpose of fuel.
- **Woolen Cloth:** To prepare the woolen clothes for the members of the royal family, 3 pao of wool was collected from each household. The cloth was made by the peasants through forced labour. Mostly this task had to be done by the weavers of Tangtsey.
- **Sheep and Goat:** There was a tradition to conduct the census of the goat and sheep and after every ten animals, one had to be handed over to the Raja. These

animals had to be kept under the supervision of the royal shepherds, and at the time of emergencies, meat, butter and wool were procured from them.

- **Cash:** Every household had to pay one "Jao" annually to the king. Beside, the villagers were responsible to repair and renovate the Mane and Chhortens, without any honorarium and free of charge. Moreover those villages wherein big Gonpas are situated, like Hemis, Chemrey, Thiksay, Pethub, Phiyang, Likir, Lamayuru, Karsha and Rangdum were granted the payable dues and the Stewards of the Gonpas were responsible to collect the dues. But the correct figure of the income is not known. Besides the above-mentioned income the Raja was having some miscellaneous income too, through other sources:
- **Tea:** The royal trader "Lobchhak" used to go from Ladakh to Tibet for trade purposes after every three years. The "Lobchhak" had to be provided transportation from Ladakh to Lhasa and Lhasa to Ladakh free of cost. In return to the concession, he was responsible to arrange the tea for the royal family for the whole year.
- **The Royal Traders:** No body was allowed to proceed to Chanthang and Lhasa for trade except the royal traders. Mostly the Arghon traders were authorized to go there. They had to pay 3000 Jao as advance amount and had to receive double of the amount at the time of return.
- **Tax on the Goods:** The Yarkendi traders, who brought their goods to sell in Ladakh, had to pay tax, but the correct figure is not available. However, there had been increase and decrease in the total amount of income subject to the quantity of goods. The approximate income was in between twelve thousand to thirty thousand.
- **Services During War:** The weapons and ammunition had to be stored in the royal arms store. During the

external invasion or attack every household had to provide one soldier each, his food and clothes but the arms had to be provided by the king. The soldiers were mostly untrained.

- **Royal Posts:** After the Raja, there was a Kalon or Prime Minister and there were many other Kalons or Lonpos under him as head of the provinces and the Namberdar of the villages were under him. They were not paid any salary from the royal treasury. However, every officer had to receive the "Rasum" from his subordinate officer and the grass-root level officer had to receive it from the peasants.

2. The Administration of Wazir Zorawar Singh: Wazir Zorawar Singh never interfered in the administration of Raja, during his first invasion. However, he imposed a sum of 9000 to Raja Tundup Namgyal as annual tribute and restored him his territory. During the next invasion, when he deposed Raja Tundup Namgyal and appointed Mourup Stanzin as nominal king and doubled the amount of tribute to 18,000 annually.

3. Magna Thanedar and Wazir Ratnu: After the third invasion, the administration of Ladakh had come completely in the hand of the Dogra rulers of Jammu.

(a) The Nobles like Kalon and Lonpo, etc. had to pay the tax at the rate of rupees 14, 25, and 30 per household. Finally, Wazir Ratnu and Magna Thanedar imposed the land revenue tax. They made the census of the region, made the grading system and imposed the revenue tax on different grades as per the following rates:

(b) The peasants were categorized in three groups. First "gama", i.e. middle; Second "Phetma", i.e. half and the Third; "Yan Phetma", i.e. one fourth and were imposed tax at the rate of 9, 3.8 and 10 percent respectively.

(c) The regions of Skurbuchan and Nubra being very fertile, so he increased the tax at the rate of 3.4, 4.1 and 20 percent respectively.

(d) In the areas of Rupsho and Tangtsey the agricultural productions were minimum. The peasants were dependent on animals, only. Hence, the tax was fixed as per the quantity of the animals but the rate and correct figure is not known.

(e) The taxes on grain, woods and butter were not fixed. It is said that tax had to be received at the level of the expenses of the government employees, as per the past practice. This was in addition to the cash revenue.

(f) During the rule of Buddhist kingdom the goats and sheep which were under the care of the royal shepherds were owned by the government and were kept continuously under their care. They were supplied as per the requirement of meat for the government employees. The shepherds had to keep in tact the exact number of the animals as it was earlier.

(g) During the reign of Buddhist kings the royal traders received Rs. 3000 as advance and had to pay back the double of the amount. This system also continued during the Dogra's period.

(h) The toll tax on the goods of the Yarkendi traders remained the same as per the past practice.

(i) The tradition of the Buddhist regimes to make the census of the animals and to receive one animal after every ten goats or sheep was banned.

(j) The concessions granted in the past by the Buddhist kingdoms to the Gonpa's were continued in the new system, and the land was not included in the list. They were kept tax free.

4. The Amendment of Mehta Basti Ram: During the period of Mehta Basti Ram, the goats and sheep owned by the government were put under the care of the shepherds, who had to pay annually 1 seer butter per goat, 1 seer Pashmina per he-goat or she-goat, 1 seer wool per sheep. This was the old system and no amendment was made in this respect.

5. The Amendment of Mehta Manggal: As per the proposal of Magna Thanedar, the land revenue system continued for about twenty years. Later Mehta Manggal made some amendment in it. He continued the grading system and rate of revenue tax started by Magna Thanedar and Wazir Ratnu was renamed as "real" and those, where the payment of revenue was ceased or included in the list during the previous time or the land which was demarcated after the said period, all were added, the land revenue tax of the two crops villages was increased. He made reforms in other revenue arrangements. The above-mentioned fact indicates that the early Dogra administrators followed the principles of Buddhist kingdom and gradually made reforms in the revenue systems which improved the state income. Thus the differences between the harsh and lenient views were removed. The efficiency and far sighted policy of these officers is praiseworthy. The later administrations and internal arrangements are based on principles formulated by Mehta Manggal.

6. Mr. Johnson's Revenue Improvements: Mr. Johnson who like Mehta Manggal was very popular, efficient and good strategic administrator. He made wide reforms in the revenue systems.

1. The tax was imposed on Mansar village which is in between Naris Korsum and Lhasa like an island.
2. The "Charu" was collected from Rupsho and Tangtse. Lamb skin is called "Charu", and by joining them jacket is prepared.
3. Salt tax was imposed on the areas of Rupsho, Hemis and Rong, who used to take the benefits of salt from Thugjay Lake.
4. Nitre and coal were imported from Nubra valley and "Hartal" from Lingshed village. He imposed "Rasum" tax on these articles.
5. Soda, which is locally called "Phuli", was procured from Nubra and it was given on contract.
6. "Nagtsur" is a colour; the mine of nagtsur was properly guarded.
7. He introduced the system of cleaning the borax.

8. He made reforms in the systems of the iron mining and imposed tax.
9. He fixed the rate of "Zare-murakab" on the horses of transportation and fixed "Zare-mehtarana" on the animals, which entered Ladakh from Kargil and Kashmir.
10. The traders of Tibet who used to bring wool and salt in Ladakh and in return got the purchase of grain of Ladakh. He imposed import tax on the goods.
11. He increased the agricultural revenue.
12. Foodgrain were distributed from the government stores to the peasants for seeds.
13. Rasum in cash instead of kind was fixed on the animals owned by the state.
14. The gift items received by the government employees had to be deposited in the state treasury.
15. Reforms were made in the service conditions of forced labours utilized by the government employees.
16. Instead of cash as interest on the advance amount paid to the state traders, he preferred to receive pashmina.
17. Beside the revenue in kind, he passed on the order of purchase.

7. Land Settlement of Pandit Radha Kishen Koul: Pandit Radha Kishen Koul did the land settlement in 1940, but there had been a common hatredness against this system and the peasants complained against it. Consequently, instead of introducing the new system, he continued the old system with slight modification and increase in the revenue.

8. The 'Bachh' System of Mr. Klark: Mr. Klark introduced the new "Bachh" system with slight modification in 1958, but the complaint of the peasants about the harsh system of the "Bachh" continued. Later Mr. Talbot with the assistance of Choudry Khoshi Mohammad properly did the land measurement and repelled the complaints. He imposed tax on pasture lands.

After Mr. Klark many Wazirs came, but they were not popular as compared to their predecessors. Finally, Choudry Khoshi Mohammad Mohtamim Bondabast and Wazir, made the legal land settlement of Zangskar and Ladakh under the supervision of commissioner of settlement Mr. Talbot. He made reforms in the system of forced labour and the arrangement of halting places.

Atrocities on Ladakhis by the Dogra Rulers

The Ladakhi people faced the autocratic rule of Dogra rulers. People suffered untold miseries at the hands of Dogra invaders and the despotic government officials posted in Ladakh. The poor Ladakhis had to feed the greedy government officials out of their hard-earned produce and money. Under the "Res" (forced labour) system each family had to provide men and animals for transportation of government officials, and their goods, without payment. Moreover, they had to provide butter, milk, egg, cock, vegetables and other products, free of cost. Even they had to carry the dogs and wives of the Dogra officers. There was harassment, victimization, and maltreatment by the Dogras. The poor village horse rider had to come down from his horse and bow to government officials, otherwise he had to face the punishment, abusing and accusing was common, and unparliamentarian and foul languages against mother, sister and daughter were frequently used. Some of the foul languages inherited by the Dogras are still prevailing in Ladakhi society. They terrorized the people and gave capital punishment without trial.

According to a Dogra officer Ganga Ram Naqashi, "Kalon Rahim Khan of Purig had been severely punished and his limbs were cut off the body and to dip the stump at once into the boiling oil, and the executioner had also to cut off his nose, ears, and tongue and had been left in the open field to die. Similarly many other Ladakhis were severely punished. It is said that at some important places limbs of the human organs like head, hand, etc. were kept hanging for public display, so as to terrorize the common people." Ganga Ram Naqashi further says that "ten thousand people alongwith women and children were gathered in the fort of Khapulo. The next day the men and women were gang raped, Wazir also came there and Holi was played. The Baltis felt it very much as hard as bullets."

It is clear from the above statements that the Dogra soldiers crossed all the limits and did all sort of inhuman activities and atrocities on oppressed Balti people of Khapulo and the neighbouring areas. From 1830 to 1842, Ladakh remained a battle field for the Dogras and the poor villagers were mistreated and suffered a lot at the hands of the Dogras and because of psychological pressure they became lazy and coward.

They destroyed the monuments and set on fire some of the important historical buildings like Karsey Khar, Parsi-Khar, Sot, castle of Pashkyum, Kharpochhey Skardo, and even the historical mosque of Karpo-Khar. Similarly, they partially damaged the Chemday Gonpa and Singgay Palace Leh. Dogra invaders looted all the monuments and valuable goods of Gonpas and castles (except Hemis) like silver and golden stupas, small statues, prayer bowls, valuable utensils, furnitures, carpets, ornaments and other valuable articles. They shifted them to Jammu loaded on horse back several times. They also looted pashmina, fine wool and cattles. They even showed disrespect to the religious places like mosque, Imam Barah and Gonpas. They kept their animals like donkeys in the main hall of Lamayuru Gonpa and used it as stable and Imam barah Skardo was used as a residential quarter for the soldiers.

However, at the later stage from 1898 to 1966, most of the Dogra administrators like Mehta Basti Ram, Mehta Manggal, Mr. Johnson and Syed Akbar Ali Wazir among others did some welfare activities. Mehta Manggal for the first time made reform in tax system. The border between Tibet and Ladakh was demarcated. He constructed sarais at every destination so as to facilitate the travelers and traders etc. by constructing khuls at various places. He founded new colonies like Ranbirpura, Rampur, Partapur and Rambirpura, Daras, etc. and settled the homeless people there. He planted trees in Ladakh at every possible places, where there was possibility of irrigation, and raised the greenery. Some of the gardens and parks like Mangalchak at Martselang and Mangla Bagh Leh are after his name and still well maintained. Since 1923, when Syed Akbar Ali was the administrator of Ladakh the post of Thanedar was re-designated as Wazir. He introduced "Chadar" instead of perak among the Muslim women and advised them to maintain cleanliness. But they paid less attention towards the promotion of education in Ladakh.

After Independence in July 1949, the first Prime Minister Pt. Jawaharlal Nehru along with Sheikh Mohammad Abdullah and Mrs. Indira Gandhi visited Ladakh in the month of June, during the Hemis festival. The dignitaries came on horseback from Leh via Thiksay and stayed for the night in a camp at Ranbirpur in the Bagh of one Aziz Mohammad and next day they proceeded for Hemis. After the Mela when they returned from Hemis, the prominent local people arranged a tea party for them at Choglamsar Bagh. The people apprised him about the hard topography and tough situation faced by them politically, economically and socially. Though there were many other welloff Ladakhi people who wanted to get the political reign in their own hands but the public requested Nehru ji and Sheikh Sahib, to assign the local leadership in the hands of Kushok Bakula. The people also at large showed their resentment, that they are not ready to accept none as their leader except Kushok Bakula. On the request of the public, Jawaharlal Nehru asked Kushok Sahib to come forward for the service of the Ladakhi people. Since then the local leadership is rendering containuously their services, according to their capacity, for the upliftment of the poor and oppressed people of Ladakh.

The Contemporary Leaders of Ladakh

7

Padma Bhushan K.G. Bakula Rinpoche (1917-2003)

K.G. Bakula was born in a royal family at Matho palace in 1917. His father Sh. Nangwa Thayas was a descendant of the Namgyal dynasty and his mother Ishay Wangmo was a princess of Zangla Khar. When he was a child of six years, he was recognized by the 13th Dalai Lama as the 19th reincarnation of Bakula Arhat, and was subsequently enthroned at Pethub Gonpa. He received his basic monastic education at Pethub Gonpa under the care of Geshay Ishay Tundup, a well-known Buddhist scholar. Then he proceeded to Lhasa for higher studies in 1927. There he remained very busy in seeking religious education and Buddhist philosophy for fourteen years under the supervision of learned Buddhist scholars of Tibet, at the renowned Drepong Lasaling Monastery. He got the degree of Geshe Lharampa with distinction from the Drespung Lasaling Monastery. After having completed his monastic studies with distinction in Lhasa, he returned back to Ladakh in 1940. Here he started to preach the noble teachings of Lord Buddha and morale values to the people of Ladakh region, pointing out social evils such as smoking, alcohol, gambling, polyandry, and inequality in the society. After independence when the Maharaja of Jammu and Kashmir decided to accede to India, Ladakh being a remote hilly district of J&K automatically became a part of India. In 1947-48, when the Pakistani raiders were on their way to Leh by Skardo route, Kushok Bakula sent his political advisor, named Pandit Shridhar Koul Dullu to Delhi with a request asking for reinforcements to the very small contingent of the Dogra forces deployed in the Zorawar Fort at Leh. The request was promptly acceded to and a Battalion of 2/8 Gorkha Rifles under the command of Major Hari Chand reached Leh via Manali. The Pakistani raiders were pushed back when they had reached within 8 km of Leh Airfield. He also helped the Indian army in every possible way. He converted a major portion of the Spituk Monastery into an army store, and first aid center. He provided rations to the Indian army personnels. In July 1949, Pandit Jawaharlal Nehru, the first Prime Minister of India along with Sheikh Muhammad Abdullah and Smt. Indira Gandhi visited Ladakh. Consequently Hemis Tsishu and Bakula Rinpochhe came in close contact with the dignitaries. While returning from Hemis on horse back, a welcome party was organized on the bank of Indus River at Choklamsar garden. Some of the landlords and moneylenders also tried to get a political favour from them but in vain. Since the poor Ladakhis were disgruntled with them because of their atrocities during the pre-independence period. At Choglamsar garden a big group of Ladakhi senior citizens approached the Prime Minister Nehru and requested that they would accept none but K.G. Bakula Rinpochhe as their sole leader. Hence, Nehruji and Sheikh Abdullah could not deny the mass appeal and asked K.G. Bakula to be the leader of the Ladakhi people, so as to uplift them socially, economically, educationally and morally. Now Bakula Rinpochhe assumed the dual role of political leadership of Ladakhi people in addition to his religious duties as the Head Lama. He would have never accepted this new role if Prime Minister Jawaharlal Nehru had not pressured upon him to do so, as per the public opinion. Later a friendship developed between the two and Nehruji had a great regards and respect for him. On his death UPA Chairperson Sonia Gandhi had expressed deep concern in these words, "He had a very close association with my family starting with India's first Prime Minister Jawaharlal Nehru himself. Indira Gandhi and Rajiv Gandhi had profound respect and regard for him. His death was therefore a personal loss for me." After taking the responsibility, he toured every part of the region on horseback, since there was no means of modern communication. He educated the people to make them aware about their rights, eradication of social evils and poverty, value of modern education. He freed the people from the debt and subjugation of landlords, moneylenders and from atrocities of government officials. Some educated youths came forward to help Kushok Bakula in social and political affairs, among them only Sonam Wangyal emerged as a leader of the oppressed people and became MLC, MLA and Minister in the J&K Cabinet.

Togdan Rinpoche, Khanpo Rinpoche, Bakula Rinpoche, Sheikh Jamaldin and other Congress Leaders at a Public Meeting

Bakula Rinpochhe was the architect of modern Ladakh. He strode over Ladakh like a colossus for more than four decades and added new dimensions in the public life by reminding the people of Ladakh that without becoming the masters of their own destiny, Ladakh cannot become a prosperous region. He was a legendary figure whose activities were confined not only to Ladakh but also encompassed the whole country and many countries of the world. That is why in recognition to his outstanding services to the nation and humanity he received awards from several countries including the prestigious Padma

Bhushan and Polar Star from the Government of India and Mongolia respectively.

K.G. Bakula Rinpochhe was a member of the Jammu and Kashmir Legislative Assembly from 1951 to 1967 and served as Deputy Minister, Minister of State and Minister holding important portfolios in the State Government from 1953 to 1967. He had been a member of the Fourth and Fifth Lok Sabha from 1967 to 1977, representing Ladakh Parliamentary Constituency of J&K state. He was a member of the consultative committees for Defense, Education and Planning and was also associated with several Parliamentary Committees. He was appointed member of the Minorities Commission in 1978 and served the downtrodden people of the country for over one decade. He served as Indian Ambassador to Mongolia for ten years from 1990 to 2000, and did remarkable job in strengthening the relation between the two countries. It is said that when he joined as Indian Ambassador in Mongolia, it was a Communist ruled State, but because of his interaction and spiritual teachings political changes began rapidly in the country and it became a Buddhist ruled state. The Mongolian people from all corners were coming to seek his blessings. Even after he completed his diplomatic assignment, he retained his links with Mongolia where he had set up Pethub Monastery for the Buddhist monks. Admiring K.G. Bakula's life and achievements, His Holiness the Dalai Lama has said, "that Bakula Rinpochhe dedicated his life to the cause of Buddha Dharma and service to the humanity." His Holiness also said that Bakula Rinpochhe's contributions to the revival of Buddhism in Mongolia, Russia and China are particularly praiseworthy.

According to the government ordinance of 1950, no temple, mosque or monastery could keep land beyond 182 kanals and that exceeding this limit would be confiscated and distributed to the landless. If implemented, this would have harmed the monastic institution of Ladakh, because the monks in Ladakh lived in these monasteries and were totally dependent on this land for their survival. Hence, a delegation headed by K.G. Bakula Rinpochhe met the prominent central leaders including the first Prime Minister of India Pandit Jawaharlal Nehru. They convinced the leaders, resultantly the monasteries in Ladakh were kept out of the purview of the ordinance. In 1959, when the Chinese occupied Tibet hundreds of Ladakhi Lamas had to return home. At that time, there was no arrangement or facilities for higher studies in Ladakh. Bakula Rinpochhe explored other avenues for higher studies within India. Bakula Rinpochhe submitted a proposal to the Government of India in 1962, which was accepted and Jawaharlal Nehru, the then Prime Minister of India, accredited its management to the Department of Culture of government of India. It became a full-fledged institute of Buddhist Studies. It is situated at Choglamsar and is known as the Central Institute of Buddhist Studies Leh. Long back he started the campaign to achieve the Union Territory status for Ladakh with different names, like Central Administration and NEFA type administration. The movement for Union Territory status for Ladakh is still continuing and is in progress with the support of different political parties and religious organizations. Since the movement is inter-linked with the Kashmir issue, so it can take some more time to be matured. However, his noble support and guidance was crucial for the formation of Ladakh Autonomous Hill Development Council. He prepared young leadership to shoulder this responsibility. Since the people of Ladakh have achieved the Scheduled Tribe status for several Ladakhi tribes, it was perhaps not possible without his guidance and moral support.

K.G. Bakula Rinpochhe founded the Ladakh Gonpa Association, an apex body of all the Monasteries of Ladakh and guided its activities as its President for several decades. It was due to his untiring efforts that a part of Wazir Bagh in Leh town was allotted for the construction of Chokhang Vihar, the present headquarters of Ladakh Buddhist Association. He brought the statue of Jowo Rinpochhe from Tibet and installed in the Chokhang Vihar. He also established the Ladakh Buddhist Vihar in Delhi. It is not out of place to mention here that the Buddhist of Leh established an organization in 1938, namely "The Youngmen Buddhist Association". In 1948,

Kalon Tsewang Rigzin was its President and he re-named it as Ladakh Buddhist Association. K.G. Bakula was also associated with this organization and did remarkable job for the promotion of Buddhist culture, society and religion.

K.G. Bakula was a secular leader. Being a pious Buddhist spiritual leader, he was having a great respect and regards towards his Muslim brothers. During his public meetings, he always used to give emphasize on communal harmony and brotherhood. He often used to call meetings at his monastery in Sankar, to which Muslims were always invited. In fact, many of his close associates, advisors and political workers were Muslims who stood by him despite many odds. Among them Kh. Abdul Haq, Kh. Abdul Sattar, Kh. Ghulam Sultan Shangku, Haji Muhammad Hussain Aabedi, Haji Ghulam Muhammad Barcha, Kh. Ghulam Rasool Betong, Haji Hussain Muhammad Pharka, Sheikh Jamaluddin and Akhon Muhammad Raza, etc. are worth mentioning. It is because of his visionary leadership that Ladakh today has become a pride of the nation for its unique culture, tradition, peace and harmony among its people. This great political and spiritual leader breathed his last at his residence at Saket in South Delhi on Tuesday, 4th of November 2003 at the age of 86. On 7th of November, Rinpochhe's body was brought to Leh in a special Indian Air Force plane. Thousands of people gathered at the airport and throughout the entire route to Leh. They could not hide their emotions, as hundreds of men and women were crying for the loss of the great spiritual leader. His mortal remains were kept in a Dukhang (main Hall) of the Pethub monastery, where thousands of people paid homage to their favourite leader. After fifteen days of prayers and rituals at Pethub Monastery, the body was cremated on 16th November 2003, with full state honours. Hundreds of prominent state, National and international leaders participated in his funeral, and paid homage to the departed soul.

Bakula Rinpochhe will always be known for his integrity in public life. He was an eminent political and spiritual leader who performed his key role without any fear or favour. The passing away of K.G. Bakula Rinpochhe is an irreparable loss not only to the Buddhist community but equally to the Muslims of Ladakh. Ladakh has lost its most eminent leader whose life and works shall always continue to inspire the present and coming generation. He will be remembered as a great visionary who paved the way for laying the foundation of a resurgent and vibrant Ladakh and for maintaining communal harmony and brotherhood in the region.

Sonam Wangyal (1925-1998): He was born at village Chemre on 26 January 1925 in a very poor family. As an assistant of Ven. K.G. Bakula, he rose to become a great figure in the political and economic development of Ladakh in the second half of the 20th century. In his political career, he was first appointed as President District National Conference Leh, which later merged with Indian National Congress. He was nominated as a member of Jammu and Kashmir Legislative Council and then was elected twice as member of the Legislative Assembly. He served the people as minister in the G.M. Sadiq and Mir Qasim's cabinet. He is known as leader of the oppressed people and is especially remembered for redressing the social and economic injustices in Ladakh, bringing to an end the system of forced labour, and freeing the common people from the burden of debt and high interest that had kept them close to starvation.

Sonam Wangyal was brought up in a rural background, and his family faced great hardships in his youth. He also noticed the hardships of the poor people around him, who were the victims of the autocratic rule of the Dogra regime. People suffered untold miseries at the hands of unscrupulous moneylenders and the despotic government officials posted in Ladakh. More than ninety per cent people lived on agriculture, and the farmers had to feed the greedy government officials out of their hard-earned produce and money. As stated earlier under the "res" (forced labour) system each family had to provide men and animals for transportation of government officials and their goods without payment. Moreover, they had to provide butter, milk, eggs, cock, vegetables and other local products free of cost. Even they had to carry the dogs and wives of government officers. There was harassment, victimization and maltreatment by the landlords, village functionaries and government officials. The poor village horse rider had to come down from his horse and bow in respect of the government officials especially Police, otherwise he had to face the punishment. The visit of officials to the villages was feared and hated, and corruption was rampant. The landlords and moneylenders exploited the less fortunate with loans of grain in times of hardships, but the interest was so high that the debts only grew and could almost never be paid off.

In the Ladakhi society of those days, the common Ladakhi had not enough to eat, and most of the people were half starved. Sonam Wangyal often contemplated helplessly about how to relieve the distress of the stricken people, and wished for a savior to come and rescue his people. In October 1947, Pakistan invaded Kashmir, reaching as far as to Ladakh. To defend the Ladakh region, a volunteer force was raised under Pandit Shridhar Koul, popularly known as Pandit Dullu. He embraced Buddhism and developed close relations with the Buddhists of Ladakh. He was the sole education officer in Ladakh region at that time, and exercised a great influence on the local population. At that time young Wangyal approached Pandit Dullu and expressed his desire to join the volunteer force, which was known as the Home Guard. Military training was given to the force. Koul inquired about his family position and social background. In the course of their discussion, the problems of Ladakh were raised. Pandit Dullu persuaded Wangyal that he should first complete his studies and then devote himself for the service of the oppressed people of Ladakh. Sonam Wangyal readily agreed to the advice of Pandit Dullu and taking a letter from him in the name of Pandit Nehru, the then Prime Minister of India, he proceeded towards Delhi. Sonam Wangyal trekked to Manali on foot in May, on his way to Delhi. The snowbound Rothang and Baralacha passes were not fully open and he had to walk continuously for one week on snow. After forty-five days, he finally reached Delhi, where he had to stay for one week in the refugee camp at Birla temple. He succeeded in getting an appointment with Prime Minister Nehru. Sheikh Muhammad Abdullah, the then

Chief Minister of Jammu and Kashmir and his colleague, and freedom fighter Mirza Afzal Beg were also present in the Prime Minister's office. Wangyal presented the letter of Pandit Dullu to the Prime Minister Nehru, who went through the letter and recommended to grant a scholarship, so as to continue his studies. Beg Sahib managed to send the young man to Srinagar by truck, where he was admitted in the S.P. High School. Two other Ladakhi students, namely Tashi Rabgyas and Mourup Gurmet were also studying in the same school. As Wangyal was from a poor family and had virtually no monetary support from home, he had to face lot of hardships to continue his studies.

At Srinagar Sonam Wangyal met Ven. K.G. Bakula, the great leader of the poor Ladakhis. He had embarked on a political career to serve the people of Ladakh. In July 1949, Pandit Nehru and Sheikh Mohammad Abdullah had visited Ladakh. Some Ladakhi representatives had requested them at Choglamsar garden to persuade the young head Lama to assume a political role in Ladakh. During that period K.G. Bakula was in need of an educated youth to assist him in day to day political and social work. Tashi Rabgyas, Mourup Gurmet, and Sonam Wangyal discussed in depth as to who would voluntarily give up his studies to work for Rinpochhe. Wangyal was chosen for the task. After his matriculation, he left for Leh to work with Bakula Rinpochhe. He had to face lot of difficulties to cross the Zujila Pass, because of the heavy snow fall. At that time Ladakhis had to face great difficulties due to imposition of heavy revenue taxes, and the callousness of the moneylenders had added to their sufferings. Wangyal had the opportunity to meet people through Ladakh, and closely observe the plight of the farmers and poor villagers.

Though India was from the yoke of slavery, and independence had dawned, the people of Ladakh were not free from the clutches of the moneylenders and landlords. The government officials were exploiting the common people. Wangyal undertook an extensive tour of the villages and saw the situation by himself. Under the leadership of K.G. Bakula Rinpochhe, Wangyal awakened the consciousness of the people who were overburdened with debt. He encouraged them to fight for their basic rights. They collectively launched a campaign against the corrupt administration, the moneylenders, and other vested interests. The administration reacted and consequently Wangyal was arrested several times, and even sentenced to imprisonment. However, common sense prevailed upon the administration. Farmers were exempted from the exorbitant revenue tax, the government settled half the debt, and loan cases. Sonam Wangyal was nominated as a representative on behalf of the people to present their cases. He won about five hundred registered cases, and more than one thousand cases were settled by negotiation between the concerned parties. K.G. Bakula Rinpochhe was pleased with Wangyal's achievements and advised the people to give him further support whole-heartedly. He gained full confidence and sympathy of people and was elected District President, National Conference Leh. Later, the National Conference was dissolved and the Congress Party was established. Wangyal was unanimously elected the District President of the Party. The party focussed its attention towards social problems. Their main objective was to raise the level of literacy as only five per cent of the population could read and write in terms of modern education. They urged the people to educate their children.

In 1957, Sonam Wangyal was elected Member of the Legislative Council of Jammu and Kashmir and continued in this position until 1967. In 1967, he contested the Ladakh seat of the Legislative Assembly and was elected defeating his nearest rival by a wide margin. Following this, he was inducted as Minister of State. He was well-known among the public as leader of the poor and the oppressed people. He enjoyed massive support of the people. During the next Assembly election in 1972, he again won by defeating his nearest rival by a wide margin. Although Ladakh had made considerable progress in a number of fields by this time, it was still developmentally very backward compared to other two regions of the state, the Kashmir valley and Jammu. The state government appointed a Commission headed by a former-Chief Justice of India, in order to redress the regional imbalances. In June 1968, one of the members of that Commission paid a visit to Ladakh, and took the evidence of both officials and non-officials in Leh and Kargil. The Ladakhi representatives argued forcefully that their legitimate regional aspiration had been ignored. Among the commission's recommendations were the establishment of Degree College at both Leh and Kargil; to improve electricity supplies; and to develop the transport infrastructure of the region. Ladakh had also long deserved Scheduled Tribe status that encompasses many benefits and reservations and to redress and correct earlier imbalances and discrimination.

At that time people in the North East states and along the Himalayas were declared Scheduled Tribe, but Ladakh was ignored. In 1982, a campaign was launched in this regard. Wangyal took an active part in the movement. Both Muslims and Buddhists of Ladakh participated fully in the movement. Some Congress leaders like P.T. Wangyal, Tashi Targyas, Tsering Sampail, Haji Mohammad Hussain Aabedi, Nisar Hussain Siksa, and Nurboo Gyalchan were arrested and imprisoned, and later released after forty days, when Ghul Shah's government came in power in Kashmir. Similarly to pressurize the government to fulfill this long standing public demand, Sonam Wangyal went on hunger strike for sixteen days in January 1984. Later he again went on hunger strike for five days. Mrs. Indira Gandhi, the then Prime Minister of India, visited Leh and assured the protesters that Ladakh will be granted Scheduled Tribe status very soon. She asked Wangyal to withdraw his hunger strike by offering him a glass of soft drink. On her return to Delhi, she announced the intention of the government to grant the Scheduled Tribes status to the people of Ladakh; however this decision was not implemented until 1989.

Homelessness also became a serious problem in Ladakh. As a reflection of the world-wide phenomenon of the people migrating from the rural to urban areas, many people came from villages to Leh to seek jobs, and so on. Wangyal formed an organization called the Homeless Persons Association to tackle this problem. Hundreds of people were benefited. In

1989 after a communal clash between the Buddhists and Muslims, the Ladakh Buddhists Association (LBA) launched a campaign to press the government to grant Autonomous Hill Development Council and Union Territory Status for Ladakh. Sonam Wangyal was invited by the President of the LBA to extend his support and join the campaign. However, Wangyal was dismayed to learn about the LBA's plan to impose a social and economic boycott against the Muslim minority. Although he was in favour of the U.T. demand, but he opposed the communal division outright, and told the President and others that the imposition of an economic and social boycott was in contravention of the spirit of the Indian constitution, and the country's democratic and secular traditions. He also felt that it was against the traditions and ethos of Ladakhi life, which advocates religious tolerance and communal harmony. Moreover, it violated the religious tenets. He also felt strongly that Ladakhis could not afford to mix religious communalism with politics. Wangyal proposed the involment of both Muslims and Buddhists in the movement, and offered his services, to sit on Dharna and go on hunger strike. The Ladakh Buddhist Association, however did not agree with him, and ostracized him by declaring a strict social boycott against him. They were determined to isolate the Muslims and to impose social and economic boycott against the community, which lasted after four years. Wangyal was very glad in 1992, when the LBA finally had come back to the path he had championed and lifted its boycott against the Muslims before the Hill Council status was granted, but he felt till his death that the age-old traditionally amicable relations between the Buddhists and the Muslims had been sadly damaged.

Sonam Wangyal has earned a place in the history of Ladakh for his successful efforts to bring basic economic justice, democratic rights, and educational opportunities to the common people in Ladakh. He will be remembered for his sacrifices to uphold communal harmony and secular ideals in Ladakh. That is why, he is considered the champion of secularism and communal harmony. Many prominent citizens and scholars felt that the Ladakhi people at the helm of affairs did nothing to honour this great leader he was not given due status what he deserved. The author, being a part of the Ladakhi heritage, put forward the demand that at least a leading Government Institution or colony should be named after Sonam Wangyal or endorse him for a befitting posthumous award.

Padmashri Sonam Nurboo (1909-1979)

Sonam Nurboo was born on 27th of July, 1909 in Nyachu family of Skara. His parents were farmers by profession. he was an upright and hard-working student. Right from his childhood he showed keenness to go to school and was sent to Government Middle School Leh wherefrom he passed his 8th class examination and went for further studies at Srinagar. He passed his matriculation in 1929 from Sri Pratap High School Srinagar and also did his FA degree from Srinagar. After passing his graduation from Jammu in Science subject he was selected for the training of Naib Tehsildar. During the training, an advertisement regarding admission for Engineering invited his attention and he opted for it. He was selected for Engineering degree to be done from England. The government recommended Mr. Nurboo's case to England with some financial grant. He got the degree of Bachelor in Engineering in 1942 from Sheffield University. On his return from England he was appointed Assistant Engineer in Baramulla on 26th July, 1942. In the wake of independence, Sonam Nurboo's service was sought to construct a makeshift Airfield at Leh to counter the "Qabaili war."

In the month of February 1948, Sonam Nurboo accompanied by Major Prithichand along with a small contingent of 20 jawans crossed the Zojila on foot in sub-zero temperature. The party reached Leh on 9th March 1948 after facing great hardships in the way. Soon after his arrival at Leh, Sonam Nurboo undertook the task of construction of an airfield for the Indian army on a sandy plain called Abi-Chhenmothang. He worked day and night to complete the construction of the airfield in record time, as there was a great danger of Leh being captured by the Pak raiders. May 24, 1948 was a memorable day in the history of Ladakh, when the first Dakota aircraft of the Indian Air Force was landed at the newly constructed airfield by Air Commodore Maher Singh. Major General K.S. Thimayya who accompanied him promised the local commander and the people that more aircrafts would be sent soon carrying troops along with arms, ammunition, medicines, etc. In due course, more Dakotas landed with troops and thus Leh was saved from the Pak raiders. In the year 1950, Sonam Nurboo was elevated to the post of Divisional Engineer and was posted at Ramban division. During the early fifties, Sonam Nurboo took in hand the survey and construction of Leh-Srinagar highway. Toiling day and night he got it completed within record time. After serving at Kishtawar, Anantnag and other places in Kashmir he was promoted to Superintending Engineer on October 4, 1958 and posted in his hometown at Leh. As an Engineer, he did remarkable job throughout Ladakh. The Airport Leh, Stakna Hydel Project and Srinagar-Leh road were constructed under his supervision, for which the people of Leh are still grateful to him. In recognition to his distinguished services in the region, the Government of India conferred him the prestigious Padma Shri award. He is known as the architect of modern Ladakh. He was retired from the government service as Chief Engineer in 1963. He was soon re-employed in the Border Road Organization as Chief Engineer of Project Cheetak in which post he remained for three years. In 1965, the state government retrieved his service and appointed him as Development Commissioner of Leh. Later the Government of India appointed him as Ambassador of India in Mongolia. He strengthened the diplomatic relations between the two countries working there for about six years. Later in 1975, when Sheikh Mohammad Abdullah's government came in power in Jammu and Kashmir, Sonam Nurboo was inducted in his cabinet, and was allotted the most privileged portfolio of Public Works Department.

Sonam Nurboo was a man of dedication and devotion with the qualities of straight-forwardness, honesty, agility and ethical values. He was having least interest for personal benefit. He remained in chase of the Projects till they reached to the completion. Sonam Nurboo will be remembered forever as a role model in the Ladakh's history. When he died in February 1980, thousands of Ladakhis, State Government dignitaries and officials participated in his funeral. He was cremated at Skyachaks Leh, with full State honours. After his death his only son Pintoo Nurboo was elected MLC and was inducted in the Sheikh Abdullah's cabinet as Deputy Minister for Tourism and Protocol. Presently, he is a Member of Legislative Assembly from Nubra Constituency.

Pintoo Nurboo

Pintoo Nurboo was born on 2nd July 1948 in the Nyachu family to Padmashri Sonam Nurboo and Smt. Shema Pal. He was the only son of his parents and was educated at Born Hall School Sonawar, Srinagar from Primary to Higher secondary class. Later, he went to Delhi and got admission in Karorimal College wherefrom he did his graduation. He was doing MA in Political Science from Delhi University, but in the meantime, he was selected to undergo training in Tea Plantation management in Assam. After the completion of the said training, he was appointed as assistant Manager at Assam Tea Plantation. He worked there sincerely and efficiently for four years from 1969 to 1972. Having got training in management, he wanted to establish his own Hotel at Leh, consequently he resigned from the post and became busy in construction of Shambala hotel.

Ladakh was open for foreign tourists since 1974 and his efforts bore fruits and his hotel business flourished. In 1980, his beloved father Sonam Nurboo expired and Sheikh Mohammad Abdullah got him elected as Member of the Legislative Council and was elevated to Deputy Minister Protocol. Later Sheikh Abdullah too passed away in 1982 and his son Farooq Abdullah became the Chief Minister of J&K who elevated him as Minister of State for Tourism. In this capacity, he did so many remarkable jobs for the state. The project cable car was one of them. In 1983, he fought the MLA election as an NC candidate against Congress candidate Sonam Gyalchan Vakil but lost the election. After Sonam Gyalchan Vakil Tsering Samphel was elected MLA. But neither Sonam Gyalchan nor Tsering Samphel were inducted in the cabinet, as both of the members were from opposition Congress. Consequently, from 1984 to 1996, there was no Minister in J&K cabinet from Leh region. Ladakh was in a great loss. In 1996, he fought the election on NC mandate against Congress candidate Tsering Dorjay Lakruk and lost the election. In 1989, due to some differences with the NC government, he left the party and joined the BJP. In 2002, all the parties, national as well as regional, were amalgamated in LUTF. He was elected as MLA un-contested from Nubra constituency. As a Member of the Legislative Assembly he served the people of Ladakh very honestly and sincerely. According to him, it was because of his efforts and pressure that NC government endorsed the issue of ST status to the Central Government with recommendation. In the J&K Assembly, he pleaded the point that Ladakh should not be considered mere as District but as an important region. It was a trade centre in the past and historical gateway to the central Asian countries, and strategically it occupies an important place. The then Chief Minister Mufti Mohammad Sayeed principally agreed with his views.

Pintoo Nurboo visited China, Russia, Mongolia, Sweeden, Germany, France, Belgium, Sri Lanka, Thailand, Hungary, Singapur, Pakistan, Dubai, Sharjah, Canada, and USA. He attended several National and International seminars on Kashmir apart from Pakwash conference at Islamabad and Sri Lanka and conference on Kashmir dispute in Canada. He also attended European Parliamentary conference at Brussel in Belgium and presented his views. He had been a Member National Integration Council twice and emphasized the people to maintain communal harmony and brotherhood between the two major communities, i.e. Hindu and Muslim. According to Pintoo there have been some politicians in the society who instigate the sentiments of the innocent people, and create communal tensions in the region to grind their own axe, especially during parliamentary elections. People remember him as a sociable, soft spoken, gentle man of high principles.

Phuntsog Namgyal

Phuntsog Namgyal was born on 17th December 1937, at Sumoor Nubra. His father Kunzang Dorjay was the Block President of Indian National Congress, Nubra. He was a highly qualified person in Bothi Language. His house in the village Sumoor is named "Stakre", which means the Tiger and this has a history behind it. The title of Stakre was granted to his great grandfather by the Raja of Ladakh as far back as 1830 in recognition to his bravery shown by him in fighting the forces of Mirza Haider of Turkistan, who had invaded Ladakh. His elder brother Lt. Col. Tsewang Rinchen, has had a distinguished military career, who was conferred twice MVC, and one SM by the Government of India for his bravery during Indo-Pak wars. In 1948-49, when the Pakistani raiders blocked the gate of Nubra and consequently threatening life of the people of Nubra (Ladakh). The second MVC was awarded to him in 1971, after liberating Turtuk region in Nubra. Namgyal aged fifteen and his brother Chewang Rinchen aged seventeen, joined the Nubra guard to defend the country. And probably Namgyal was the youngest one among the guards. His brother Chewang Rinchen was later regularized in the Indian Army as Jamadar at the age of seventeen and half and was the youngest JCO in the Indian Army. Later, when he was awarded MVC at the end of the Indo-Pak war in 1948-49, he became the youngest winner of MVC. Namgyal received his primary education at Sumoor Nubra and then came to Leh to seek admission in the middle classes. He passed the middle standard examination from Govt. Middle School Leh and then proceeded to Srinagar for Higher studies and passed the matriculation from Bisco School Srinagar. After qualifying the B.Sc. Agriculture in 1959 from Agriculture College Ludhiana, he was appointed as Assistant Agriculture Officer at Leh. In 1968, he was deputed to Andhra Pradesh Agricultural University for doing M.Sc. and qualified the postgraduate in 1969, and promoted as District Agriculture Officer. He did government service from 1959 to 1969. In the meantime, the post of MLC was vacated due to the appointment of Sonam Nurboo as Indian Ambassador to Mongolia. Many friends and well-wishers approached Namgyal, and asked him to resign from the government service, and contest the election of Member Legislative Council. Finally, he resigned from the government service in 1969 and agreed to contest the election and was elected as a Congress candidate. He retained the seat for full ten years. Later he contested the parliament election twice. He won the first election and lost the second one. After winning the first Parliament election, he was inducted in the cabinet of Prime Minister Narsimha Rao in 1988 as Deputy Minister for Surface Transport and Parliamentary Affairs. In 1989, he was elevated as Minister of State for Petro-chemical and Parliamentary Affairs. He did remarkable service to the people of India in general and the Ladakhis in particular. It is because of his sincere efforts that he formed the Co-operative society in Leh, airline services and introduced L.P.G. bottling plant. He participated in the tripartite talk for grant of Scheduled tribe and Hill Council status for Ladakh. As a Member of Parliament he was member, Consultative Committee on Defence, Transport and Civil Aviation. He visited Mongolia as member of the Asian Buddhist conference for Peace, in Geneva Switzerland, representing Congress party in a committee, headed by President Dr. Shankar Dayal Sharma to North Korea on the occasion of 75th birth anniversary of President Kim-il-Song, visited Combodia and Vietnam as a Member of Parliamentary Committee. Other countries he visited are England, France, Germany, Sri Lanka, Thailand, Malaysia, Singapore, Hong Kong, China, and Russia. Presently, he is once again the Member of the Jammu and Kashmir Legislative Council and is one of the senior living Congress leaders at National level. He acted as Officiating Chairman of J&K Legislative Council for seven months in 2007-08. He got constructed a two storey building out of his MP LAD fund, as sarai to accommodate the people of far flung areas in Leh town. His elder daughter is a doctor by profession and the younger daughter did M.A. in sociology and qualified NET.

Kushok Togdan Rinpoche: Chos-je Togdan Rinpoche is the spiritual leader of Drikung Kargyud tradition. Actually Chos-je was sent from Drikung Thil monastery in Tibet to places such as Mount Kailash, Tsari, Lachi, and Ladakh, etc. Since the previous incarnation of Togdan Rinpoche was born in Ladakh, it became the tradition that his successive re-incarnation would be appointed as the Chos-je for Ladakh. His predecessor was a nephew of Raja Sonam Namgyal born to a lady of Stok called Gupupa Ama Shema.

Togdan Rinpoche is the re-incarnation of the great Indian Maha Sidha Hungchen Kara, who centuries later incarnated as Kongbo Togdan Tulku, a disciple of H.H. Drikung Terton Rinchen Phuntsog (1509-57). His previous six re-incarnations were born in Tibet and 8th in Ladakh at Stok. The present Togdan Rinpoche with his religious name Konchok Stanzin Thubstan Stanpai Gyaltsan is the 9th re-incarnation. He was born in a poor family of Konchok Tsultim and Skalzang Dolma in 1938 in Durbuk village situated 110 kms. away from Leh. He lost his mother when he was just two hours old. He was fed by his aunt with the help of goat's milk. It is said that when he was one and a half year old he left a clear impression of his footprint on a boulder where he was standing, which can be seen today. Several miraculous impressions and natural things were also happened in his family which left an imprint of his Superiority in the society.

The previous Skaybgon Chetsang Rinpoche, Shiwe Lodros recognized him as the incarnation of Togdan Rinpoche. In 1943, he was enthroned as Chos-je Togdan Rinpoche in Shachukul monastery which is one of the three main monasteries of the Drikung Kargyud sect in Ladakh. The monastery is located very close to his birth place. He received the traditional education at the very young age and in 1952, he accompanied by his tutor Gergon Konchok Sonam and travelled to Drikung monastery in Tibet where he received higher education in various fields from many spiritual leaders. Upto 1954, he studied in the Philosophical College known as Drikung Nima Changra. He became very popular within a short time. When China took over Tibet in 1960, he came back to Ladakh along with his tutor and many other Ladakhi monks. Since then, Rinpoche has been carrying out his responsibilities for fifty Drikung monasteries in Ladakh while maintaining the Drikung Kargyud tradition there. Rinpoche holds the special transmission of Gong Chig, Yamnataka, Phowa and Dharampalas of Drikung Kargyud. Besides, being an important transmission holder of Drikung Kargyud, Rinpoche also holds the transmission of Rinchen Ter-Zod which is considered mainly Ningmapa tradition. In the beginning of 1967, Rinpoche arranged for the Rinchen Ter-Zod empowerment to be given at Tso Padma (Rewalsar), one of the most sacred places of Guru Padmasambhawa, where H.H. Dudjom Rinpoche gave this empowerment to a great assembly consisting of 30 Tulkus and several thousands people. Consequently, H.H. Dudjom Rinpoche initiated him as his successor for imparting this great empowerment of Rinchen Ter-Zod. Years later, Rinpoche discovered several sacred hidden places and also revealed some mind treasured texts. His collected works that comprise of one volume, contains a short commentary of Gong-Chig. He is also working on a small history book namely "Kunsang Melong" which is yet to be published. After 1960's, Rinpoche had been the only spiritual leader of the Drikungpa school, who holds all kinds of oral and empowerment transmission of Drikung Tradition. He has given several empowerments and oral transmission to the present Drikungpas living in India and abroad. He gave H.H. Chetsang Rinpoche, the oral transmission of Rigzin Chostaks works. In 1974, Togdan Rinpoche invited Khyunka Rinpoche to Ladakh where he started a meditation centre at Chushul. Later on, this meditation centre was shifted to Lamayuru. After repairing the monastery of Atitse in 1981, Rinpoche established a school for young monks. Atitse monastery is situated north-west of Lamayuru.

In 1978, under the supervision of Togdan Rinpoche, a spectacular reception ceremony was held at Leh for H.H. the Drikung Skyabgon Chetsang Rinpoche who is the overall head of Drikung Kargyud. In this reception ceremony the monks of Phiyang, Lamayuru and Shachukul monasteries participated. This was the first visit of Chetsang Rinpoche to Ladakh having miraculously escaped from Chinese occupied Tibet only three years back. Thus, the Chetsang Rinpoche and Togdan

Rinpoche jointly worked for strengthening of the Drikung Kargyud in Ladakh. In 1979, under both the spiritual leaders, 800th anniversary of the foundation of Drikung Thil monastery by Skyoba Jigsten Sumgon in 1179 was celebrated at Phiyang monastery. In 1985, H.H. Chetsang Rinpoche also visited Ladakh, marking a most auspicious event because this was the first meeting of the three spiritual leaders. Chos-je Togdan Rinpoche had been the President of All Ladakh Gonpa Society during four years from 1972 to 1975; he attended World Buddhist Conference held in Taiwan; Spain, Germany, Switzerland, France and America.

In 1967, the political situation of Ladakh turned towards a new direction. This led to form Ladakh Action Committee which would make agitation against the government for fulfillment of various demands of Ladakh region. Togdan Rinpoche was unanimously elected as the Chairman of the Ladakh Action Committee. Under that auspices, the State Government was forced to accept ten demands of the Ladakh Action Committee and this way Kushok Togdan Rinpoche became a known political leader beside his high religious position. The success of the Ladakh Action Committee was highly honoured and appreciated by the people. K.G. Bakula Rinpoche the then President of Ladakh Gonpa Society presented a memento to Togdan Rinpoche on behalf of himself and the people of Ladakh.

While recognizing the penchant of social welfare, political aspiration and religious tolerance in Togdan Rinpoche, the Chief Minister of J&K State, Syed Mir Qasim appointed him as Vice Chairman of Ladakh Development Board, which he held for four years. During that period many developmental works were taken up in Ladakh. Due to repeated efforts by Togdan Rinpoche several developmental schemes were executed in far off places in Ladakh. The most prominent achievements were projected such as Durbuk canal, Alchi Bridge, upgradation of High School Timisgam and many lower high schools, Medical Aid Centres at Timisgam, Sumoor, Man, Merak and Skurbuchan, etc. In 1970's, local Congress was divided in two groups, viz. Congress "A" and Congress "B". Togdan Rinpoche contested the Leh Assembly election as a candidate of Congress "B" against the Congress "A" candidate Sonam Wangyal and lost the seat. In 1974, when Sheikh Mohammad Abdullah came in power, he introduced many policies in his administration and under such policy, the Vice Chairmen of some of the Boards were abolished including Ladakh Development Board. In recognition to his social services and to strengthen the National Conference Party at Leh, he was entrusted the Presidentship of the Party at Leh. Togdan Rinpoche made his best efforts to strengthen National Conference in the District and remained as Head of the Party in Leh till 1989. The success of Tsettan Namgyal as MLA from Nubra constituency directly goes to the credit of Togdan Rinpoche. The services rendered by Togdan Rinpoche in the capacity of President, National Conference, Leh strengthened the party in Leh. He was nominated as MLC in the J&K Assembly and later elevated as Minister of State for Ladakh Affairs and Planning in the cabinet of Chief Minister Dr. Farooq Abdullah. As a Minister he took various steps for speediest development of Ladakh. He tried his best to enhance budgetary grant for Ladakh region. Thus, since 1960's Rinpoche served selflessly the people of Ladakh in various capacities in the State Government until recently when he submitted his resignation on 19th September 2003 from his post of Minister of State for Ladakh Affairs and Planning, which he held for six years. He said he has done so keeping in view the sentiments and aspirations of the people of Ladakh, who are demanding Union Territory status for Ladakh. He had been an active member of the Ladakh Union Territory Front and recently resigned from its primary membership. Presently, he is holding the dual post of President Ladakh Gonpa Association and Ladakh Buddhist Association Leh. Distancing from politics, he intends to establish Nalanda School to serve the Dharma and Buddhist community.

Kushok Nawang Chamba Stanzin (Khanpo Rinpoche)

Kushok Nawang Chamba Stanzin was born at Chushot at Bilupa house in the year 1944. He was recognized as the Khanpo Rinpoche at the age of five and was shifted and enthroned at Thiksay monastery. He received his basic monastic education under the care of his religious teacher

Kachen Lobzang Zotpa, a scholar of Thiksay Gonpa and then proceeded to Lhasa for further monastic studies, where from he qualified for the Geshes degree from Daspung monastery but could not continue the higher studies, because of the Chinese occupation of Tibet. He returned back to Ladakh to perform the religious duties. He is the 9th reincarnation of Khanpo Rinpoche of Thiksay monastery. Eight other reincarnations are: 1. Stot Changsem Sherap Zangpo, 2. Chhosje Jamyang Lotus 3. Paldan Sherap, 4. Sharpa Chhosje Lobzang Chinba, 5. Gyalrsas Jigmat Namgyal, who was the son of King Tsewang Namgyal IInd with his second wife Tsering Khatoon, 6. Gyalrsas Nawang Namgyal, was the younger brother of King Nima Namgyal, 7. rJe Chamba Chhognis, 8. rJe Chamba Chosphel and finally Kushok Nawang Chamba Stanzin.

It was Changsem Sherap Zangpo who introduced and propagated the Gelukpa sect in Ladakh. He was born in Thiksay Village to father Tashi and mother Palzom. Later, he went to Tibet for higher studies and came to know about Galdan Gonpa and rje Lama Tsongkhapa. He became a true disciple of Tsongkhapa and he got the knowledge of "Sutra" and Tantra from him, popularly known as Stot Changsem Sherap Zangpo. Changsem and one of his collegues reached Ladakh with a small statue sent by Tsongkhapa to King Takpa Bum Ldey. They presented it to the king, who kept it in Pethub Gonpa. Later, Changsem started his mission. First of all he got constructed the Stagmo Gonpa. His disciple Spon Paldan Sherap constructed the Thiksay Gonpa. The Diskit Gonpa was constructed by a Raja of Nubra namely Neema Takapa under the supervision of Changsem Sherap Zangpo. Moreover, Changsem Sherap Zangpo got constructed Gonpas at various places like Charasa and Ahinsa in Nubra, Chhazar, Phugtal and Karsha and Zangskar Wakha, Kartsey, Tsangra, and Amdhi in Purig and Lingshed in Sham. Later, a Raja of Nubra Tsewang Raftan and his queen constructed the Lhakhang and Dukhang Kagyat. In 1770, King Tsewang Namgyal handed over the Diskit Gonpa to Kushok Khanpo of Thiksay.

Kushok Khanpo Chamba Stanzin did remarkable job in the field of religion and improved every system in the Gonpa. He introduced common kitchen system for the Lamas. He got constructed a 45 feet high statue of Chamba in the sitting position in the year 1979, and the "Tashish Rapnas" of the statue was performed by H.H. the Dalai Lama in 1981. He established monastic school and library within the Gonpa. Where the young monks are being imparted monastic education and trained in religious activities. Kushok Khampo got contructed a palace for H.H. Dalai Lama under the foothill of Diskit Gonpa where Dalai Lama stayed for the first time in July 2003. He also got constructed 100 ft. high statue of Gyalwa Chamba at the hill of Diskit Gonpa. It was started in 2005 and took five years to complete. Thus, "Rapnas" was performed by H.H. the Dalai Lama on 24th July 2010. H.H. the Dalai Lama also recognized a boy as re-incarnation of Kachen Lobzang Zotpa, the tutor of Khanpo Rinpocle and named Khantol Stanzin Zotpa Gyatso. He had been the President of Ladakh Gonpa Association for many years from 1992-97, and served the Buddhist community, and fought for the cause of Gonpa's for many years. Later, on the request of some people, he came in politics and contested the Assembly election in 1967, against the Congress candidate Sonam Wangyal and lost the election. Later he was elected president of District Congress Committee Leh and served the people. He was the member of many delegations to Jammu and Delhi, to discuss the long standing demands of the Ladakhis and present the memorandum to the Central and State leaders. He was also a member of the tripartite talk held in New Delhi in October 1993, in connection with the grant of Hill Council status to the Ladakhis. He had been a close associate of Dr. Farooq Abdullah, the then Chief Minister of Jammu and Kashmir, who offered him the post of MLC and Minister in the J&K cabinet, but he rejected the offer. Togdan Rinpoche and Tsettan Namgyal were inducted in the J&K cabinet, on the request and recommendation of Khanpo Rinpoche. It shows that he is not a power hungry politician, instead he is a king maker. Later, he was elected as Member of Parliament for Rajya Sabha in 1998 and served the people for full five years.

He spent the Member Parliament LAD funds for construction of hospitals, community hall and water supply schemes. Recently, he retired from the party politics and decided to dedicate himself for the cause of Buddhism in Ladakh.

Thufstan Tsewang

Thufstan Tsewang was born in the Lonpo family of Shay on Ist September, 1947. His father Sonam Tsephal was a school teacher during the post-independence period, and served the people. In those days, education was a neglected sector and this neglect still continues. Probably, he is one of the oldest persons in the region. His mother Smt. Nurzin Wangmo was a princess of Matho Palace, an offspring of the Namgyal dynasty. Thufstan received his basic education at primary school Shay and then shifted to Srinagar to receive middle education, under the care of his maternal uncle Rev. K.G. Bakula, who had been a Minister in the J&K cabinet at that time. Thufstan has to move from Srinagar to Jammu, with the move of the Civil Secretariat and finally passed the middle school standard examination from Tyndle Bisco School Srinagar. After passing middle school examination from Srinagar, he was enrolled in the Mahabodhi intermediate college Sarnath, where from he passed the matriculation examination under the U.P. Board, with good marks. He passed the higher secondary Part-II examination from the Delhi United Christian Higher Secondary School and then he was admitted in the Ramjas College of Delhi University in 1964 for higher studies, where from he qualified the graduation in 1967. Later, he was enrolled in the law faculty of Delhi University and completed the LLB in 1970. He practiced law at Jammu, under the care of Justice R.P. Sethi. In 1971-72, he started a movement for grant of Central Administration to Ladakh, when Syed Mir Qasim was in power in J&K. He was sent to jail, along with other colleagues.

It is not out of place to mention here that for the first time, the Ladakhis demanded NEFA type administration and then Central Administration, and now demanding Union Territory status for Ladakh but it will take time to be matured, because of its linkage with the Kashmir issue.

Thufstan Tsewang CEC alongwith EC'S

In 1975-77, he worked as Public Relation Officer to Sonam Nurboo, then Public Works Minister of J&K, for about two years in a very efficient manner. In 1978, he was selected as Programme Executive in All India Radio Leh and worked on the said post, very honestly and sincerely for about ten years. However, he resigned from the said post in 1987 to assume the post of Director in LEDEG (Ladakh Ecological Development Group) a local NGO. Besides, he was elected as President Ladakh Buddhist Association and served the Buddhist community for about eight years with merits. He married with princess Sarla Tsewang and became the son in law of late Raja Kunzang Namgyal of Stok, the offspring of Namgyal dynasty. He is having one son and one daughter and they are studying in Delhi. Thufstan Tsewang is a fearless, soft spoken, straightforward, gentle, able and honest statesman, and commands a high respect and regards in the society. He served the people of Ladakh in different capacities, in a very efficient manner and guided the poor people on the right path. He played a vital role in the capacity of LBA President, during the agitation of 1989 for the common cause of the Ladakhi Buddhists and against the discrimination of the Kashmir government. A social and economic boycott was imposed against the Muslims and it was lifted on November 29, 1992 during the tripartite talk in New Delhi, because the State and Central leadership asked the LBA leaders to remove the differences and to create traditional brotherhood and harmonious relations. He led many delegations from 1989 to 1995 to Jammu, Srinagar and New Delhi, in connection with the grant of Scheduled Tribe and Hill Council Status to Ladakh and to discuss the long standing demands. Finally, Hill Council was granted and he became the first Chairman and Chief Executive Councillor of Ladakh Autonomous Hill Development Council on 5th September 1995, and remained on the said post for about nine years upto 2004, and did remarkable constructive and welfare activities in the District at his command. He resigned from the said post to contest the Parliament election of 2004, and won the election by defeating his nearest rival Hassan Khan with a good margin. Though he lost the 1999 MP election with the said person, it is because of his sincere efforts, that the plight of the Buddhists of Ladakh changed economically, socially, educationally, and politically under the banner of LBA. In recognition to his services rendered to humanity in the capacity of LBA President, the Mahabodhi Society Leh conferred on him the "Humanity Service Award". Moreover considering his outstanding public services, in different capacities, the Indira Gandhi Indian Farmers Journalists Association awarded him the "Indira Gandhi IFJA Award". He is the sitting Member Parliament from Ladakh for the last four years and has done many welfare activities in the Ladakh region, by utilizing his MP LAD fund. As an MP, he led the Indian Parliamentary delegation to South Africa. He was a member of the Parliamentary delegation to Myanmar and Mauritius. Under the leadership of Somnath Chatterji the Hon'ble Speaker, he was a member of the Parliamentary delegation to Vietnam and Bangkok. Moreover, he remained the Member of the Parliamentary Standing Committee on Defense, Science and Technology, Environment and Forest. He is a Member of the Parliamentary Consultative Committee on Rural Development. He is also the President of Ladakh Union Territory Front, a local party and under his leadership, the party won a great victory during the council election of 2006.

Rigzin Spalbar

He was born in Chushot Leh and received the primary education in Leh itself. He later was enrolled in Ladakh Institute of Higher Studies and Vishesh Kendriya Vidyalaya Delhi, wherefrom he passed the 11th class. He qualified for the graduation from the Kirorimal College of Delhi University. At that time only a few students, from Ladakh were studying at Delhi. Rev. K.G. Bakula, Lama Lobzang and P. Namgyal, etc. were the prominent and popular Ladakhi leaders in Delhi and he was in close contact with these dignitaries and got the opportunity to meet the central leaders and ministers in various delegations, to present the problems faced by the Ladakhi people and indirectly got the leadership qualities and training.

Rigzin Spalbar CEC and Rigzin Jora Minister alongwith H.H. Dalai Lama at an Inaugural Function

After graduation, when he came back to Leh, he established a travel agency, namely Silk Route Travels at Leh. During this period, he was taking active part in Youth Congress activities and was elected the President of District Youth Congress Committee Leh and worked whole heartedly for strengthening the Congress party and did remarkable job during the MP and MLA elections. In 1989, he was elected

General Secretary of Ladakh Buddhist Association Leh and worked for a long time for the welfare of the Ladakhi Buddhists and LBA movement, so as to make the Ladakhi Buddhists aware of their rights and duties. He was one of the Members of the Ladakh Coordination Committee, to achieve the Hill Council status for Ladakh, and participated in tripartite talks at Srinagar, Jammu and Delhi along with other dignitaries. After the approval of the council Act by the President of India, in May 1995, the council election was held in Leh and he was elected Councillor uncontested, from the Lamayuru constituency and was sworn in as a Councillor at Polo ground Leh, on 3rd September, 1995.

Again in 2000, he was elected as a Congress councillor from upper Leh Constituency and was elevated as Executive Councillor Education, under the Chairmanship of Thufstan Tsewang. He worked as EC Education for three years and proved one of the best and brilliant EC, who put the whole education system on the right track and the Board results under him, improved year by year. He was elected Chairman and Chief Executive Councillor in June 2004 when Thufstan Tsewang was elected as Member of Parliament. He was the Chief Manager for the parliament election and the Congress workers and leaders worked under him in a team spirit and won the election. He has proved himself one of the best administrators and dynamic leader in the LAHDC Leh. Though, he remained as CEC, for a brief period but he did remarkable job during his chairmanship. For instance road and bridges were constructed at many places in the district, nine high schools were upgraded as higher secondary schools, four blocks have been created, an MOU was signed with the TATA group and hundreds of teachers and other officers and officials were promoted in their respective cadres. Since there was Congress Government at the centre, and State, and at Leh itself. There was a good relation and understanding between the State Government and LAHDC Leh. He got drafted the Vision 2020, which is perhaps a guideline for the council. In 2005 council election, he was got elected as councillor from the Sku-Markha constituency and is playing a vital role as the opposition leader in the council. Being a very good orator and debater, his speeches had been highly impressive during the general council meetings. He was appointed General Secretary of the District Congress Committee Leh, when Mr. Tsering Sampel was the Distt. President but after his appointment as Member SC, ST, Commission, he was elevated as President Congress Committee Leh in 2007, and continued on the post till November 2010. The LAHDC Council election of 2010 was fought under his leadership and Congress achieved a land slide victory over his rival BJP. He himself was elected from two constituencies from Sku-Markha and Lower Leh. He was elected un-opposed from Sku-Markha. After the council election he was unanimously elected Chairman of the LAHDC Leh once again and presently is performing as Chief Executive Councillor with guts and in a very efficient manner.

Nawang Rigzin Jora

Nawang Rigzin Jora was born on 2nd February, 1958 at village Nimmu, Leh. His father Phuntsog Stobgais was an agriculturist. He received his basic education in Leh and did graduation from renowned institution of Delhi's St. Stephen College. He is having two children, a son and a daughter. After completion of his studies, he was affiliated with the tourism sector. Later he started his political career under the banner of Indian National Congress and was Joint Secretary District Congress Committee Leh in 1998. He had been the General Secretary of Ladakh Buddhist Association and launched an agitation under the aegis of LBA to achieve the status of Hill Development Council for Ladakh. He was one of the members to participate in tripartite talks at Srinagar, Jammu and Delhi, to achieve the Hill Development Council status for Ladakh, and presented the views before the government in a very efficient manner. Finally on May 9, 1995 President of India approved the "Ladakh Autonomous Hill Development Council act". As a result, on 3rd of September, 1995 under the supervision of the Governor of J&K, Gen. K.V. Krishna Rao swearing in ceremony for the first Ladakh Autonomous Hill Development Council was held at the Leh polo ground and Mr. Thufstan Tsewang was elected as first Chairman and Chief

Executive Councillor of the Council. Mr. Jora had been councillor and Executive Councillor Education from 1993 to 2000 and was re-elected as councillor in September 2000; he also was Executive Councillor PWD.

Nawang Rigzin Jora Minister of Urban Development is Laying the Foundation Stone of War-Memory

He was elected unopposed, as Member J&K Legislative Assembly in 2002 General Election and was inducted as Minister of Mufti Mohammad Sayeed cabinet as Minister of State for Public Works on 2nd November 2002. Later, considering his honesty and efficiency, he was elevated to the cabinet rank as Minister of Science and Technology, Labour and Employment and Information Technology on January 14, 2003. He became Minister of Power in November 2005 and Minister, Industries and Commerce in 2008. In the general Election 2008, he was re-elected as Member J&K Legislative Assembly, by defeating his nearest rival Sh. Thufstan Tsewang. He was inducted in the Cabinet of Mr. Omar Abdullah as Minister for Tourism and Culture in January, 2009, and did remarkable job to boost the tourist industry in the State of J&K. That is why the CNN-IBN has conferred on him the award for best Tourism Minister in India. As a Minister he has taken various steps for speediest development of Ladakh region. He is considered the ablest Cabinet Minister Ladakh has ever produced. But recently in the month of January 2013, he was shifted from Tourism to Urban Development & Urban

Local Bodies Ministry in a cabinet reshuffle. Mr. Jora has command over many languages and is bold enough to present the cases and problems faced by the Ladakhis, in the cabinet and J&K Assembly. He is one of the brilliant, honest and efficient ministers in the present cabinet and is also considered as Mr. Clean among the cabinet Ministers. It is one of the characteristics of Mr. Jora that he does efforts to solve the problems of the people irrespective of his political affiliation, caste, color, creed or religion. Thus, since 1990's he is serving selflessly the people of Ladakh and State Government. He toured foreign countries like, Canada, England, France, Belgium, Luxemburg, Thailand, Netherland, Switzerland, Germany and Portugal. He attended many National and International seminars and presented papers. As a politician and statesman, Jora Rigzin earned the regard, respect, aclaim and admiration of his collegues, bureaucrats and polity. He has a very clear and distinct vision of different politico-socio-economic situations with good communication and rapport building skills. He is an active social worker with mass support of people of Leh and Kargil.

Tsering Dorjay Lakruk

Tsering Dorjay was born on 24th of December 1948 at Lakruk house Sankar in Leh. His father Tashi Namgyal was a progressive farmer who did remarkable job in producing various kinds of vegetables in Leh. Tsering Dorjay received his primary education at Diskit Nubra and middle education at Middle School Leh. He passed matriculation from Govt. High School Leh in 1965, under the J&K Board of School Education, Srinagar. Later, he proceeded to Srinagar, enrolled in S.P. College Srinagar for higher education and qualified for graduation in 1970. After graduation, he joined State Bank of India Leh branch and worked there for about six years, resigned from the post in 1976, and worked for a Swiss travel agency and traveled to many foreign countries, in connection with the business. He was an active youth leader and took part in the scheduled tribe movement in 1982. He had been President Youth Congress District Leh for about six years, from 1983 to 1987, and did remarkable job to make the people aware of their rights. Besides, he had been Vice-President of Ladakh Buddhist Association from 1988 to 1995, and was an active member in 1989. Buddhist agitation, against the indifferent attitude of the Kashmir Govt. and to fulfill the long standing demands of the Ladakhi Buddhists, he worked sincerely for the cause of the Buddhist community and to create awareness in the field of social, political, economic, and cultural and education. He participated as a member of the LBA delegation to Srinagar, Jammu and Delhi, headed by Thufstan Tsewang. He participated as a member of the LBA delegation in the tripartite talk, from 1989 to 1995, in connection with the grant of Hill Development Status for Ladakh. In the said talk, the State and central leadership asked to remove the differences with the Muslims of Leh and to create harmonious relation between different communities in the region. Government said "Unless or until the Muslims would not cooperate the movement, the Govt. could not give any kind of assurance of your demands". Thus on November 29, 1992 during the tripartite talk in New Delhi, the LBA lifted the three years old social and economic boycott. And the Muslims of Leh, under the leadership of Mohammad Akbar Ladakhi wholeheartedly participated in the struggle of greater autonomy, popularly known as Hill Council status to Ladakh.

The second tripartite talk was held in New Delhi in October 1993. In the said meeting the Union Home Minister S.B. Chavan, formally announced that the demand of "Autonomous Hill Development Council" would be soon considered. Finally on May 9, 1995 President of India approved the Council Act and after the election of the 26 councillors, the swearing ceremony for the first Ladakh Autonomous Hill Development Council was held at Polo ground Leh, on 3rd of September, 1995 and Thufstan Tsewang was elected the first Chairman and Chief Executive Councillor of the LAHDC Leh. In September 1995, Lakruk was elected councillor from the upper Leh constituency but resigned in 1996 due to offer of MLA election from Pradesh Congress Committee J&K, and won the election by defeating his nearest rival by a good margin. He represented the people of Leh in the J&K assembly from 1996 to 2002 and did remarkable job for the welfare of the people of Ladakh. As an MLA he had been the Secretary of the J&K Congress Legislature Party and remained Member of the consultative committee for Planning, Power development, and Ladakh affairs, and served the people of J&K in a very efficient manner. The most important LAHDC Act, had to be rectified within one year, after the popular government came in power. The resolution was handed over to a select committee and ultimately the bill was passed. Secondly, the J&K National Conference submitted the Autonomy resolution in the house, the Congress and other like-minded members opposed and showed resentment against the Autonomy resolution and it could not be passed. He had been an active member of the Action Committee on ST and worked whole-heartedly to achieve the goal under the leadership of Rev. K.G. Bakula. Mr. Dorjay was elected President Ladakh Union Territory Front in 2002 and worked on the said post till he was sworn in as Chairman and Chief Executive Councillor of LAHDC Leh after the land slide

victory to his party in the council election. As Chief Executive Councillor, he participated in many seminars at National and International Level and presented his papers on social, political, cultural, educational and economical scenario of Ladakh. But in 2009 council election he lost the seat from Fiyang Constituency. Presently he is an active member of BJP Leh.

Ven. Lama Lobzang

Ven. Lama Lobzang is the son of Norbu Tsering of Skara Leh. He was born in 1931 in Kau family at Leh. Basically; he is a Buddhist Lama and belongs to the "Boto" community of

Scheduled Tribe of J&K State. Presently he is putting up at Ashoka Mission, Mehrauli New Delhi, where from he guides, helps and serves the Ladakhis to solve their problems, especially to enroll the patients at the AIIMS and other Hospitals for better treatment. He is equally popular among the Buddhists and Muslims of Leh for rendering his noble services.

He was enrolled in "Pethub Gonpa" as a young Lama and received basic religious education there itself and then proceeded to Lhasa (Tibet) for higher education. He got intensive training in Buddhist monastic life, both in Theravada and Mahayana. He is well-versed in English, Hindi, Tibetan and Ladakhi. He was a disciple and close associate of Kushok Bakula and got him appointed as founding General Secretary of Ladakh Buddha Vihara, New Delhi who served the Ladakhis there for more than 20 years. While staying in Delhi he got lot of knowledge and experience in various fields, which proved very beneficial to him in his life.

In recognition to his services in different fields, the Government of India was kind enough to appoint him on the following high offices. He had been Member High Power Panel on Minorities, Scheduled Castes, Scheduled Tribes and other weaker sections, from 1980 to 1983.

He worked as Member (Non-Statutory) National Commission for Scheduled Caste and Scheduled Tribes, from 1984 to 1992. During these periods, his unique contributions were two "Padyatras", one for 37 days from Delhi to Lucknow, covering 10 districts and a distance of 740 kms and the other for 14 days from Nasik to Pune, covering 3 districts and a distance of 280 kms. The Padyatras enabled the Commission to have a direct and first hand assessment of the programmes for alleviating poverty among the Scheduled Castes and Scheduled Tribes.

Later on, after amendment of Article 338 of the Constitution of India the President of India appointed him as a Member of the (Constitutional) National Commission for Scheduled Castes and Scheduled Tribes from October 1995 to 1998 and again from 1998 to 2001. He was again appointed as a Member, National Commission for Scheduled Tribes, Government of India, from 2nd March 2004 to 1st March 2007.

Ven. Lama Lobzang held the following social and religious positions in India and abroad:

1. President, Ashoka Mission, Mehrauli, New Delhi.
2. Vice-President, Mahabodhi Society of India.
3. Vice-President, World Buddhist Sangha Council (Hqs. Taipei, Taiwan).
4. Vice-President World Buddhist Supreme Tathagata Followers (Hqs. Seoul, South Korea).
5. President, India-Nepal Human Development and Friendship Association, New Delhi.
6. Founding General Secretary, Ladakh Buddha Vihara, Delhi, from 1963 to 1986.

In his capacity of a well-known Buddhist scholar, Ven. Lama Lobzang participated in many International Conferences on different occasions—

1. Sixth Buddhist Synod, Rangoon, in 1954.
2. Conference of the World Fellowship of Buddhists, in Bangkok as a leader of the Indian delegation in 1966.
3. World Conference of Religions for Peace, Moscow, in 1977.
4. A delegate to the Republic of Sri Lanka, January 1978.
5. Conference of the World Fellowship of Buddhists, Tokyo, in 1978.
6. World Conference of Religions for Peace, Nairobi, in 1984.
7. World Council of Religions and Peace, Seoul, South Korea, in 1984.
8. World Congress of Religions, New Jersey, USA in 1985.
9. Led a delegation of Buddhist monks and important laity welcomed by the President of Sri Lanka in July 1988. Hereafter also attended the ceremony of the

exposition of the Holy Tooth relic of the Tathagata Buddha at Kandy.

10. World Council of Religions and Peace, Melbourne, Australia, in 1989.
11. Bodhi Tree Planting ceremony, Nihonji temple, Tokyo Japan, in 1989.
12. International Conference on Peace and Security of Asia with special focus on Tibet, Tokyo Japan, in 1990.
13. Film Premiere on His Holiness the Dalai Lama, Frankfurt, Germany, December 1994.
14. Inauguration of Old Age Home at Hachioji, Tokyo, January 1995.
15. Film Premiere of "Siddhartha". A Life in Light, Frankfurt, Germany, Dec. 1995.
16. Sacred Fire Offering ceremony at Agon Shu Temple, Kyoto, Japan in February 1997, February 1998, February 1999 and February 2000.
17. Sixth Executive Committee Meeting of the World Buddhists Sangha Council, Manila Philippines, April 1997.
18. Third General Conference of the World Buddhist Supreme Tathagata Followers at Colombo and Kandy Sri Lanka, in July 1997.
19. Fourth Inter-Religious conference organized by the Inter-religious Federation for World Peace, Washington DC, USA, November 1997.
20. World Culture and Sports festival 1998 and convocation on the Family and World Peace and Unification International, New York city USA, in June 1998.
21. World Culture Festival 1999 organised by the Family and World Peace and Unification International, Seoul, South Korea, in February 1999.
22. Meeting of the World Buddhist Sangha Council, Colombo, in April 1999.

23. Conference of the World Buddhist Supreme Tathagata Followers Kandy, Sri Lanka, in March 2000.
24. Seventh General Conference of the World Buddhist Sangha Council, Taipei, Taiwan, in November 2000.
25. International Conference of the Maha Bodhi Societies World Wide, Colombo, in July 2001.
26. International Conference on Religious Cooperation, Taiwan, September 2001.
27. The General Conference of the World Buddhist Sangha Council Singapore, in November 2001.
28. Conference on 'Forging Path to Peace at a Time of Global Crises' Seoul, South Korea, 29 April to 2nd May 2004.
29. Conference of Inter-religious and International Federation for World Peace, Seoul, South Korea, from November 30 to December 4, 2004.
30. International Celebration of the 88th Birthday of Rev. Takeyasu Miyamoto, one of the senior most religious and social leaders of Japan at Tokyo, 14th May 2005.

Besides attending the above-mentioned international conferences, Ven. Lama Lobzang organized the following National and International Programmes and Conferences at different places in India:

1. Organised Inter University Seminar, at Indian Institute of Advanced Studies, Shimla in 1974.
2. Organized All India Frontier Buddha Sammelan in New Delhi in September 1978.
3. Organized International Buddhist Conference, in New Delhi, in September 1978 as Chief Organizer.
4. Invited a high level Buddhist delegation consisting of three top religious leaders (Mahanayakas) and important laity from Sri Lanka, who called on the President and Prime Minister of India in March 1988. This visit had a great impact on the people of Sri Lanka.

5. Indo-Sri Lanka cultural Interaction, Parliament House Annexe, New Delhi, 1990.
6. Organized an International Conference on the occasion of the 60th Birth celebration of His Holiness the Dalai Lama in Delhi, July 1995.
7. Invited a high level Buddhist delegation from Sri Lanka who met the Prime Minister of India and visited Buddhist holy places of India.
8. Convener, International Conference on 'The Heritage of Nalanda' at Nalanda, from February 12 to 14, 2006.
9. Member, National Committee for the Celebration of the 2550th Anniversary of the Mahaparinirvana of Bhagwan Buddha, Ministry of Culture, Government of India, 2006.

Ven. Lama Lobzang has been doing an extraordinary service to the poor and suffering people of Ladakh and the entire Himalayan region for the last many years by organizing medical camps at Leh once a year and sometimes twice a year with the assistance of renowned specialists belonging to different disciplines. They have been mostly drawn from AIIMS who are extending very valuable cooperation to him in this great humanitarian service by giving treatment. Various surgeries have been carried out successfully in diverse fields in circumstances not conducive to advanced surgeries. Besides thousands of patients suffering from various types of diseases have received free outdoor treatment in these medical camps. Thus all these indoor and outdoor patients were saved from incurring expenditure on travel and treatment in Delhi. Lama Lobzang has also managed to conduct such medical camps at Kargil, for the last few years, so as to provide similar facilities to them. Lamaji has been similarly helping thousands of patients over the years by personally taking them to AIIMS and also to other Hospitals like Dr. R.M.L. Hospital and Safdarjung Hospital every single day while in Delhi and arranging best possible treatment for them both indoor and outdoor. A good number of patients from Ladakh and other Himalayan regions are indebted to him for saving their lives with the cooperation of the Hospital authorities and specialists. This selfless service and contribution of Lamaji is significant enough to elicit undiluted appreciation. He also mobilized the patriotic people of Ladakh for cultural and strategic social integration with India in view of the geopolitical importance of the region. He made efforts along with other political and religious heads of Ladakh towards declaration of the indigenous people of Ladakh as Scheduled Tribes and also worked for their social and economic upliftments of SC, ST and other weaker sections.

Ghulam Abbas Aabedi

Ghulam Abbas Aabedi is the son of Haji Mohammad Hussain Aabedi and the grandson of Haji Ali Mir Aabedi of Pari, Kharmang. His father, Haji Mohammad Hussain Aabedi, had been a Congress leader and close associate of Rev. K.G. Bakula. Ghulam Abbas Aabedi was born at Thiksay in 1968. He was enrolled in Govt. High School Thiksay for Primary, Middle and High School education and passed the matriculation and 12th class examination from Govt. Higher Secondary School Leh. During the school days he won the students election and became the Students Union President. Later, he proceeded to Srinagar to seek higher education and passed the graduation in B.Sc. geography. Here also he was elected the President of the Ladakhi students studying in Srinagar. After graduation, he was enrolled in Aligarh Muslim University and did MA in Sociology. He had been President Ladakh Imamia Youth Federation Leh, and served the community for many years, with merit. He came forward for the rescue of the downtrodden and disabled persons. He enrolled some blind students from Ladakh in Blind School Aligarh. Presently they are receiving higher education there. One blind girl student has done her postgraduation in Urdu and qualified the NET. Another blind student is studying in BA. In 2001, he was nominated as Councillor among the Shia Muslims of Leh, and later elevated as an Executive Councillor in the LAHDC Leh. Abbas Aabedi worked as Executive Councillor Health and was also holding the portfolios of Tourism, Fisheries, Social Welfare, PDS, and minority affairs, etc., under the Chairmanship of Thufstan Tsewang and Rigzin Spalbar respectively.

He is the first Muslim politician from Leh region, who got the status of a Deputy Minister in the council. He contested the Council election twice in 2006 and 2010 from Chushot constituency, and won the elections. In 2006, he was in the opposition because Congress could not win more than two seats in the LAHDC election, and he was one of them, but in 2010 election the Congress party gained a victory by winning 21 council seats out of 26.

Abbas Aabedi E.C. with Mufti Syeed Chief Minister

Rigzin Spalbar became the Chairman and Chief Executive Councillor of the LAHDC Leh and Abbas Aabedi was once again inducted in the council as Executive Councillor for CA&PD with the other portfolios of Cooperative, Higher Education, Sports, Fisheries, District garage, and Minority affairs. Some genuine and long standing demands of the people were fulfilled during his period; this includes formation of Chushot block and six panchayati blocks for Chushot. High School Chushot Shamma was upgraded as a full fledged higher secondary school. Besides two more high schools at Chushot Gongma and Yokma were upgraded. Inter village road connectivity improved tremendously with the construction of new link roads and three of the existing village roads were black topped. Drinking water facility improved a lot with the provision of hand pump to almost every household in the village. Moreover, a big project to supply drinking water under greater water supply scheme to the villagers is under progress. The Igoo-Phey land under command area has been distributed among all inhabitants of Chushot. A big fish pond is being constructed at Chushot Shamma and so many private fish ponds have come into existence. Beside the poor and needy people are provided every kind of help and guided in every possible manner. He served the people of his constituency satisfactorily and in a very efficient manner. Therefore the people of Chushot preferred to re-elect him in the council election. In recognition to his best and outstanding services to the public, he was conferred the Bharat Jyoti Award by Indian International Friendship Society New Delhi in the year 2006. The other recipients of this award from J&K state include Dr. Karan Singh, Mr. Muzaffar Hussain Beig, Dr. Abdul Hamid Zargar and Dugchen Rinpochhe. Abbas Aabedi is a good orator and parliamentarian. He is a bold, courageous, straightforward and fearless person and presents the various problems and demands of the people in the general council meetings and before the State and Centre dignitaries in a very efficient manner. He participated in several National and International seminars at Srinagar, Jammu, Mumbai, Delhi and Pune and presented his views.

Mohammad Akbar Ladakhi

M. Akbar Ladakhi was the son of Haji Ghulam Mohammad Chodhary and grandson of Akhon Abdul Hussain of Tsendo, Baltistan, who used to come at Leh for trade purposes during the pre-independence period. His trade flourished and later permanently settled at Thiksay. His father Haji Ghulam Mohammad Chodhary, married with a lady of a noble family of Saboo called Ayu Kalon, who converted to Islam and performed pilgrimage to the holy places of Islam. Akbar Ladakhi's father and grandfather were the richest person among the Muslims of Ladakh during the post-independence period, who extended all sort of cooperation for organizing Muharram procession in Leh and establishing Maktabas in different Muslim villages. Akbar Ladakhi received his primary education at Imamia Public School Leh located at Chutay-Rantak and upper primary education at Middle School Leh and after passing matriculation he was enrolled in SP College Srinagar and then proceeded to Lucknow for higher education, where he was in close contact with the poets and scholars of the past that is why, he was having a good taste for language, literature, poetry and history and especially he loved the Balti Ghazal. He was a free minded person and never cared for the strict religious rules. He was also a great lover of sports and always encouraged the young players to excel in games as well. He also played an important role in promoting polo games in Leh and used to attend all major matches at Leh polo ground. Being an active politician he remained linked with G.M. Sadiq's Democratic National Conference for several years. Later, when G.M. Sadiq under the Congress banner, became the Chief Minister of Jammu and Kashmir, he was appointed as Information Officer and elevated as SDM, PRO to Public Works Minister, Assistant Commissioner Revenue Leh, Dy. general manager Tourism Corporation and Under Secretary Ladakh affairs. After retirement from the service, he was elected as President Ladakh Muslim Association Leh and remained on the said post for several years and served the community as per his strength and valour. In the capacity of President LMA, he played a vital role for strengthening the relation, between the Ladakhi Buddhists and Muslims. He headed the community during the tripartite talks from 1989 onwards and finally supported the case of LAHDC, whole-heartedly. During his Presidentship, the Muslims of Leh had to face a social and economic boycott, imposed by the majority community, continuously for three years from 1989 onwards and it was lifted during a tripartite talk in New Delhi on November 29, 1992. Thus, the differences with the Muslims of Leh were resolved and harmonious relations were created. After the approval of the Council Act by the President of India in May 1995, the first Council election was held in September 1995. Mr. Akbar Ladakhi was elected un-opposed from the

Chushot Constituency and appointed as the first Muslim Executive Councillor under the Chairmanship of Thufstan Tsewang. Though a great leader Mr. Akbar Ladakhi would have done much more for the Ladakhi community but unfortunately he did not keep well during his tenure and could serve in the council for only less than one year and passed away on 28th of June 1996 leaving a great vacuum in the Muslim society of Ladakh.

Tsering Samphel

Tsering Samphel son of late Sonam Wangyal was born at Hemis Shukpachann now settled at Mohalla Khakshal, Samkar Leh. He received his basic education from the school of his village and got the higher education from the Sampuranand Sanskrit University, Varanasi and Punjab University, Patiala. He is well versed in Urdu, Hindi, English and Bhoti languages, and is one of the good orators of the region. Initially he worked as a petition writer, but soon he joined the politics and served the people under the leadership of K.G. Bakula Rinpochhe. Samphel was elected Member Legislative Assembly of J&K state Assembly from 1987 to 1990, and served the people of the region in a very efficient manner. He had been President District Congress Committee Leh from 1990 to 1996 and from 2004 onwards for a long period and mobilized the party in the region and won many Assembly and Parliament elections, under his leadership. He had been Co-founder of Lamdon Model Schools in Ladakh, a non-profit educational movement presently having 3000 students on roll in classes Nursery to 12th class in a dozen of schools all over Ladakh, and served as President/Secretary of the Lamdon Social Welfare Society Leh for 17 years from 1971 to 1987. Tsering Samphel did remarkable services to the Buddhist community, in the capacity of President LBA (Ladakh Buddhist Association) Leh from 1997 to 2004. Once, during his Presidentship when a delegation of Ladakh Muslim Association met with the H.H. The Dalai Lama at Jiwatsal during the course of his address, he convened Tsering Samphel and said to him, "These minority Muslims of Leh are my possession, I am handing them over to you. Treat them nicely and sincerely and whenever a tension arises between the communities, solve it amicably." No doubt he did a lot for the promotion of communal harmony and brotherhood in the region.

Tsering Samphel had been Director Leh Nutrition Project from 1987 to 2004, an oldest NGO in Ladakh working on child rights, water harvesting with focus on artificial glaciering, health education, Women Development, Tribal Welfare and communal Harmony. He had been Founder Secretary Ladakh Co-operative Transport Society, with 900 trucks and Trippers owners as member with an annual turnover of ₹ 15 to 18 crores.

He had been Member Working Group constituted by Planning Commission, Govt. of India for 10th Five Year Plan for formulation of strategy for empowering the minorities. He was Member Northern India Advisory Committee of SIDBI (Small Industries Development Bank of India) from 1997 to 2001 and Member Jammu and Kashmir Khadi & Village Industries Board from 1987 to 2002. He was associated to many organization like:

1. Member Asian Buddhist Conference, Mongolia.
2. Member International Association for Ladakh Studies, USA.
3. Member Board of Management, Central Institute of Buddhist Studies, Ladakh, Ministry of Culture, and Govt. of India from 1997 to 2004.
4. Member Task Forces of various Ministries.

Tsering Samphel participated in conferences and seminars at National and International level with presentation of paper and lectures as social and political activist. He had been one of the participants in the Prime Minister's Round Table Conference held in February, 2006 in New Delhi towards peaceful resolution of Kashmir issue. He also attended the workshop organized by Uppsala University in Sweden in September, 2006 on conflict Management in special reference to Kashmir. He also participated in few rounds of tripartite talk in New Delhi from 1989 to November, 1992, to achieve the Hill Council status for Ladakh. He was imprisoned in

Central Jail Leh, during the struggle for Scheduled Tribe status for Ladakh, along with P.T. Wangyal, Haji Hussain Abidi, Nurboo Gyalchan, Nisar Hussain, Tashi Targes Dimbir, and was released after 48 days by G.M. Shah's Government. He participated in so many delegations under the leadership of Kushok Bakula Rinpochhe, and P. Namgyal at Srinagar, Jammu, and Delhi to present the charter of demands of the Ladakhi people before the State and Central dignitaries. Presently, he is functioning as Member, National Commission for Scheduled Tribes and is doing an excellent job for the welfare of the down-trodden people of India. He is very gentle, humorist, soft spoken, straightforward and a bold person.

Smt. Spalzes Wangmo

Smt. Spalzes Wangmo is the daughter of Tashi Tundup Sergar of village Chemday. She had been General Secretary of District Congress Committee Leh, under the leadership of Kushok Bakula Rinpochhe and Sonam Wangyal. Spalzes Wangmo was born at Chemday and did her schooling from Welham girls High School in Dehradun. She completed her graduation from Government Girl's College Chandigarh, Punjab University, after that she pursued a law degree from Law campus centre in Delhi University and subsequently practiced in Supreme Court for a period of two years.

She also taught in the far-flung remote region of the Nubra valley in Ladakh, where she was involved in numerous social work and adult literacy campaign. In 1995, when Ladakh acquired the Ladakh Autonomous Hill development council, she became one of the first women councillor, and thereafter was subsequently nominated and served efficiently as a member of the Hill Council for the last fourteen years. During this period she raised important issues like equality, women's rights and protection. She held the post of General Secretary, District Congress Committee, Leh and the President Mahila Congress Committee, Leh for many years, and mobilized the cadre strength of women Congress Members to thousands. Smt. Spalzes Wangmo was also the member, state Red Cross society of the government of J&K. She is also a member of the International Association for Ladakh Studies and attended an

International Conference in Aarhus University, Denmark, where she presented a paper on "Women and Development in Ladakh". She can speak Hindi, Bhoti and English languages and is having good command over English language. She is a good speaker and is bold enough to raise the issues concerning the empowerment of women and upliftment of the society. A sociable, straight forward and kind lady is presently working as Member, National Commission for Minorities Government of India, since 6th March 2009, and is serving the people in a very efficient manner.

Agha Syed Ibrahim Shah Musavi

Agha Syed Ibrahim Shah Musavi was the son of Agha Syed Kazim Shah Musavi, his father Syed Kazim Shah was born in 1909 at his native village Akchamal-Kargil in a Syed family. Later on he shifted to village Chhoskor and permanently settled there along with his family. Syed Ibrahim Shah received the basic education from his father and then proceeded to Najafe-Ashraf in Iraq for higher Islamic studies. He spent about twelve years for his studies there and gained knowledge in various Islamic subjects. Besides Urdu and Purgi, he was well versed with Arabic and Persian languages as well and was a good speaker. He was very bold, straight forward and popular among the public.

Agha Syed Ibrahim Shah participated in state politics in 1950 and became the President of the Tehsil National Conference Kargil. Prior to him Agha Syed Mehdi of Saliskot was the 1st President of this party. Hence, Syed Ibrahim Shah had been the 2nd president of National Conference in Kargil. He was elected twice as Member of the State Legislative Assembly un-opposed during the year 1951 and 1957 and served the people of Kargil. His tenure as MLA was during the regime of Bakhshi Ghulam Mohammad, Kh. Shamsuddin, Kh. G.M. Sadiq, and Syed Mir Qasim. In those days, the two senior leaders and MLAs K.G. Bakula from Leh and Agha Ibrahim Shah from Kargil were very popular in the region. In 1962, he was appointed as Vice-Chairman Ladakh Development Board Kargil and remained on the said post till 1967. In 1971, he was elected as President District Congress

Committee Kargil, after the amalgamation of the J&K National Conference in National Congress. In 1972, he was elected as Member Legislative council and retired from the post of MLC in 1978. Thus, he served the people of Kargil for many decades in different capacities and contributed a lot to spread the modern education. Since in the past the people were orthodox and were not in favour of the modern education. He is the person who enlightened the flame of modern education in the far flung areas of District Kargil. What Kargil today is, it is because of the sincere contribution of Agha Ibrahim Shah. The senior most political leader of Kargil, the first MLA of the region, who served the Kargilis for 15 years as MLA and six years as MLC, passed away on 31st of October, 1999 by leaving a great vacuum in the politics of Kargil. He had two sons. The elder son Syed Hassan retired as Assistant Labour Commissioner and younger Syed Hussain as teacher.

Congress delegates of Ladakh region Headed by Sonam Wangyal and Agha Ibrahim Shah MLAs with J&K CM, Mir Qasim

Kacho Mohammad Ali Khan (1921-2002)

Kacho Mohammad Ali Khan was born in 1921 at village Pashkyum Kargil. His ancestors belonged to Rajput clan of Rathore family of Rajsthan. Kacho Ahmad Khan the grandfather of Kacho Mohammad Ali Khan was deputed by the then Maharaja of Kashmir to administer Ladakh and Baltistan. His father Kacho Mirza Mohammad Khan a police

Officer namely Thanedar was also deputed by the Maharaja of Kashmir to administer the region from Zojila to Fotola.

Kacho Mohammad Ali Khan received his early education from Tyndal Bisco Memorial School, Srinagar. He did his FA from Sri-Pratap College Srinagar. After completing his studies he joined the British Army and fought against Japanese forces at Burma border during the Second World War. After the war he left the British Army and joined Revenue Department as Naib Tehsildar and was posted at Nyoma in 1962, during the Indo-Chinese war. He performed his duties very honestly and efficiently.

During and after the Indo-Pak war in 1965, when he saw the pathetic condition of the people of Kargil, he resigned from the government service and joined active politics in 1967. He fought assembly election from Kargil constituency in 1967 as an Independent candidate and won the election with good margin. During that period Ghulam Mohammad Sadiq was the Chief Minister of Jammu and Kashmir, who included him in the State cabinet and gave the portfolio of Health and Medical education. Later, keeping in view his efficiency, honesty and straightforwardness, he was given the important portfolio of Excise and Taxation and he was able to raise revenue of 21 crores for the State Government. Again, during the period of Syed Mir Qasim, Chief Minister of J&K he continued with the same portfolio. In 1974, when Sheikh Mohammad Abdullah became the Chief Minister of the State, he was given the portfolio of Irrigation and Flood Control. In short he was MLA Kargil from 1967 to 1977 and Minister in the state cabinet holding different portfolios from 1969 to 1977. He was Member of Cultural and Peace Commission at the Central level. He participated in a conference on Peace Mission in Iraq as a Member of Indian delegation in 1978. He was responsible for creating and providing political space to Indian National Congress in Kargil District of J&K through his statesman like qualities. During the regime of Sheikh Mohammad Abdullah, he was invited to join the J&K National Conference. But Kacho sahib preferred to be a Congressman. He was honoured and awarded for his excellence in his job and uprightness and honesty by G.M. Sadiq, the then Chief Minister of J&K. For this very quality of his, he is still, even after his death is respected at the State and Central level across political parties.

Kacho Mohammad Ali Khan did a lot for the welfare of Kargil. He is solely responsible for providing a post of Surgeon and Gynecologist for the first time at District Hospital Kargil. After his exit from the ministry these posts remained vacant for a long time, until his son Dr. Kacho Mohammad Hussain joined the District Hospital and made it fully functional with active support of 121 brigade Kargil. Education was always on his list of priorities. He would advocate and mobilize support from the State Government, for promotion of education for all. He facilitated the process of providing electricity to almost all the villages of Kargil district for the first time, through providing diesel generators sets under rural electrification scheme. During a major famine in Kargil, he provided all kinds of possible support to the affected communities and helped them to overcome this distressing period. His basic vision was to promote equitable and sustainable development of the people of the region. The Kurbathang project, providing sustainable source of livelihood to the people of Kargil is one of the many examples of his long-term vision. He was also involved in the process of implementing the Iqbal Hydel project and Suru Hydel Project for the District. He always believed in promoting and maintaining cordial relations with the Central government. He had a good understanding of national and international affairs. He was one of the persons responsible for not letting Kargil affected by militancy despite provocations. He always maintained the communal harmony and respect for different religions, culture and regional balance. The popular leader of the region, Kacho Mohammad Ali passed away on 19th May 2002 after a brief illness. His son Kacho Mohammad Hussain is planning to establish a hospital in his memory at village Pashkyum in the years to come.

He is survived by three sons and one daughter, eldest daughter Mrs. Zahra Begum is married in Kargil to Wazir Mohammad Ali. His eldest son Kacho Mohammad Hussain is a doctor and working at District Hospital Kargil as Surgeon specialist. Another son Kacho Manzoor-ul-Hassan is running a petrol pump at Kargil. His youngest son Kacho Mohammad Feroze is an Engineer and works in the field of development.

Alhaj Munshi Habibullah (1923-2001)

Munshi Habibullah was born on 2nd May, 1923 in a prominent and well-known trading family of Ladakh. His father Munshi Aziz Bhat was the official Petition Writer of Maharaja Hari Singh for Ladakh Wazarat and the owner of Munshi Aziz Bhat Trading Company. Munshi Aziz Bhat brought him up in an educational environment. He studied up to 5th standard at Government Primary School Kargil and went to Skardo (Baltistan) for further studies. He qualified the Middle Standard examination from there and was appointed as a teacher in Middle School Skardo and worked wholeheartedly for the betterment of education in this far-flung and backward area. After serving several years as teacher, he was forced to resign from the government service by his colleagues and friends and joined the politics, because they saw in him the leadership qualities. Hence, he laid the foundation of J&K National Conference in Kargil and he became the first President of the party. Later, National Conference was merged with J&K National Congress and he joined the party in 1955, under the aegis of Bakhshi Ghulam Mohammad. He was nominated as Member J&K Legislative Council in 1955 and served the people of Kargil in a very efficient manner for two terms till 1965. In 1965, he was elevated to the post of Vice-Chairman Kargil Development Board, with the status of Deputy Minister in the Government of G.M. Sadiq and continued on this post till 1975. Keeping in view the interest of the people of Kargil and his political strategy, he joined the J&K National Congress and was elevated as Deputy Minister in the cabinet of Chief Minister Sheikh Mohammad Abdullah, with the portfolio of irrigation and flood control and continued on the post till 1982. He was again elevated as Minister of State with the portfolio of Animal Husbandry and Power in the cabinet of Dr. Farooq Abdullah and continued till 1983. In the year 1984, he again fought the Assembly election from Kargil constituency and won the election with good margin by defeating his nearest rival. This time he was appointed as Cabinet Minister for Forest and Ladakh Affairs in the cabinet of Chief Minister Ghulam Mohammad Shah and continued on the post till 1986. Thus, he made a history to become the first Cabinet Minister from District Kargil and served the people of Kargil in every field with merit. It is because of his noble efforts that he was able to create a separate District for Kargil in 1979 and the pace of development in the region was enhanced. He is considered the pioneer of modern education in Kargil, especially women education. He had been member and representative from Ladakh in the J&K Hurriyat Conference from 1992 to 1995. He was founder member and first Secretary of prestigious Islamia School Kargil. His contributions for the development of religious institutions in the region are laudable. He had been Convener All Ladakh Action Committee for the struggle of LAHDC status for Ladakh. He visited Saudi Arabia, Muscat, Oman, Iran, Iraq, Syria, and Afghanistan and performed Hajj and Ziarat in 1999. In recognition to his excellent performance in the J&K Assembly, he was conferred the "Best Legislature Award" in 1982. In memory of his ancestors, "Munshi Aziz Bhat Museum" was founded in 2001 by his family with the collaboration of Kargil Social and Cultural Organization. Presently one of his sons Gulzar Hussain Munshi is the Ex-Officio Director of the said museum. Munshi Habibullah was very much active in state politics till his old age. But alas, one of the senior most and beloved leaders of Kargil, he passed away on 25th of October 2002 at the age of 79, by creating a great vacuum in the political and social field of Kargil. After his death the members of the family established a School, called Munshi Habibullah Mission School Kargil to honor the departed soul.

Munshi Habibullah is having four sons and five daughters. His elder son Abdul Aziz Munshi retired as Additional Secretary Revenue Department J&K, second son Sajjad Hussain Munshi is presently working as Administrator Kargil Municipal council, third son Gulzar Husain Munshi is a master in civil engineering from Delhi College of Engineering and a diploma in Musicology from Mansfield College Oxford, England. He is presently working as Executive Engineer in Rural Engineering Development Department Kargil, the fourth and youngest son is working as Youth Co-coordinator Nehru Yuva Kendra, Ministry of Youth Affairs and Sports Government of India New Delhi. Among his daughters four are government school teachers and the youngest one is the first M.Phil lady from District Kargil and is presently working as Block Development Officer in Rural Development Department Kargil.

Qamar Ali Akhon

Mr. Qamar Ali Akhon was born in Akhonpa's family in village Tsangra on 15th May, 1957. Tsangra is situated at a distance of 58 km from Kargil Town. His forefathers came from Kharmang Baltistan as preacher and settled at village Tsangra. Qamar Ali is the 5th generation of the old Akhon family. He received his basic education from primary school Tsangra and did his matriculation from high school Sankoo. In 1973, he lost his father when he was reading in 3rd primary, thereafter his elder brother Talib Hussain Akhon took all the responsibility on his shoulder to support the family and giving the education to Qamar Ali Akhon and his younger brother Dr. Mohammad Jafar Akhon. Highly impressed with the diligent and educational aptitude in Qamar Ali, the renowned religious leader of Sankoo block, Agha Syed Haider Rizvi assisted in sending him to Srinagar for higher studies by providing financial assistance. Consequently, he did his graduation in Arts subject from Kashmir University, and later did the LLB Hons from Lucknow University.

Qamar Ali Akhon is regarded as an active political leader among the young generation of Kargilis. He is considered to be a matured politician after Munshi Habibullah, Kacho Mohammad Ali, Agha Syed Ibrahim Shah, and Kacho Hassan Khan. In politics, he fought the Parliament election for the first time against Congress candidate P. Namgyal and lost. Having allegiance with National Conference, and Agha Syed Haider Rizvi, he was fortunate enough to have a ready made vote bank in the Suru valley and the then Chief Minister Dr. Farooq

Abdullah observed in him the political qualities and put his candidature for Member Legislative Assembly in 1986, against Congress candidate Kacho Mohammad Ali and declared elected with comfortable margin. Again in the year, 1996 Qamar Ali was elected MLA as a candidate of J&K National Conference by defeating Congress candidate Kacho Ghulam Hassan Khan and was elevated to the post of Minister of State for Works and Power, in the Farooq Abdullah's cabinet.

Qamar Ali alongwith other dignitaries visits the new site of the University at Kargil

Since the political leaders of Leh constituted the LAHDC Leh in September 1995, the Kargili leaders were suspicious about its success that is why they delayed to constitute it for a long period of nine years and finally constituted LAHDC Kargil in the year 2003. Qamar Ali Akhon became the first Chairman and Chief Executive Councillor of LAHDC, Kargil. He failed to prove the majority in the General council meeting by one vote only and had to resign. During the Assembly election of 2009, he fought the election on NC mandate against Independent candidate Haji Nisar Ali, and won the election with good margin. He was elevated as Minister of Transport and Public Distribution, in the Omar Abdullah's cabinet, and is serving the people very sincerely and honestly. The day to day work of Consumer Affairs & Public Distribution and transport department' is managed in a manner that no file remains unattended after 12 hours. The disposal is made puzzle quick. Moreover the office hours in the ministry are utilized in full form from 9.30 am to 5 pm attending public causes. He is sober, sociable, soft spoken and sincere, and always keeps ready to serve and solve the problems of the people of the area. His dream is to take Kargil at heights in all spheres of life. He has an aspiration to make aware all Kargilies about education, who hitherto remained neglected so far. The only aim of his life is to serve poor, downtrodden and oppressed people of the state in general and those hailing from Ladakh in particular. He rendered unblemished services to people by travelling across the state in far flung areas to know and redress their grievances on spot. He attended National and International seminars at Delhi, Hyderabad, Srinagar, Jammu, and Bangalore and presented papers. His autobiography, based on his political and social experiences is under publication. In recognition to his excellent services to the people he was conferred the "Gavru award". The Speaker and Chief Minister of J&K appreciated his performances during the year 2010-11.

Alhaj Ghulam Hassan Khan

Alhaj Ghulam Hassan Khan was born at village Silmo (Kargil) at the house of Haji Ghulam Mohammad. His father and grandfather were the prominent persons of Kargil. He received his primary education at Kargil and qualified matriculation from Government High School Kargil, through J&K Board in the year 1956. Later he proceeded to Srinagar for higher education. He did graduation from Kashmir University in 1960. It is not out of place to mention here that he was the first graduate from district Kargil. It indicates that the people of the region were not aware about the value and importance of education in the past.

After graduation, in 1962 he joined the J&K Police service as Inspector and served the Police Department very honestly and efficiently for about 35 years in different capacities and finally retired as D.I.G. Police in 1995. He had been very honest, active, efficient and sincere officer. Hence considering his distinguished and meritorious services in the Police Department, the Government of India conferred on him the President Police Medal in 1995.

Sheikh Ahamad and Hassan Khan MP alongwith Farooq and Omar at a Press Conference

Kacho Ghulam Hassan Khan joined the politics after his retirement from the Police service and fought the assembly election on Indian National Congress mandate from Kargil in 1996 but did not succeed. Again in the year 1999, he successfully won the parliamentary election as a National Conference candidate by defeating his nearest rival Thufstan Tsewang with a huge margin and served the people of Ladakh very efficiently for full five years term from 1999 to 2004. He fought the parliamentary elections in 2005 but lost to Thufstan Tsewang, because of the division of his vote bank by Mr. Wazir Ali. It was in 2009 that Mr. Hassan Khan won the parliament seat from Ladakh defeating his nearest rival P. Namgyal, a Congress candidate. He is a good orator and fearless parliamentarian and has raised the important issues of the people of Ladakh region in the parliament from time to time. He is straightforward, sociable, articulate and man of versatile qualities having interests in varied range of fields.

Besides being a good parliamentarian, he has also shown his concern towards various cultural and environmental issues affecting the region and has been actively raising questions and starting debates through his writings.

Hassan Khan had been Member Standing Committees on Transport, Civil Aviation, Defense, Forest and Environment, Science and Technology, Labour and Employment, Textile and Handicrafts. He represented Kargil in the Round Table Conference on centre-state relation headed by Justice Sagheer Ahmad and presented a paper, as per the aspiration of the people of Kargil for amicable solution of the Kashmir problems. He had been the Member of the Government of India's Haj Delegation to Saudi Arabia, headed by the then Union Minister Syed Shahnawaz Hussain in 2000. Mr. Hassan Khan attended many National and International seminars, especially on Indo-Pak peace Seminars at Singapore, Delhi and Jammu. He had been the first Ladakhi Muslim who attended at the shrine of Hazrat Shah Hamdan at Khatlan in Uzbekistan in the year 2009, as an official delegation with the President of India. He offered "Chadar" and recited Sura Fateha there. Since Ladakhi Muslims are having a deep regards, respect and attachment towards Shah Hamdan, who had visited Kashmir thrice from 1377 to 1382, and is considered to be the first, among the Muslim preachers, who visited Baltistan and Ladakh.

Hassan Khan as a Member of Parliament served the people of the region whole-heartedly, sincerely and impartially and has spent his M.P. LAD funds on upgradations of buildings for various institutions, providing ambulance and machines to the Hospitals, computer for schools, community halls, cultural and other developmental activities. He did efforts to provide due representation in Army and Para Military Forces to the Muslim youth of Ladakh and his main aim is the connectivity of Ladakh region, throughout the year with rest of the country, by air and surface Transport and also within the region to connect the remote areas with the town and cities. That is why; he is doing efforts to connect the region with Kashmir and Himachal Pradesh through tunnels at Zoojila and Baralacha. Besides, the upgradation and regularization of Air field at

Kargil is on top priority of his agenda. Since good education is need of the hour, hence he is in favour of quality education for the young generations. His noble efforts for the promotion of communal harmony and brotherhood in the region are worth mentioning and appreciable. Mr. Hassan Khan has one son and two daughters. Both the daughters are doctors by profession and his son Feroz Ahmad Khan is a politician having allegiance with J&K National Conference and presently, is an MLA from Zangskar constituency. Mr. Hassan Khan is a high status leader, that the Ladakh in particular and Kashmir in general has ever produced.

Haji Azgar Karbalai

Azgar Karbalai is the son of Sheikh Ghulam Abbas of Baghe-Khomeni in Kargil town. He was born at Karbala in Iraq, and educated at Karbala itself in an Iranian Institution, therefore by associating himself with the holy city of Karbala he uses Karbalai as surname and later received religious and formal education in Kargil. He is sober, sociable, farsighted and a very good orator. Being a son of a religious preacher he inherited this art from his ancestors. Karbalai rose to limelight during the conflict that erupted due to the ideological differences between two schools of thoughts Islamia School and Imam Khomeini Memorial Trust (KMT). KMT found a young, energetic and dynamic leader in Karbalai, since then he has been a veteran for KMT camp and over the years has led the Trust successfully. He was one of the founding members of Imam Khomeini Memorial Trust Kargil, established in 1989, and also had been the general Secretary and Vice-Chairman of the said organization for many years. He is also the founding member and Chairman of Mutahri Educational Trust, established in 1984, which is one of the leading institutions having fourteen branches of schools at different places in Kargil. The Board result of the Mutahri Public School remained excellent for last many years. In 1994 the first batch of students from the school appeared for their matriculation examinations through J&K Board and during the last few years produced many brilliant Lecturers, Doctors, Engineers,

Advocates, Executives and Ph.D scholars. Presently, he is the Patron of the said educational trust.

In 2004, he had been the Member of the Indian Haj Delegation to Saudi Arabia headed by Jinabe Ghulam Nabi Azad, the then Chief Minister of J&K. He also attended the death anniversary of Imam Khomeini in Iran twice. Besides Saudi Arabia, Iraq, Iran, he visited Pakistan, London, Sri Lanka, Brussels, and France, in connection to find out the solution to solve the Kashmir problems. Azgar Karbalai attended the seminar of Sadh Bhawna in Leh and Kargil during the tenure of Lt. General Arjun Roy GOC, 14 INF Div Leh. He presented papers and his views in these seminars were appreciated.

Azgar Karbalai CEC Kargil

Initially, he had been associated with the K.M.T. organization and did religious services but later people compelled him to come in politics. He won the Kargil hill council election twice. He had been chairman and Chief Executive Councillor LAHDC Kargil for four years from 2004 to 2008, under Kargil alliance by defeating his nearest rival Qamar Ali Akhon in a vote of no-confidence. He is not affiliated to any registered political party but supports Congress from outside. Azgar Karbalai is considered an able, brilliant, young and energetic administrator. He maintained a good discipline and improved work culture among the employees of the hill council. He paid surprise visits in the district, encouraged the efficient and honest officials by awarding merit certificates and awards and punished those who failed to achieve the targets and did not perform their duty sincerely and practice corruption. The following developmental works in the District Kargil were undertaken in hand during his tenure as Chief Executive Councillor Kargil. Beside political and social gatherings, he also speaks in religious functions in a very efficient manner, and arrests the attention of the gatherings.

1. It was during his tenure that Prime Minister sanctioned 64 MW Chutuk hydel project at the cost of ₹ 640 crore.
2. Kargil-Zangskar road was improved by spending ₹ 128 crore so as to enhance and maintain better communication and transportation facilities.
3. ₹ 39 crore have been earmarked to construct the Parkachik irrigation canal.
4. Eight Higher Secondary Schools were upgraded and were provided better infrastructure. Kargil Tourism Development Authority was set up to promote tourism in the region.
5. In order to preserve the historical and religious monuments steps have been taken and repair and renovation of Karpo Khar and Kartsey Khar and face lifting of Daropadi Kund in Matain have been made.
6. 200 KV radio transmission was inaugurated by the then Chief Minister Ghulam Nabi Azad, and News in "Purgi" language from All India Radio Kargil was introduced for the first time.
7. To open Kargil-Skardo road, he met with the then President of Pakistan Gen. Pervez Musharraf and Dr. Manmohan Singh, the Prime Minister of India and requested for early action in this regard.

Karbalai gave first preference to education sector and opened primary schools at the remote corners of the region. He upgraded 100 primary schools to middle and many middle schools were upgraded as high schools, so as to enlighten the flame of education in every remote and dark corner. He also got established a Campus of Kashmir University in Kargil, so that the poor students could be benefited and the emphasis was given on quality education and prepared Kargil educational strategy. His main aim was to make Kargil a role model and model District in the whole State. Karbalai maintained communal harmony in the region and during his speech at Imam-barah Leh, he invited H.H. the Dalai Lama to visit Kargil, so as to strengthen the harmony and brotherhood. He fought two council elections and won; and lost the parliament election in 2009.

Kacho Ahmad Ali Khan

Kacho Ahmad Khan is the son of Kacho Sher Ali Khan of Yurbaltic, Sot Kargil. He was born on 13th April 1944 at Yurbaltic, Sot in a Kacho family. In Baltistan and Purig the rulers like Raja's are called "Kacho". His ancestors were the Raja of Sot and they suffered a lot in the hands of the Dogra invaders. The castle was burnt to ashes and looted the belongings and other valuable assets. Besides the common people many members of the royal family were assassinated. Similarly one of the rulers of Purig Kalon Rahim Khan, who revolted against the Dogra to liberate the Ladakh from their clutch was caught decisively and severely punished in an inhuman manner. Probably Kalon Rahim Khan was the first Ladakhi ruler who revolted against the Dogras for the cause of independent Ladakh, but due to lack of support he failed in his mission.

Kacho Ahmad Ali CEC Kargil alongwith Jinabe Farooq Abdullah and Omar Abdullah CM J&K

Kacho Ahmad Ali Khan is a man of soft nature and humble person. Being a son of a noble family, he was having all sorts of facilities. So during his childhood, he used to serve lunch to the poor and hungry children of his village and did efforts to eradicate their problems. He remembers the day when he saw an old couple sitting outside in the sun daily right from morning to evening without food. They had no barley to eat. Ahmad Ali was moved to hear this and he provided some barley flour for the poor couple. After middle standard examination, when he returned from Kargil town to Sot, he met a lady, who was hungry for few days and requested for some food. Knowing her problem, Ahmad Ali managed some barley flour to the lady. It indicates that during post-independence period the people of Kargil were very poor. They were having no work to do to earn and feed their family. When he was studying at Srinagar, he came home for summer vacation in the month of August 1965. There was chaos and crises in Kashmir because of the infiltration of the Pakistani Gorillas in the valley. But the situation was quite normal and peaceful in Kargil. In spite of that, the Army started crackdown and house to house search terrorized the people especially women and children. They were beating the innocent people mercilessly. Many villages of Kargil like Drass, Hardas, Poen, Pashkyum, Batalik and Silmo, etc. suffered a lot, when the army reached his village; Ahmad Khan being an educated person approached the Indian Army and offered refreshment and manpower to them and convinced them about the loyalty of the inhabitants. Thus because of his sincerity and cleverness the people of Sot were saved from the ill-treatment and terror of the Army. Again in October 1971, when he was posted in Zangskar as Agricultural Extension Officer. He was in Kargil in connection with some official work, when the Indo-Pak war started. The border people of village Sot were highly afraid. Out of fear all the people gathered at Kacho's house. Ahmad Ali thought it his first and foremost duty to maintain a good liaison between the civil population and Army. He managed to serve food and refreshments to the army jawans passing through his village and provided portars, ponies and donkeys to carry the loads at the post at the mountains. Thus the people of Yubaltik Sot played a vital role in helping the army during the emergencies. This was because of the noble efforts of Ahmad Ali. Ahmad Khan qualified matriculation Board Examination from High School Kargil and proceeded to Srinagar for higher education and joined S.P. College Srinagar. Later he did B.Sc. Agriculture from Agriculture College Wadoora Sopore. Basically, he was appointed as an Agriculture Assistant. Later he preferred to join Rural Development Agency and worked on various posts in the capacity of BDO, DPO, ACD, and CPO and was conferred KAS cadre. He took the voluntary retirement four years earlier as Dy. Secretary Housing and Urban Development, Civil Secretariat J&K, because of the pressure and demand of the people of Sot and the Scholars of Islamia School Kargil to join politics to lead the people of the region.

After retirement from the government service he joined National Conference Party and fought the LAHDC Kargil's Council election from Sot constituency and was elected uncontested. Later he was appointed as Executive Councillor in the first council, under the Chairmanship of Qamar Ali Akhon, but he resigned from the post because of the failure of the NC party in the "No confidence motion" moved by the opposition under the leadership of Mr. Azgar Karbalai. He did remarkable services to the people of Kargil in general and to the people of his constituency (Sot) in particular. Therefore, he was re-elected un-opposed from Sot constituency in the Council election of 2008. This time his party got an absolute majority and he was unanimously elected Chairman of LAHDC Kargil and assumed the post of Chief Executive Councillor LAHDC Kargil. Under his leadership district Kargil achieved a lot in every field, as being the government there of the same party at District and State level.

Being an administrator earlier he proved to be a great leader and worked dedicatedly for the development of District Kargil. He made special effort to improve the education scenario in the region and has also showed great concern for women empowerment at a larger level. Under his leadership Kargil district made good progress. It was because of his progressive thinking that he commands the respect and support of the Islamia School as well the youths of Kargil. Needless to mention, both his sons qualified for the KAS.

Haji Mohammad Abbas

Haji Mohammad Abbas was the son of Haji Mohammad Ibrahim Ibcho of Braqboo Kargil. His mother Nasima was a gentle and kind lady, who brought him up with love and affection. His father Haji Mohammad Ibrahim was a Mail Overseer in the Postal Department during the British regime. He was born in 1929, received his basic education from Kargil itself and then did his F.A, from Lahore University during 1946. In the beginning, he worked as a teacher in Education Department for a brief period, then resigned from the post and joined Police service. After serving at different places on different ranks in the Police Department, he was retired as Senior Superintendent of Police in the year 1984. As a Police Officer he served at Leh, Kargil, Jammu, Rajouri, Anantnag, Baramulla, and Pulwama with honesty, efficiently and merit. He was enjoying regards, respect and reputation in Leh and Kargil. The Ladakhi people knew him as Thanedar Abbas, Dy. S.P. Abbas and S.P. Abbas. He was sociable and supportive. After retirement he took keen interest in social activities and began to serve the people in different ways. He was one of the members of Kargil Action Committee, and played a vital role in minimizing the communal tension of 1989 in Ladakh, and also preventing Kargil youth from indulging in anti-National activities during the Kashmir turmoil. He participated in tripartite talks in Delhi along with other members of the delegation to resolve the problems faced by the people of Kargil.

In 1996, the Jammu and Kashmir National Conference offered him the mandate from Zangskar constituency. He fought the election against Congress candidate Kacho Mohammad Ali and won the election and became M.L.A. for the first time. Similarly, in 2003, he again fought the election on N.C. mandate from the same constituencies against Congress candidate Mr. Ghulam Raza and defeated him, while in rest of the constituency N.C. lost all its seats. As a Member of the Legislative Assembly he served the people of Kargil in a very efficient manner and has taken various steps for speediest development of Kargil.

He performed Haj in 1985 and again performed Umrah and Ziarat in 2000. But unfortunately on 10th of April 2006 he passed away at Jammu as a sitting M.L.A. and left a vacuum in Kargil politics. Among his offsprings he is having one son and two daughters. His son Dr. Mohammad Raza Abbasi is serving as Deputy Director in Sheep Husbandry Department. The elder daughter Najama Bano is a Principal of a Higher Secondary School and the younger daughter Nargis Bano is Child Development project Officer in the ICDS Department. Haji Md. Abbas will always be rememberd as an honest Police Officer and politician.

Tsettan Namgyal

Tsettan Namgyal was born on 2nd of January 1966 at Tiagar Nobra. His parents have come from two noble families of Leh. His father Wngdus Nurboo from Shangara family and mother Shema Tsering Dolkar from Kalon family. His ancesters were holding high posts in the royal court. The Shangara family remained the member of the "Lopchhak", i.e. trade mission to Lhasa. Presently his family resides at Tirith Nubra. He received his early education from Bisco School Srinagar and qualified matriculation from the said School and did graduation and postgraduation in Geology from Jammu University. After completion of postgraduation, he prepared for Civil Service examination. He was associated with an NGO for hardly one year, when he was offered mandate by J&K National Conference from Nubra constituency. He fought Assembly election against Congress candidate Stanzin Dorjay in 1996 and won the election. He became minister of State for tourism in the Cabinet of Dr. Farooq Abdullah for about 3 years and rest of the period as Minister of state for Agriculture from 1996 to 2002. Though being a senior member of NC and minister he was strengthening his position in the party, but unfortunately he has to resign from the Party and Ministry, because of the amalgamation of all parties in Union Territory Front.

He could not fight election at this time, because the LUTF unanimously elected Pintoo Nurboo as MLA Nubra, and Nawang Rigzin Jora as MLA, Leh without contest. Thus he has to sacrifice his political career for the cause of UT movement.

MLA Nubra Tsettan Namgyal and E.C's alongwith CEC Rigzin Spalbar at an arrow shooting function

But according to Tsettan Namgyal that was a mockery, the elected members never spoke a word in the Assembly in favour of UT and within years they along with their old colleagues went back to their parent organizations, whereas Tsettan Namgyal had to wait nine years. In 2011, he revived the National Conference party in Nubra Block and was back to his parent organization. He is a young, energetic and highly educated leader. In 2008 general election he again fought the Assembly election as an independent candidate, with the support of LUTF against Congress candidate Tsewang Rigzin and was defeated. He did good efforts to improve the quality of education in Nubra, construction of link roads and irrigation canals funded by ADP and NABARD, and provided generators and other needful equipments to the far flung villagers under his CCDF fund. His main aim is to open the old border routes, like Nubra-Khapulo and Nubra-Yarkend, so as to restore the old Silk route trade. This trade has proved very beneficial for the people of Nubra in the past. Besides, many relatives of the people of Nubra reside outside the border. With the opening of these routes they can meet with each other and bilateral relations can be developed further.

Haji Nisar Ali

Haji Nisar Ali was born on 7th of June 1966, at village Karith block Shargol, in Kargil. He received his basic education at Middle School Karith, Higher Secondary education at Kargil and was a student of ARSB College Delhi. Before joining politics he did social services to the people of Ladakh under the guidance of his uncle Haji Hassan. He helped those people to get Visa and passport who were desirous to proceed for Haj and Ziarat and guided the poor and needy patients to be hospitalized in Delhi for treatment. He had been caretaker of the Mutahari School Book Department and remained attached with Roohani Tour and Travels for several years. In 2002, he fought the assembly election from Kargil constituency as an independent candidate and won with good margin, but in 2008, he could not retain the seat again. Though he won the election as an independent candidate but he gave absolute support to the Congress party in all spheres. He was inducted in the Mufti Sayeed's cabinet as Minister for Social Welfare, Minister for Rural Development and Minister for Youth Affairs, Sports and Technical Education and earned the regard, respect and acclaim of both bureaucracy and polity in the State as the cabinet Minister. He had been in the political arena for the past two decades and has a thorough and sound understanding of its functioning, demography of Jammu & Kashmir, voter base and opposition strengths and weaknesses. He has good organizational skills and party infrastructure building and manages the party as a structured organization. He has worked extensively at the grass-root level and has a clear understanding of problem areas, needs and possible solutions, and has a very good communication and rapport building skills.

As a Minister of Social Welfare, he introduced a structured approach to determine the requirements, purchases and staff, for anganwadi and enrolling members to the scheme. He assessed the current staff structure and created and filled all the posts needed to run the Ministry at different levels including districts and blocks and established 1000 new anganwadi centres. He got assessed properly the pensioner scheme, revived the current members in the scheme, assessed and added 1.25 lac new members in this social welfare scheme and gave special prominence to the aged, helpless, handicapped and widowed women.

In Technical Education Department, there were just 9 Polytechnic Institutions before he joined the Ministry. He interacted with all the key officials, students and also officers at all levels including Deans, principals, faculty and staff and ensured that every district of J&K should have at least one Polytechnic Institute. It is because of his noble efforts that now Jammu & Kashmir have 22 Polytechnic Institutes. He introduced many trades which were needed to keep pace with changing needs for the young students, and upgraded the lab facilities.

As a Sport Minister, he assessed the functioning of the department and introduced many sport activities on a regular basis at zonal levels. He assessed and interacted at all levels, created the needed physical Education trainer posts and ensured all the higher secondary schools and the college level institutes in the State had proper PT department, fully equipped and had Physical Education Trainers. Haji Nisar Ali as Sports Minister of J&K represented India at Athens in Greece during the closing ceremony of Olympics in 2004. Since Olympic Games started in 1904, and completed 100 years in 2004, hence, he got the opportunity to participate in golden jubilee celebration. He performed Haj and Ziarat several times and visited Saudi Arabia, Syria, Iraq, Iran and Greece. Presently, he is a leading member of Indian National Congress.

Nurboo Gyaltsan

Nurboo Gyaltsan was born at Khaltsey in the year 1943. His father enrolled him in the Primary school of the village, wherefrom he passed primary and went to Timisgam High School for further studies. After qualifying matriculation from that school he went to Srinagar and passed the graduation in arts from S.P. college Srinagar. He did L.L.B. from Aligarh Muslim University. The credit of being the first Advocate from the region goes to him, who joined District court at Leh in 1969, since then he is doing practice in the court. He had been a founder member of the Lamdon Social Welfare Society Leh. He remained as its honorary President for 9 years and served the society.

S. Dorjay, T. Samphel, Abbas Aabedi and Nurboo Gyaltsan alongwith Jhon Mecon Senator USA

The society also established Lamdon Model School Leh which is presently one of the leading private schools of the region. Once in his prime youth he fought the Assembly election as an independent candidate but lost. He was general Secretary of Ladakh Buddhist Association for many years and served the community. He had been an active member of the Indian National Congress and remained as its District President for many years. He is one of the members who was detained in the prison along with other collegues while struggling for Scheduled Tribe status for Ladakh during 1972 and was released after 48 days when G.M. Shah came in power with the support of Congress. He along with Thufstan Tsewang and Tsering Samphel raised voice against the atrocities of Kashmir Government and demanded "Central Administration for Ladakh in 1970's when Syed Mir Qasim was in power, but it could not get a mass support like the U.T. movement of today. However, he participated actively in every movement of the Ladakhis like grant of S.T., Regional autonomy and U.T. status for Ladakh. He fought the Council election from Khaltsey constituency twice and got elected once, was elevated as Executive Councillor for Public Works and served the people with merits. Considering his best services to the people and party, the local Congress leaders recommended his name as a candidate for M.L.C. He was got elected in 2009. Since then he is serving the people in every field as per his capacity. Presently, he is one of the senior leaders of the local Congress party. He visited France and Bhutan and participated in many National and International seminars. He is humble, gentle, softspoken and sociable; people like his nature and behaviour very much.

Kacho Gulzar Hussain Khan

Kacho Gulzar Hussain Khan is the son of renowned scholar and historian Kacho Sikander Khan. He was born in District Budgam Kashmir, where Kacho Sikander Khan was posted as Tehsildar in 1970's. It is not out of place to mention here an outstanding contribution of Kacho Sikander in the field of history and literature. Kacho Sikander Khan was the son of Kacho Isfandyar Khan of Yokma Khjarboo. After completing his education from Sri Pratab College Srinager, he joined the Revenue Department and worked on different posts very efficiently and honestly like, Naib Tehsildar, Tehsildar, Sub-Divisional Magistrate, and Settlement Officer and finally retired as Assistant Commissioner in 1980.

A lover of art and culture Sikander has all along been urging revival of cultural heritage of the region in particular and of the country through glorious path of love and brotherhood and racial, regional, and communal harmony, and deeper human values. He is the author of many valuable books like *Qadim Ladakh*, *Nurboo Zangpo and It-thog Lhamo*, *Ladakh in the Mirror of her Folklore*, and *Afkare Pareshan*. In recognition to his outstanding services to the language and literature, the Jammu and Kashmir Cultural Academy conferred him the "Life time achievement award." Besides, he won awards from Uttar Pradesh Urdu Academy, Jammu and Kashmir Cultural Academy and District Administration, and lastly the State award from the Governor of J&K. He attended many National and International Seminars and presented papers. He was interviewed several times by the Media persons to present talks on Radio and TV. He performed Haj and Ziarat in 1990. After a brief illness, he passed away on 12th June, 2007. His elder son Kacho Isfandyar Khan is an IAS Officer.

Kacho Gulzar Hussain is the youngest son of Kacho Sikander Khan. He received his basic education at Higher Secondary School Kargil. Then he proceeded to Delhi for further studies and graduated from Delhi University. Later, he did his postgraduation from RICM Chandigarh.

After completion of his studies he joined politics and became the youngest councillor in the first Ladakh Autonomous Hill development council Kargil in 2003 and elevated as Executive Councillor for Agriculture under the Chairmanship of Haji Azgar Karbali from 2004 to 2008. He served the people of Kargil very sincerely and honestly in the capacity of Executive Councillor. He worked for the welfare and upliftment of the farming community of the District tirelessly and dedicatedly. He is associated with many NGO's and Societies also. His father influenced him greatly due to which he developed great interest in Ladakhi culture and literature. He attended several national and international conferences and presented papers relating to Ladakh folk literature and culture and on Kashmir issue. He regularly writes columns for several national and state newspapers and has written articles for many magazines on Geography and Culture of Ladakh. He has been nominated as man of the year by the American Biographical Institute for the year 2000. He has given talks and interviews on All India Radio Kargil and has written plays and features for the radio several times. This literary taste has been inherited in him from his scholar father. Nowadays, he is working on much research based works on the silk route. He is also working on the challenges faced by the Ladakhi youth in the era of development and invasion of different culture on Ladakh.

Nasir Hussain Munshi

Nasir Hussain Munshi is former Executive Councillor and sitting councillor in Ladakh Autonomous Hill Development Council (LAHDC), Kargil. Being a postgraduate in Journalism and Mass Communication, Nasir started freelancing for All India Radio Kargil and Doordarshan in different capacities and in the year 2001 he was awarded for the Gandhian Philosophy programme under public broadcasting awards by Prasar Bharti Broadcasting Corporation of India for the Programme "Ruhani Rehnuma". Nasir also worked with some prominent NGO's of Kargil in the past years. Nasir wrote many articles for the print media and produced many documentaries for All India Radio and Doordarshan as well on the socio-economic, politics and cultural aspects of Kargil which include *Badalte Rukh*, *Dardoon Ka Safar*, *Suru Behta Hay*, *Sham-e-Gharibban aur Subh-e-Nau*, *Mewa-e-Sangistaan*, *Waadi-e-Purik*, *Balti Lok Versa* are the prominent carried out in Programme *Tasveer* on state hook-up by Radio Kashmir Srinagar. He also worked as stringer/films resource person engaged by Regional News unit Doordarshan Kendra Srinagar. He joined politics in the year 2003 as he contested the LAHDC Elections from Gundmangalpore Constituency as an independent candidate and defeated his contender Agha Sayed Kazim by a margin of 534 votes out of a total casted vote of 1645. In December 2005, he was elevated as Executive Councillor and assigned with two important portfolios, Public Works and Power Departments. Later he was assigned to look after as officiating Chairman/CEC in LAHDC Kargil in addition. He discharged his duties as Executive Councillor Works and Power till the commencement of LAHDC Elections in July 2008.

Again in the year 2008, he contested the elections from the same constituency as independent candidate and defeated his competitor National Conference candidate Agha Syed Hussain Mutamadi (former Member Parliament Ladakh), and is contemporarily a sitting councillor in the opposition.

He joined Indian National Congress in the year 2010 as President District Youth Congress Kargil and later elevated as working President.

Nasir's foray into politics is not coincidental. He comes from a political family and it was at the insistence of the locals that he joined politics full time and was elected to LAHDC Kargil for the second consecutive term. He is the eldest son of Haji Sanaullah Munshi and nephew of prominent political figure of Ladakh Munshi Habibullah. He was born in Kargil on 6th November 1971.

Aziz Mohammad Qari

He was born on 17th August 1930 at village Pandras of Dras Sub Division, which is considered the 2nd coldest place in the world. The people have to face a very rough, and tough hard life. In Dras mostly the Dard origin people live, there. The Dardi people speak Shina dialect. They have preserved their old tradition and culture till now. His father Haji Abdul Rehman was a religious preacher of the village having good knowledge in Quaranic education and was a Hafize Quran. So, he was designated as Qari. Aziz received his Primary education at Government Primary School Pandras and upto middle standard at Lower High School Kargil itself where his grandfather Haji Ghulam Mohammad was a renowned businessman. He went to Srinagar for further education. He passed 10th class from Govt. Hari Singh High School Fateh Kadal Srinagar. Being a student of farflung area; he was awarded ₹ 12 p.m. as scholarship to continue his education in the college. Later on, he qualified B.A. and B.Ed. from Kashmir University. In the beginning he was in Government service in Defence and Revenue Department and finally he opted for the post of Teacher and served the backward people of Dras for many years in different capacities. During this period the education standard of Ladakh region was very poor, partly due to the topography of the area and secondly poor attendance of students due to limited number of Schools at long distances. In recognition to his best services in the field of education the state Government conferred him with the-State Award. Later leaders of J&K National conference, advised him to resign from the Government service and join the politics. Accordingly to guide the people of Dras in the political field he resigned from the post of Head Master and joined Jammu & Kashmir National Conference as an active member. Considering his services in the party and to give representation to the people of Dras in the council he was elected as Member Legislative Council in 1978 by the J&K National Conference Party. He was re-elected as Member Legislative Council Kargil in the year 1996 and retained the seat till 2002. In 1983, he was elected as Provincial President National Conference of Ladakh region and worked on the said post till 2006. He served the people of Kargil in general and Dras in particular in a very gentle and efficient manner and made a good rapport among the masses. Presently he is a senior leader of J&K National Conference. He is a good speaker and knows Shina, Balti, Kashmiri, Persian, Urdu and English languages. As a poet he has written many poems in Urdu, Persian, Kashmiri and Shina languages.

Agha Syed Jamal Minji Kargil

Agha Syed Jamal is son of Agha Syed Akbar Shah who was born in 1940 in a noble family of Sadaad at village Minji of Kargil District. He received basic education from Govt. Primary school Minji, now upgraded to High school. He spent few years of his childhood at village Akchamal and Chutumail for Islamic Studies under the guidance of Hujjat-ul-iIslam Sheikh Rahmatullah and Sheikh Mohdmad Mufid respectively. In the year 1960 he went to Najaf-ul-Ashraf for further Religious Education and at Najaf; he was associated with the known Ayatullah Hakim's family while studying at "Madrasai Haji" Najaf-ul-Ashraf (Iraq).

During his stay in Najaf he was partly involved in social work to help the Indian Islamic students with regard to their visa problems, admission in different Institutes and providing them Shehria (scholarship) etc. and in this way he remained helpful to the Indian Students. After 7 years of Islamic Studies Agha Jamal came back to his native place Minji Kargil in the year 1967 and joined politics as an active worker in Indian National Congress under the leadership of Agha Ibrahim Shah, the then Member Legislative Assembly and in 1968 he was appointed as Block President Congress–I. In 1969 he became District President Congress–I Kargil and served as District President PCC for about 25 years.

In the year 1988 Agha Syed Jamal was elected as Member J & K Legislative Council for a period of six years. He was also Member of J&K Pradesh Congress working Committee during the said period.

He was elected as Councillor in the Ladakh Autonomous Hill Council Kargil, and served as Councillor for 5 years from 2003 to 2007. In 2011 Agha Jamal was elected as Vice President Jamiet-ul-ulma Madrasai Isna-Asharia (Islamia School) Kargil.

After the sad demise of Sheikh Ahmed Muhammadi President Jamet-ul-ulma Madrasai-Isna-Asharia (Islamia School) Kargil in the year 2012, Agha Syed Jamal has been given the responsibility to act as President Islamia School in place of Sheikh Ahmed Muhammadi by the elected members of the institution and presently he is the acting President Jamet-ul-ulma Madrasai-Isna-Asharia (Islamia School) Kargil. He is a soft spoken, sociable and straight forward and being a religious leader, is a good orator. He served the backward people of Kargil in different capicities in a very efficient manner and is very popular among the masses.

Comparative Studies of Past and Present

8

In Ladakh the State and Central Government both have taken numerous measures to overcome the problems. This has both, positive as well as negative effects on the local population and the same is reflected in diverse forms including in culture and ecology. Some of the notable events, chronologically placed in the recent history of Ladakh had a variety of impact on the life and culture of Ladakh. More notable of these events could be Chinese aggression 1962, Liberation of Turtuk region from Pakistan 1971, Opening of Ladakh for domestic and foreign tourist 1974, Creation of separate District for Kargil, 1979, Emergence of Non-Government Organization, since 1980 onwards, Agitation for creation of Ladakh Autonomous Hill Development Council and Union Territory since 1989 onwards, Declaration of eight ethnic groups as Scheduled Tribe on 7th October, 1989. Patch-up between Ladakh Buddhist Association and Ladakh Muslim Association, 1993. Formation of Ladakh Hill Development Council, 1995. Leh is predominantly Buddhist district while Kargil district is Muslim dominated. Let us now visualise today's Ladakh on the basis of socially, economically, politically, educationally, spiritually, morally, ethnically, aesthetically and so on.

Social System and Behaviour

The ancient people were very simple and innocent and were having the sense of love, regard and respect to the senior and literate people. The common people were having no extra work except farming. Not to speak of government employment, even people could not have the labours job. However, there were some traders, who used to go Changthang and Kargil loading their merchandise on ponies and donkeys. Due to idleness, the common people gathered at the village "Pandal" or at a central place, where they heard the news of different places, discussing the social, religious and other common problems and doing efforts to find out the solutions. Whenever, a traveler or trader came from Kashmir, Tibet, Manali or Baltistan, people still gather around him to know the new developments and news and listen to him for hours together. Sometimes they are astonished to hear about motor, ship, radio, telephone and engine, etc. There was no system of hiring labours and workers like today, instead having a good tradition in the village society to support each other in performing the agricultural and other works, free of wages. There was shortage of money in the society, due to unemployment. The only source of income was agriculture. They used to sell cattle, grain, plants and trees to fulfill other requirements of a family. A person who possessed one hundred rupees is considered a rich and powerful man and called "Gyatumpa" which means master of hundred rupees.

During the Dogra rule they were ill-treated and harassed. One noble of Chiktan Kalon Rahim Khan was severely punished. The Dogra rulers made the society coward and dull. Even the villagers were afraid of a government peon or a police constable till a decade's back when they used to come in the village to deliver a summon. Even the capitalist and rich people exploited them, they had to perform the agricultural work in his fields as a forced labour. But nowadays every Ladakhi is aware of their right and duties and they never bothered of the Government employees. This is because of the noble efforts of Kushok Bakula and Sonam Wangyal, who freed them from "Kar-Begar" and other similar problems. In the past, Ladakhis were very innocent, honest and trustworthy. They used to hate the liar and uncultured people. Honest people were highly respected. The promise made between one another is properly fulfilled. Theft cases were very rare and the houses were not locked like today, instead, a wooden hook was in use. This can be opened by every one except animals. People were very strict to moral values. During the reign of King Nima Namgyal in 1715, two Italian Priests Father Dezidary and Emanuel Ferrari visited Ladakh. Father Dezidary has stated in his travel note that the Ladakhis are noble, gentle, trustworthy and straightforward. They are sociable and cheerful. Similarly, in the year 1812, an officer of East India Company Meer Izattullah visited Leh, he writes, "I have never seen a person carrying weapon in Leh, and Leh is free of criminals, culprits, robbers, dacoity and violence. All the foreign visitors have mentioned in their travel notes that the Ladakhis are honest and peace loving people whereas their remarks about the neighbouring regions are quite reverse.

The Ladakhis are honest and truthful as compared to other communities and nations. Patience and tolerance are inseparable from Ladakhi way of life. Most of them do not smoke. Tobacco smoking is considered a vice and sin. However, they are fond of taking snuff in leisure hours. Apart laymen, some of the Lamas also make use of snuff.

The dialect of the Ladakhis is called Ladakhi. Bhoti is their written language and it is little different from Tibetan and is a mixture of Tibetan and Ladakhi. The Bhoti language is being spoken with little differences right from Baltistan to Tibet. Bhoti being the religious language of the Ladakhi Buddhists, most of the common people in the past knew to read and write the Bhoti but whenever they received a letter in English or Urdu, they had to face problems in finding a literate person to read the letter. Hence one had to go from door to door and village to village to find out a literate person and some time reaching the office where from the letter was issued. But luckily, today every body is literate in the family and the problem has been solved once for all.

The Social and Religious Festivals

Social festivals and functions in the village were very simple, except a very few outsiders like relatives, only a handful of villagers gather at the function. The number of participants, including both the sexes used to be 100 at the most. But today the friends and social circle are enlarged and the numbers of guests are crossing the mark of 1000. It is difficult to accommodate in the house, hence big shamiyanas are erected outside the house in the fields. The Ladakhis are very cheerful people and try to make any event as gaiety. This cheerfulness is manifest in their singing and dancing. This is usually performed in groups. In olden days the king's gloom was also dispelled by "Takshos" (dancing girls), such females represented good families and felt proud of their dancing skills. The Ladakhis are very fond of archery and often organize the "Dartses" (archery competitions) in every village which continues for whole day. Prizes are given to the winners. The Dartses is of great importance; it includes amusement, entertainment, competition, outing, community feeling, unity and integrity. In the past the "Argon Dartses" was very popular in Leh town. Members of all the communities were participating in it. But it has ceased to organize now, for not known reason. The archery competitions are also organized by the Lamas of different Gonpas. They also perform dramatic gesture to provide humour to the spectators and the occasion becomes full of fun and laughters. The Ladakhi songs throw lights on the social, cultural, historical, political and religious aspect of the land, and reflect the emotional, romance and feeling of the lovers. In the past, the folk songs were not recorded but transmitted verbally from generation to generation. But presently the poets have recorded their poems and the Cultural Academy Leh has published hundreds of books on various songs. The flower festivals of Nubra, Wakha-Mulbek, Darchik-Garkhon, and Shakar-Chiktan are very popular in Ladakh. The young and beautiful girls collect the flowers in the morning and offer at the religious places and later participate in the dancing programmes, and the special song of flower festival is being sung jointly.

The mask dance which is known as "Chhams" is organised in all the Gonpas called "Gustor or Tses-chu". It is based on religious philosophy and reflects the victory of the truth over evils. It is also said, that these mask dances are performed to make people familiar with the devil faces, which one has to face in the next world. It also reflects the assassination of King Lhang Tarma, an enemy of Buddhist Dharma in Tibet, by a saint Lama Spalgi Dorje. The Hemis Tses-chu or Mela Hemis, which is very popular among all the festivals, is celebrated in the month of June to commemorate the birth anniversary of great Buddhist saint Padma Sambava. Thousands of local and foreign tourists participate in the Mela. The Tourism Department of Jammu and Kashmir organizes Ladakh Festivals at various block headquarters of Leh and Kargil in the month of September. The main objectives of the festivals are to preserve the culture and transmit it to the next generation. Secondly to motivate the tourists to visit the different blocks and retain them for some more time in Ladakh. Beside this, the Singgay Khababs, Sindhu Darshan festival is being organized at the bank of Indus at Shay Manla in June every year. Beside the local people thousands of tourists and devotees from the plain areas, especially the Sindhis participate in the festivals. In the morning, prayers are performed by the saints of different religion and the festival starts by unfurling the National flag. Cultural programmes of various states are performed by the professional artists. The Sindhis take bath in the River Indus and take the water to their various destinations, since the water of Indus is sacred both for Sindhis and the Buddhists. It was started for the first time during the BJP rule by its Home Minister Lal Krishana Advani in 1997. Since then it is continuing every year with great zeal.

Beside the above festivals, the Buddhists of Ladakh celebrate the Buddha Purnima, Gochhak, Moslam Chhenpo, birth anniversaries of great saints and Losar. On the occasion of Buddha Purnima a grand public meeting is held at polo ground Leh and scholars throw lights on the life and achievements of Lord Buddha. The Losar is the red letter day for the Buddhist of Ladakh, they celebrate it with great pump and show. In the morning people go to the Chokhang to pay homage and offer "Khatak" to the statue of Cho-Rinpoche. Later the function starts. Here is a legend about the celebration of Losar. Though the Buddhists of the Himalayan region,

China and Tibet celebrate the Losar on the 1st day of the 1st Bodhi month. But in Ladakh it is celebrated on the 1st day of the 11th month, i.e. two months earlier of the Tibetan Buddhists. History reveals that king Jamyang Namgyal came to know through his spies, about the suspicious activities of the Baltis at the border. Perhaps they wanted to invade Ladakh. King Jamyang could not make a compromise with the safety and security of the country. So he decided to celebrate the Losar two month's earlier, keeping in view the significance of the security of the country and to leave for Baltistan for a war. Since then it is celebrated on the 1st day of the 11th month of the Bodhi calendar. Though there are many Eids in Islam, like Eide Mailad-un-Nabi, Eide Ghadir, Eide Naroze, Eid-ul-Fitr and Eid-ul-Zuha. But the later two Eids are celebrated by all the Muslims of the world with great enthusiasm. The Muslims keep fast for one month during the month of Ramzan. When the Eid moon appears on the evening of the last day, they celebrate the Eid on the 1st day of shawal. On this day, they perform the "Nimaz" at Idgah in the morning, Pay Fitra to the poors and break the fast. Later they visit the grave-yard for "Fatiha", and visit the house of relatives and elder people to greet them.

The 2nd great Eid which all the Muslims irrespective of sects do celebrate is Eid-ul-Zuha. It is celebrated to commemorate the great sacrifice of Prophet Ibrahim at Mina, on 10th of Zilhajja. On this day also first they perform the mass prayer at the Idgah. Pay greetings to each other after the Nimaz is over by hugging and shaking hands and visit the home of friends and relatives. Later pay the sacrifice of sheep and goats, etc. and distribute the meat among the neighbours, relatives and needy people. It is not out of place to mention here, that whether it is Eid or Losar people of opposite community visit the houses of their friends and relatives to pay homage and greetings on the occasion. This is really a good sign of communal harmony.

Muharram: Ashura is celebrated on 10th of Muharram every year to commemorate the martyrs day of Imam Hussain (AS) the son of Ali (AS) and Fatima (AS) and the grandson of the Prophet of Islam (SAW) on this day Yazid the son of Maviya brutally killed Imam Husain and his companion at the desert of Karbala in Iraq. This day has a great significance in Islam and Muslims do remember the sacrifice of Imam Hussain for the cause of Islam and his achievements. Though Muharram is celebrated by all sects of Islam in one way or other but the Shia Muslims do organize Majlise-Hussaini right from Ist Muharram.

Eidul-Maildun-Nabi is celebrated on 12th Rabiul-Awal by the Sunni Muslims and on 17th Rabiul-Awal by the Shia Muslims. But the grand Ayatollah Imam Khomenei appealed the Muslims of the world to celebrate a unity week from 12th to 17th Rabiul-Awal. Since then Muslims do organize seminars, poetic symposium, quiz programme and sirati jalsa, etc. during the whole week as "Haftae-Wahdat."

Caste System

Caste system is very deep rooted in Ladakh. In the beginning, there were three ethnic groups, viz. Mon, Dard and Mongol. Later hostile activities between the Mons and Dards started and as a result, Mons were subdued and got lower status in the Dard society, like that of the Aryans treated with the Dravidian in India. Certain elements of stratification bear resemblance to those of the Hindu caste system. In its practical perspective, it does cultivate some deprivation and alienation in respect of people belonging to certain ethnic groups. Similarly, it is because of the Brahminical approach and influence that the low castes like Gara, Mon, and Beda are ill-treated in the Ladakhi society. The Ladakhis still treat them as serving class who serve them whenever required. The Ladakhis are of the opinion that the affiliation with a particular group is determined by birth and not by his change of occupation. That is why, the common Buddhist children can become Lama and Chomos but the low castes are not allowed this concession. Whereas all the Buddhists, irrespective of caste, colour and creed have access to Gonpa and can worship the God and goddesses housed therein. However, I have seen one Lama among the low castes, who spent most of his time outside Ladakh. I don't know, whether he is getting due respect and status in the Ladakhi society or not. Similar situation is prevailing in Spiti, Himachal Pradesh. According to Tashi Tsering, a scholar of university of British Colombia, "The discriminatory practice of not allowing boys from caste families to become monks has begun in recent years. According to a local bzo pa man, who led a campaign to admit their children to monasteries, in December 2006 a group of sixteen bzo pa boys were admitted to the Gaden Shartse monastery, South India. In response a public meeting was held in Spiti in February 2007, which decided that the boys must return to Spiti (*Amar Ujala* 2007a). In order to punish the families of these boys, the people imposed the social ostracism rule called me lam chu lam (literally, no sharing of hearth, fire and water). For two years they remained ostracized. During this time leaders of bzo pa families informed the media and sent appeal letters to the Dalai Lama (*Divya Himachal* 2007), the Prime Minister (*Amar Ujala* 2007b), the President of India (*Amar Ujala* 2007c) and the Head Lama of local monastery. In 2009, with letter of support from the Head Lama of the local monastery and after a public announcement by the Dalai Lama supporting the caste members, the bzo pa boys were allowed to remain monks—but only in monasteries outside Spiti—and the me lam chu lam punishment was lifted. So far, only boys from blacksmith households have joined monasteries in South India and none from musician household." The hierarchical social structure consists of two broad groups: the caste household at the bottom and the majority Chechang households on the top. Caste in Spiti is different from the Hindu caste system. In Spiti, it refers to two groups of households, i.e. musicians and blacksmiths. The later holds the lowest position in the society, even lower than blacksmiths.

According to Tashi Tsering the Tibetan Buddhism and its monastic education system came to Spiti more than a thousand years ago as part of an important development in the history of Tibetan Buddhism known as bstan pa phyi dar (Later Diffusion of Buddhism: Tucci 1933). Before the advent of Tibetan Buddhism in the region, the inhabitants of Spiti and nearby region were said to be Mon or Monpa. According to the Indian historians (Handa 2001, Gyalpo 2006, and local Tobdan 1984); although locals in Spiti today use the word 'Mon' for the Indians. Tobdan states that Mons were a mix of Indo-Tibetan race, who lived between the Indian plains and the Tibetan plateau. Today there are Mon or Monpa in Bhutan and eastern India like Arunachal Pradesh, etc. (Chand, 2009, Baker, 2004. Klimberg-Salter, 1997) argues that those people were ethnically and linguistically a part of the ancient kingdom of zhang zhung, which covered present day western and north western Tibet. A local historian S.S. Gergan is of the opinion that the first batch of people who settled in Ladakh was the Aryan tribe Mon. The last name of the Mon village ends with "Chey". Such as Terchey, Tangchey, Phukchey, Likchey and Marchelang, etc. Similarly the name of the 'Dard' village starts with "Hey". Such as Hembabs, Hanu, Hemya, Hipti, Hemis, and Himaling, etc. Petro glyphs and cave paintings, etc. throughout Spiti provide evidence of the practice of 'Bon' religion in the region before the advent of Buddhism. These eternal Bon signs of swastika and other images on rocks and caves appear to be remnants of the older zhang-zhung kingdom (Petech 1997). In the 10th century a powerful kingdom was formed in western Tibet known as Guge, covering Guge, Purang, Ladakh, Zangskar and Spiti (Petech 1997). Guge's Buddhist king sponsored the propagation of Buddhism by constructing temples and monasteries and sponsoring scholarly activities. Tabo monastery in Spiti, regarded as the oldest continuously operating Buddhist monastery in India and the Himalaya was built during this time (Klimburg-salter 1997). As a result, 'indigenous' Bon practitioners were converted to Tibetan Buddhism. Some of the notable scholars and spiritual adepts produced during these periods include a Thorn holder of Gaden Monastery; Dhangkar Paldan Gyaltsan, Rangrik Rechen Kungga Giatso, Lopon Yeshe Tsettan, Khenpo Gyatso and many others who earned the title of Kachen and Geshe, which is considered to be equivalent to a Doctorate in Buddhist Philosophy (Tsering 2000). Today, admission in local monasteries is open to all male members, except caste households.

Here are examples that Lord Buddha admitted to his order of monks people of so-called low castes along with the members of noble castes. He made no distinction between them in the rank of monks. All received equal homage, reverence, and respect. For instance Upali, the barber was made in preference to all others, the chief disciple in matter pertaining to Vinya discipline. Sunita, who was honored by kings and nobles as an Arahant, was a timed scavenger. The philosophic Sati was the son of a fisherman. Subha was a daughter of a Blacksmith. Thus Buddha fought against this inhuman attitude and destroyed the barrier of caste. It was the Buddha who, for the first time in the known history of mankind, attempted to abolish the caste system and slavery and invented the higher morality and ideas of brotherhood of the entire human race, and in striking terms condemned the degrading caste system which in Indian society at that time was firmly rooted. The Buddha declared—

> By birth is not one an outcaste, by birth is not one a Brahmin, By deed is one an outcaste, by deed is one a Brahmin.

Such instances show that the portals of Buddhism were wide open to all without any distinction. The Buddha provided equal opportunities for all and he declared—

> No man is noble by birth No man in ignoble by birth. Man is noble by his own deeds; Man is ignoble by his own deeds.

Similar words have been said in Qurane-sharif in part 26, Al-Hujrat and Aya No 13. "Indeed we created you from a male and female (Adam and Eve) and made you nation and tribes that you may identify yourselves with one another, indeed the most honored of you in the sight of Allah is the most God wary among you." But it is unfortunate, that in spite of the noble teachings of every religion the caste system is so rigid in Ladakhi societies; especially in the case of intersect marriage. Though, much has been said and condemned against the inequality and caste barriers, by the saints, scholars, leaders and religious heads but the real situation prevalent is different than what the ideals speak for.

Marriage and Family

The family can be classified into three categories from marriage perspective namely monogamous, polygymous, and polyandrous. In the traditional Ladakhi Buddhist society there has, till recently, been the practice of polyandrous family. Thus the members of the polyandrous family have a common residence and jointly contribute to uplift the economy of the family; whereas the family property is not equally shared. Since the entire property of the family was inherited only by the eldest son. The rest of the brothers did not get anything out of it. All the brothers were dependent on the eldest one. However, they shared the wife of the eldest brother, it was because of the economic compulsion that kept the family members integrated and promoted polyandrous marriage. For instance, in 1938, Prince Peter made a social, education and economic survey of 6 families in Leh town, known as Thogtok, Mayay, Tsangbu, Goba, Oldan and Gatpo. According to the survey all the families were dependent on farming, none was literate and polyandry system was prevailing in all the families. After 42 years in 1981, an English Professor John Crock and Tsering Shakya, again made a survey of the above mentioned 6 families and found that out of the 36 male members of the 6 families only 18 were farmers, the rest 18 were government employees and the polyandry system of marriage was not existing among the new generations. Now this system of marriage has totally been abolished and one cannot find single instances at any corner of the region. It has become a past story. Under the new rules, the family property can be equally inherited by all the siblings and every brother has the right to have an individual wife. It has given setback to polyandrous families. It also declined because of the legislation against the system and because of the criticism by the saints, scholars and social welfare organizations.

History of Education in Ladakh

Historical sources point that Ladakh was forward in education during 10th century, when a ruler of western Tibet La-Lama Eshay Od established a university at Nyarma, Thiksay, which is 20 km away from Leh. The famous Buddhist scholar Lotsava Rinchen Zangpo was its head and administrator. The university had enrollments of students belonging to different parts of Ladakh and adjacent places. These included Zangskar, Nubra, Purig, Baltistan. Lahol-Spiti and lower Ladakh. The presence of the university made Nyarma a crowded place full of students and scholars and there was hustle and bustle in the area due to the movements of enthusiastic students. Teachings were conducted primarily in three linguistic mediums, which included Pali, Sanskrit, and Bhoti. The university did not sustain for long time due to acute financial and political problems and probably due to ideological differences. As a result, the importance of Nyarma decreased gradually and the statue of Dorje-Chhenmo was shifted to the capital Shay. The remnants and ruins of Lakhangs and other buildings of the university are still present in Nyarma which stand testimony to the glory of foregone era. However, there has been little or rather no effort to preserve these structures. The closure of the University was a sad development in history of Ladakh. Since its closure, Ladakhis found it difficult to have access to education for centuries. After the closure of the great centre of learning at Nyarma, Ladakhis had to go to Tibet to seek religious education, when Lhasa became the centre of knowledge. The practice of travelling to Lhasa for education started during the reign of King Lachen Mourup Gon and continued till the Chinese occupation of Tibet. The kings of the Namgyal dynasty failed to establish such a school or college to impart religious education to its subjects. However, the Lamas had to receive the basic education at their concerned Gonpa and then had to proceed to Lhasa for further education. Some of the Ladakhi Lamas received the highest degree of Geshes and Ladumpa, etc. Most of the common people remained illiterate, but some interested persons like traders, businessmen and prominent persons learned the Bhoti language from Lamas and other learned persons, so as to keep the trade accounts and to recite the "Pothi" during the "Tseschu" which was organized on 10th of every month. Some of the Muslim traders and prominent persons also learned the Bhoti to maintain the trade record. Some of the Shia Muslims in the past used to recite

Qasida, Marsia and Noha in this very language. The people of Purig were having a Maktab in every village, where the Akhon used to impart Persian and Quranic education to the people. Moorcroft (1820-21) has stated that he found one or two persons in every village of Purig, who knew to speak Persian or Hindustani language. Similarly in the Muslim inhabited areas of Leh district the Akhons also imparted Quranic and religious education to the masses. The Akhon's style of teaching was very informal and personal. Therefore a formalized education through organized curriculum for Islamic teaching could not emerge in Ladakh. The first institutionally organized effort at imparting Islamic education started only in the post-independence period when Islamia School Kargil was established. After basic Islamic education at the institution, students proceeded to Iraq and Iran for higher studies in Islamic education.

The Dogras also did nothing for the promotion of education, after annexing of Ladakh with the Government of Jammu, through a treaty of peace signed on 17 September 1842. However, they opened a Pathshala in the name of Shashtiri School in 1874 at Leh, where Sanskrit and Hindi were taught and the local language Bhoti was ignored. Hence, the Pathshala was viewed with suspicion by the local population. They thought it is a beginning of a process intended to transform the Buddhist community into Hinduism. Hence the local people stopped enrolling their children in the Sanskrit School. According to the Diary of British Joint Commissioner from Ist to 15th October 1882, Govt. of India FGN-A, political-E Nov, 1882 55-58; "the Sanskrit School which was started a few years earlier, has only 5 students left. Consequently, it has closed now. The main purpose of opening the school by Jammu Raja is to convert the Buddhist into Hinduism."

The Tyndale Biscoe School Srinagar was established in 1881. Five years later in 1887, the Moravian Missionaries of Germany opened the Ist primary school at Leh for formal education. In the beginning the roll of the school remained very poor. Ladakhi children hesitated to join the school. Parents thought it was a conspiracy to make the people Christian. Many people thought that children will forget agricultural works and local traditions while being in the school. Thus, they could not achieve the desired objective of educating Ladakhis till 1889. In 1889, the Chief Administrator of Ladakh Pandit Radha Krishan issued an order that, every household who has more than one child will send one compulsorily to the Moravian School to seek education. Still the parents were reluctant to do so, in spite of the order by the chief administrator. Finally, the Head Lama of Hemis Gonpa Stagtsang Raspa deputed his representatives to make house to house appeal. As a result, the parents could not deny his message and had to send their children to school, which increased the roll of Moravian School. Important subjects, which were taught at the school, were English, Urdu, Bhoti, Science, Natural Study, Maths and Geography. Beside these, there was option to study Bible. Dr. Karl Marx was teaching, English, Science and Geography. Yoseb Gergan was teaching Bhoti language. T.D. Shrieve the priest of Kaylang was teaching English and Maths and the Munshi of British Joint Commissioner was teaching Urdu. Now the school was running satisfactorily, but due to ill-luck, two of its teachers Father Redsolob and Dr. Karl Marx had to face sudden death because of typhoid and it harmed the activities and system of the school. The Missionaries also did efforts to establish schools at Khalsey and Shay but could not get desired response from local population, so school had to be closed. Moreover Mrs. Dora wife of Francke was the instructor of a knitting school meant for local women. The training which she imparted is still reflected in the local Ladakhi style of knitting, which is German. The Moravian missionary School Leh continued their journey despite facing several ups and downs. The opening of several government schools decreased the roll of Moravian school gradually and the school was closed finally in 1960. After a gap of 20 years, the school was re-opened in 1980 and today it is one of the leading schools of the district. Rev. E.S. Gergan functioned as its Principal for several years. Besides many administrators the school has produced KAS and IAS officers.

In the past, there were some well-known traders and businessmen in the Shia community of Leh, like Haji Turab Shah, Syed Najaf Shah, Akhon Abdul Hussain, Haji Taqi and Haji Issa Ali, etc. These well-known traders who had their links with central Asia, and prominent personalities of Leh like Munshi Ghulam Mohammad, Master Murtaza and others felt the necessity of a school. Thus, they established a primary school, in the name of Imamia School Leh at Chutay-Rantak, in the year 1930 under the aegis of Anjuman Imamia Leh. In the beginning, they enrolled 37 students. Out of 37, there were 21 girls students. Initially, there were three teachers including a craft teacher namely Amina. Munshi Hussain Ali Maqsoom, Ghulam Nabi Hamami and Master Murtaza, etc. worked there as teacher. But later with the increase of roll, the strength of the teachers was also increased. The disciplines that were taught in the school were Urdu, Maths, Social Science, Science, craft and basic tenets of Islam and religious education. The school operated in a very smooth way and some of the prominent persons of the community like late Akbar Ladakhi, Munshi Baqir, and late Munshi Mohammad Isa, etc. had their primary education from this very school. Many other people got employment as patwari, teacher and clerks after qualifying middle standard examination from this school. But unfortunately, during the post-independence period, it could not be run properly due to various hindrance and financial crisis and was closed in 1950. If it would have continued without break the scenario of education of the Shia community would have been something different altogether. It is not out of place to refer here the story of "Hare and Tortoise", similarly the community fell asleep and could not wake up for a long time, till then the other communities established their own schools and progressed extensively. However, it was the noble efforts of Sheikh Mirza Hussain, who out of the salvage of old Imamia School Leh founded the present Imamia Model School and started its journey again from the zero point in 1992. Is it not the responsibilities of those so-called leaders and prominent personalities of the past for all these lapses? It is Allah's blessing, that the Imamia School was upgraded as a full fledged high school in 2001. Presently, it is functioning in a very efficient manner and has showed excellent results in the Board examination. Besides, the school has produced many young administrators. The school has its own library, laboratory, computer library classrooms, transport and all other modern facilities. It has a big campus at Saboothang.

The first Government School in Ladakh was opened at Leh in 1892. Francke has given his observation note about the Govt. School of Leh. He discusses that the overall performance of the school was not satisfactory. He has further observed that out of the total roll of school, which was 40, most students used to remain absent from school and less than 20 was the usual attendance of students at the school. The school was also lacking behind because of absence of trained teachers and poor pedagogy system. However, the school gradually improved. Later on with the increase in roll of the students to 60, the school was upgraded to middle standard in 1908, and an additional post of teacher was created with a monthly salary of ₹ 30. Now the total strength of teachers became three. The Inspector of school has commented at the occasion that the school will prove a boon for the inhabitants of Leh. The said school was upgraded as high school in 1950 and later as Higher Secondary School in 1975. It is true that the school proved a boon for Ladakhis, as it produced hundreds of Government officers, like doctors, lecturers, engineers, administrators, army officers, civil service officers and so on. The Government School Skardo was established in 1899 and a year later in 1900, a school was also opened at Kargil. In 1904, two more schools were opened. The Primary school Kargil was upgraded to Middle School in 1930; while Skardo Primary School was already upgraded then. Now the three Tehsil headquarters of Wazarate-Ladakh, viz. Leh, Kargil and Skardo were having one middle school each. There were forty-six primary schools and three middle schools, under the Wazarate-Ladakh during the pre-independence period. Shridhar Dullu an educationist of the past had a vital role in promoting the educational system in the Wazarate-Ladakh. He worked as Assistant Inspector of schools from 1939 to 1948 and used to inspect the schools of Leh, Kargil and Skardo, at least once a year. He used to maintain log books and gave positive or negative remarks as per the findings of the toured school. Thus, he encouraged the efficient and dedicated teachers whereas the dull one has to rectify his methodology and other activities of the school till his next visit. Pundit Dullu's contributions are still remembered in the region.

A group of Buddhist youth formed a society under the presidentship of Gay Paldan, called "Lamdon Social Welfare Society Leh". The society organized religious drama called "namthar" and plays in the Leh town and in various other prominent places, directed by Padama Shri Mourup Namgyal and collected funds of about ₹ 24,000. In the beginning, the society did efforts to pass on the messages to eradicate the illiteracy and social evils prevailing in the society like alcohol consumption, smoking, killing of animals, adulteration and polyandry system and other evils prevailing in the society. Later they established an institution in 1973, with the name of Lamdon School Leh and the enrollment at the first time were only seven. Mourup Namgyal acted as first teacher of the newly formed school. A well-known Buddhist scholar Gashes Eshay Tundup, who was patron of the society, delivered the teaching of "Lamrin". Drawing from the Buddhist traditional consideration of number 7 as an auspicious number, he, prophesized that the school will find progress and prosperity, just like the new Gonpa at Lhasa, where the initial number of students when it started was seven. His prophesy came true. Today the roll of Lamdon school is more than seventeen hundred and its branches are at 10 prominent places. Previously, the school was affiliated with the J&K Board but since 1995, they had changed it and have got it self affiliated with the C.B.S.E. Chandigarh. The first batch of matriculation appeared for the C.B.S.E. examination in 1995. Lamdon High School was upgraded in 1995 and re-named as Lamdon Senior Secondary School Leh. An honest, disciplinarian and dedicated local educationist Mr. Eshay Tundup is functioning as Principal since June 1996. Under his able guidance the school is progressing rapidly. Many of its students have qualified medical, engineering and other allied and civil service examinations. It is the leading school of Leh affiliated with C.B.S.E. Chandigarh. The school has a big campus with all modern facilities. It has residential hostels both for boys and girls, a Gonpa for prayer, library, laboratory and computer lab and the largest multipurpose hall in the district. It is situated at Takskithang Leh, just behind the Singgay palace.

The youths of Chushot Gongma, under the Chairmanship of Syed Naqi Shah established Imamia Mission School Chushot Gongma in the year 1982. The school was upgraded as high school in 1997. The school is affiliated with the J&K Board of School Education. Mrs. Uzra Rizvi is functioning as principal of the school for last 25 years and the result of the school remained highly satisfactory for last many years. The school has produced a good number of educationists, officers, and administrators. The school is having separate hostels both for boys and girls, and has used modern technology to keep it warm during the winter season. The school has a big play field, well equipped library, laboratory, computer lab and other modern facilities.

The Sunni Muslims of Leh had a Maktab at Stago-Philok Leh at the house of Akhon Ghulam Mohammad, where the local Akhons used to teach Quraan and Hadith. According to Abdul Gani Sheikh, once in the past some local Muslims were called in the court of Syed Akbar Ali, the then Wazire-Wazarat Ladakh (1866-1871) in connection with a case as witnesses. The Wazir asked them to recite "Kalima". But they could not recite and remained mum. The Wazir was shocked to know this. He convened the Molvi called Akhon locally, and asked him to establish a Maktab to impart basic tenets of Islam and Quranic education to the local Muslims. After that the Maktab functioned under the guidance of Akhons. In 1930, Syed Mohammad Sayeed, called Peer Sahib opened Madrasa Binatul—Islam, meant for girls at the house of Akhon Ghulam Mohammad of Stago-Philok. However the journey continued for a long time, but the community had to face problems occasionally to run the Maktab for want of a teacher and other reasons. Later, under the patronage of "Peer sahib" the Maktab was converted into a primary school, probably in

1936. Gradually, with the increase of roll the primary school was shifted at "Tsas-Soma" at the present site of the Central Asian Museum. In 1970, it was upgraded as a middle school and shifted at Juma Bagh and then at 'Chhagon' and finally at the present site at Murtsey. It is because of the noble efforts of Yousuf Sheikh, the then President Anjumane Moinul Islam and Dr. Noor Mohammad the then Chairman of the School, who got allotted the land from the J&K Govt. for the purpose of construction of the school. The school was upgraded as a full-fledged high school in 1980. Since then it has produced many scholars, doctors, engineers, and administrators. But it is unfortunate, that its Managing Committee during the Chairmanship of Anisur Rehman has frequently changed the principals. Just imagine, during his 7 years tenure as chairman 7 principals joined the school one after another and left the school for not known reasons, which has certainly affected the educational scenario of the institution. Many prominent members of the community have withdrawn their kids from the school and admitted in other reputed schools and the roll decreased. Presently a local educationist Abdul Wahid Sheikh is the Chairman and a local Christian lady Madam Noami Sonam functioned as its principal for more than a year in recent past. Presently the school is having all modern facilities, like computer lab, a well equipped library, Science laboratories, play field and a hall. Besides teaching-learning process, the school is taking keen interest in co-curricular activities. The school has one of its branches at village Thiksay. Recent years saw many new private schools cropping up in Leh. These are New Millennium Dambuchan, Rigjung Choglamsar, Riglam, Sidharatha Stok, St. Peter School Chushot, New Era School Murtsey, Leh Model School, Jamyang School, Sindh Public School, Delhi Public School, Thugi Dumra Spituk and so on.

Private schools also played important role in transforming the educational landscape in Kargil. The Suru valley Public School is the oldest Private school at Kargil. It was opened in the year 1983 by a group of prominent Muslims of Kargil. In 1997, first group of students matriculated from the school.

Since then, the school has been producing good result. The Imam Khomeni Memorial Trust Kargil formed "Muthahry Educational trust in 1984 under the Chairmanship of Haji Azgar Ali Karbalai. The Trust established a private school in the name of Muthahry Public School at Kargil town. In 1994, the first batch of its students appeared in the matriculation examination through J&K Board. Since then it has been producing excellent results in the Board examinations. The school has produced a good number of lecturers, doctors, engineers, advocates, executives, administrators and scholars. Presently, the school has 14 branches at different places and which function as its feeding schools. Haji Azgar Karbalai, who was the founding member and Chairman of the Educational Trust, is now its Patron.

Similarly the Islamia School Kargil has opened Jafaria School in the Kargil town, with the aim to provide quality education to its young generations. The school was established in the year 1988, under the aegis of its educational committee. The first batch of students appeared in the matriculation examination from the J&K Board in the year 2000 and showed excellent result. Since then it has been continuously producing good results. The other public schools in the district are Munshi Habibullah Memorial Public School, Sawab Public School, The Northern Public School, Sir Iqbal Public School, and Kargil Public School.

After Independence the scenario of education of the Ladakh region (both in Leh and Kargil) has totally changed. Under the new Education policy there are schools at the distance of one km, in every village, free and compulsory education is there for every child of 6 to 14 years age. Presently, there are 2 colleges, 2 polytechnic colleges—one each at Leh and Kargil. Moreover there is Central Institute of Buddhist Studies functioning at Choglamsar Leh under the Cultural Ministry Govt. of India. Recently, Goverment of Jammu and Kashmir has proposed to establish one more college and university campuses each at Leh and Kargil. The number of schools in the districts of Leh in the year 2011 is as follows: Higher Secondary School 14, High School 26, Middle

School 130, and Primary School 181, Total 351; whereas the total number of schools to impart general education in Kargil District is as under: Higher Secondary School 14, High Schools 39, Middle School 269 and Primary School—232, Total 554. It is to be noted here that though the government run schools have trained and qualified teachers and other modern facilities, yet they failed to provide quality education and to achieve excellent board results as compared to private schools. Probably it is because of lack of accountability and dedication in government schools. Thus to make the schools more effective and functional the members of the community, teachers and educational officers have to think over it very seriously and sincerely. Today's education system should be based on three "S": the school, society and students should have a very good coordination with each other. Preference should be given to the government schools while enrolling the child. Though education is a state subject but it should be made compulsory to every government officials to send at least one of their children to government schools, so that they will take more interest to improve the education system in such schools. Supervision by education officers and other dignitaries should be made functional. Log book system should be introduced. Sincere and dedicated teachers should be encouraged. Home work checking should be made compulsory. Children should be encouraged to take part in co-curricular activities and to speak at the assembly. Progress report card should be maintained and sent to the parents on monthly basis. Modern technology should be utilized in all the schools. Parents-Teacher meeting should be convened frequently, so as to discuss the problems and their solutions.

Trade and Commerce

Ladakh was a trade centre, since the ancient days. Traders from central Asian countries like Chinese, Turkistan, Afghanistan, Pakistan, Tibet, Himachal Pradesh, Punjab, Kashmir and Baltistan used to come here. The trade was wide spread and Leh happened to be the main centre of exchange of various commodities and had been the meeting place for caravaners from Yarkend, Kashgar, Kashmir and Tibet, etc.

Barter system was there and mostly they were exchanging their goods with one another. At that time the coins of different countries were available in Ladakh. Ladakh was having its own coin called "Jau", valuing equal to 4 Annas. That was the first and the last coin of Ladakh. Similarly a very few numbers of Ladakhi traders were going to Tibet, Yarkend, Himachal and Kashmir and most of the people involved in the trade as career. Tea was mostly imported from Lhasa where it used to be brought from China. During the reign of the Namgyal kings, a trade mission called "Lobchhak" used to go to Lhasa, to pay homage and tribute from the king of Ladakh to Tibet's religious leader the Dalai Lama on the occasion of the New Year. The Lobchhak offered Khatak and gifts of various kinds. According to Frederec Drew, Wazire-Wazarat of Ladakh in 1871, the post of leader of the Lobchhak was held for only one term, however, it was finally discontinued in 1940s. The leadership seems to have been divided between Leh's two wealthiest mercantile families: the Radhu family and Shangara family. Farooq Radhu was the first of Khuja family to enter the long distance caravan trade of Tibet and Central Asia. Farooq Radhu had three sons—Haider Shah, Nasir Shah and Omar Shah. All the three were engaged in trade. Similarly, some well-known Budhhist families and representatives of Gonpas were going to western Tibet and Lhasa for trade. According to the treaty of Timisgam in 1683, between king Delek Namgyal and Mughal Commander Fidai Khan, some Arghon families were permitted to go to Tibet and western Tibet to purchase fine wool and Pashmina. They are Gutu, Shangku, Sotay, Hungloo, and Kharsawar and some of them had their own residential houses at Rudok. According to my late father Haji Hussain Aabedi, he had personally seen the houses of Gutu and Shangku at Rudok during 1950's. Though the Kashmir is famous for its Shawl in the world for centuries together, but the raw materials like fine wool and pashmina, etc. are being procured from Ladakh. Syed Turab Shah and Syed Najaf Shah were the well-known Kashmiri traders, who had their trade link with Yarkend. Similarly the Punjabi traders in Leh extended their trade up to Yarkend. It is said that the Punjabi traders used to take opium from Leh to Yarkend and brought "Charas" from Yarkend to Leh. Some of the Yarkendi traders who came Leh, also used to bring "Charas". Besides, they used to bring silk, Carpets, cloth, gold, silver, pearls, tobacco, dry fruits, charas and horses. The Yarkendi traders brought the camel for the first time in Leh, loaded with mercantile goods in the year 1870. Through Chang-Chhenmo track route, this ship of desert was a surprise and a new and rare species of animal for the Ladakhis. Some of the camels still exist in Leh and the government has established a camel breeding farm at Chushot so as to preserve the species of two humped camel from extinction. The Leh-Yarkend trade route, which connects Ladakh from central Asia, is a link of one of the oldest trade routes of the world called silk route, wherefrom, the Caravans passed for centuries together. Moreover the central Asian invaders like Mirza Haider Doughlat, Sultan Sayeed Khan and others used this very route. It was the route used by the Buddhist scholars to attend the 4th Buddhist Council at Kanspura Kashmir during the rule of Kanishka (125-52 AD). Chinese traveler and famous historian Hiun Tsang also used this route. Moreover Chinese pilgrim Fahayan too used this route in around 400 AD. But the route which remained open to traders for centuries was closed for trade since 1949. Later after 13 years the Leh-Tibet route also closed. It is because of the unfavourable political relation between India and China. Whenever the diplomatic relation improves, the route could be reused again. The old silk route is famous in the world. During the British rule, in order to promote trade, they appointed two local educated youths as overseer. They were Munshi Ali Husain of Chushot and Munshi Ghulam Ali of Leh and called poney track engineers by their superiors. Their main duty was to repair and renovate the Leh-Karakuram track route. To facilitate the Yarkendi traders' two sarais were constructed in Leh at the site of present Police Station Leh and taxi stand at Zangsti, and one sarai at Safa Kadal Srinagar. Moreover, there were sarais at different quarters on the Srinagar-Leh route and some overseers were there to make repair and renovation of the sarais. The Baltistani traders brought dry fruits which are famous in the world, utensils made of serpentine stone, pots of grit stone and butter, etc.; these are mostly consumed in Ladakh itself. Moreover, they exchanged the dry fruit with the Changpas of western Tibet and got salt, pashmina and fine wool. According to Moorcroft, who visited Ladakh in 1837, nearly 600 maunds of dried apricot were exported to Lhasa. The Kashmiri and Punjabi traders used to bring utensils, ghee, butter, honey, colours, cotton, shoes, pearls, spices, sugar, rice, saffron, tobacco, oil, soap, note books, opium, etc. and mostly exported to China and Chinese Turkistan. Similarly, from Tibet, they used to import pashmina, fine wool, silver, gold, silk, sulphur, salt and sheep. According to Cunningham (1846-47), Ladakh imports one thousand maunds of tea from Tibet and China. Out of one thousand eight hundred maunds were locally consumed and the rest two hundred maunds were exported to other neighbouring countries. It is said that during the Dogra rules the government employees posted in Leh were teasing the traders by demanding money or gifts in different names. Even high officials were receiving bribes from these traders. In the past the tax on mercantile goods was received both in cash and kind by the Ladakhi rulers. The tax was different on different articles. For instance, the tax on pashmina and wool was 8 anna per one maund, 2 anna on tea and 2 rupees 4 anna on charas, 2 rupees and 8 annas on opium, and 3 rupees on saffron. The tax on one horse load rice, i.e. 120 seer was 4 seer rice. The cost of 4 seer rice was only 3 annas at that time. During the reign of the Ladakhi king the total income on taxation was ₹ 18000 per annum. It is said that the Dogra rulers received ₹ 16000 as tax in 1868. In the past, money had a great value. One could have one seer of pashmina in two rupees, one sheep in two rupees, and one yak in sixteen rupees. Today the cost of a yak is about twenty to thirty thousand. Unfortunately, the old trade routes are now closed, since last half century. This has certainly affected the economy of Ladakh. Sealing of Ladakhi borders gave a big economic setback, more so at the level of trade. Sealing of borders with Lhasa also gave a jolt to religious and spiritual life of Ladakhi Buddhists. Their monks earlier got the higher religious education at Lhasa. They considered the source of spiritual inspiration. The Ladakhis now pray that the route to Kailash Mansarovar and other trade routes to the neighbouring countries should re-open in the nearest future.

Agriculture System

Though the major part of Ladakh is having one crop only, yet the ancient Ladakhis were dependent on agriculture. Agriculture has been the major economy of the Ladakhis. It continues to form the major source of livelihood, there being only one agriculture season in a year, the Ladakhis have to be more industrious. Because of the extreme cold nothing grows in winter season. The main crop of Ladakh was barley and wheat. Grain, grass and cattles were the main source of income of the farmers. Since there was shortage of money in the society, a man with hundred rupees was considered very powerful and influential and called "Gyatumpa" meaning master of hundred rupees. Hence the common people used the grain to fulfill the domestic requirements. Even they exchanged the sheep and goats with grain from the "Changpas" of western Tibet. Moreover the Ladakhi farmers sell the grass, grain, Lucerne pasture (alfa-alfa) and cattles to overcome the financial problems and to fulfill the daily use requirements. The poor people receive grains on loan from the landlords and moneylenders to sow the seed in their fields, and mostly pay interest on it in cash or kind. In the past, there was a good tradition and custom to perform the agricultural work. The farmers were co-operating with each other in farming free of wages. During the agricultural season there were three main functionaries in the village, viz. Rarzi, Churpun and Lorapa. The shepherd who goes out on the hills and valleys with the flocks of goat and sheep is called "Rarzi". He is responsible to take the cattle at the pasture in the morning and get it back in the evening and handover to the owners. The second important functionary is the "Churpun", who channelizes irrigation to avoid any wastage of water. He maintains that everybody gets due share on his turn. He also sees that the channels are properly working without damage or leak. The third important person is "Lorapa" who is watchman of the crops. His duty is on seasonal basis right from germination till the harvesting of crop. When he finds an animal eating the crop, he informs both the owner of the crop and cattle. He keeps the animal at a particular place and does not let it free till the owner of the animal pays the penalty. The amount of the penalty goes to Lorapa. The different functionaries are paid at different rates by each house-hold. This system is in practice almost in every village even today. I have seen the farmers since my childhood following the traditional system of farming that includes local manure to be supplied on the fields through donkeys and the fields are irrigated through khuls or channels and left for 7 to 8 days to dry. In the morning of the appointed day of sowing the local manure is sprayed through "Belchas" called Khem. Soon after spring the manure in the field ploughing starts with a pair of "Dzos", and the seeds are sowed. At far off places some use the horses and yaks for ploughing. The man does the ploughing while the women plain the fields with a "T" shaped wooden instrument with the singing of particular song. Later, beds are prepared after the germination of seeds. This is followed by watering the fields. Then after 4 months harvests the crop through sickles, and thrashing is done through domesticated animals, like horse, donkey, dzo, yak and cows, etc. Later, after performing prayer the grain is taken inside to store in the house, where according to the requirement of the family flour is made at the water mill called "Rantak". Both men and women sing different songs, while performing different agricultural task. But today it is observed that the total scenario of agricultural system has changed for more than last one decade. The total system has been replaced by machines. Today, manure is supplied to the fields through tractor. Ploughing is made through tractor. Harvest, thrashing and grinding are made through different machines. Consequently, the dzo, donkeys, and different songs especially meant for different tasks have disappeared from the society. Local people hesitate to work on fields; and have no time to co-operate each other like the past, instead they utilize the services of the laborers from Nepal, Bihar and Doda. Heavy subsidy on various kinds of import like wheat, atta, rice, sugar, gas, k.oil, etc. had some negative effect on the people. Firstly, they developed a feeling of dependency on the government. The rise of such a trend started eroding the feeling of self-help. Secondly, people started detaching themselves from the native land resources as the food grains available in the market were far cheaper than the cost of production in agriculture in Ladakh. They started lacking interest in agriculture. People get readymade rations from the government store; hence less attention is given on local farming. Most of the people have transformed their lands into Lucerne fields. God forbid! If some time the flow of ration ceases to reach here, due to some disturbance or natural calamity then there will be possibility of famine like situation.

In Ladakh major portion of land is owned by the Gonpas and almost in all the villages the poor agriculturists are the tenants of the Gonpas. To be the owner of the land carries more value in Ladakhi society. Here is a history behind it. In the year 1950, the Government of Jammu and Kashmir passed a bill called large lended Estates Abolition Act, as the bill was passed without any prior consultation with the Ladakhis. They reacted against it because it directly affected the interest of monasteries in Ladakh. The Buddhists of Ladakh strongly protested against the Act. An action committee was formed under the name of Gonpa Association Leh. A delegation headed by K.G. Bakula called on Pandit Nehru, the Prime Minister of India, in New Delhi, to appraise the situation. Consequently, the Government of Jammu & Kashmir had to appoint a committee of enquiry headed by Justice Jankinath Wazir, who had been the Chief Justice of Jammu & Kashmir. The Wazir Committee visited Ladakh in 1953 and investigated the case concerning the Ladakhi monasteries. In the committee records it reports: "It was rather surprising that the tenants who were likely to gain by the operation of the Act on lands attached to the Gonpas have unanimously desired that these lands should remain attached to the Gonpa and be free of Abolition Act. The committee especially inquired of them why they were in favour of retention of the lands with the Gonpa. Their reply was that the lands which were attached to the Gonpas were cultivated by the tenants and they had to pay only one fourth of the produce to the Gonpas. The share of produce was utilized for educational, religious and charitable purposes for feeding the poor and the needy people. Therefore, they would like that the Gonpas should not be divested of these lands. Thus the Gonpa Association won the case. This was a great relief to the various Gonpas of Ladakh. As far as vegetables and floriculture is concerned, Ladakh was already having some types of flowers and vegetables like turnip, labuk, dums, salat and mustard. Moreover Ladakhis were using some wild vegetables like "zachot, han, pudina, sagani and tayat, etc. It is said that the German missionaries brought the seeds of potato and some flowers during 1887, and distributed among some of the people of Leh. Later, it is because of the noble efforts of the DIHAR and Agricultural Department Leh that they distributed the high breed seeds and vegetable seedlings among the public, which really encouraged the farmers and promoted the growth of vegetables in the area. Today almost all kinds of vegetables are being grown in Ladakh and the farmers through co-operative societies supply the vegetables not only to army but also sell in the market throughout the year on reasonable rates. Secondly, it is the boon of the green houses that the farmers grow vegetables and many kinds of flowers during winter also and the seedlings are being prepared in the green houses. The flowers of Ladakh are one of its chief joys at all events. Ladakh now has different kind of flowers at the meadows on high hills and also valuable herbs.

Animal Husbandry

Animal husbandry is one of the occupations of the Ladakhis. The number of live stock reared by a family indicates the economic status of its members. The people of Changthang called Changpas are very famous for live stock like sheep, goat and yak, etc. The Changpas keep their livestock on highland pasture for grazing purposes, and move from place to place in search of good pasture, and where grazing facilities exist. Since ancient times, Changpas are very rich people in the western Tibet. They produce fine wool and pashmina in large quantity. The shawl industry of Kashmir is dependent on the raw pashmina of Changthang. History reveals that the Kashmiri kings like Sultan Sikandar Khan, Zain-ul Aabedin, and Adam Khan, etc. invaded western Tibet especially Kugay to obtain fine wool, pashmina, cattle and yak, and drew them towards Kashmir. The pashmina wool is in great demand in Kashmir where best quality of shawls are made out of it. In other parts of Ladakh, in addition to goat, sheep, pony, donkey and horses they have kept dzo, dzomo, common cow, jersy cow, yak and demo. Horse, pony, donkey and yak are used for transportation. Dzos are used for ploughing the fields and dzomo and cow are the milch cattle. Previously the milk production in Ladakh was very poor but now most of the people in the Indus belt have kept jersy cows, milk production has increased to some extent. They are supplying milk to the people of town on reasonable rates. Moreover, most of the people have turned their crop field into lucino and growing alfa-alfa in abundance, and fodder problems for livestock have been checked. After 4 weeks of sowing, the local women start weeding the fields. The grass and weeds are used as fodder. Ladakhis are fond of gur-gur tea, which requires a huge quantity of butter in every family. This butter is locally produced with the milk obtained from the domesticated animals. Their dung is used as fuel during winter. Woolen cloth is made out of the wool procured from sheep and goat. The Ladakhis themselves spin and weave rough kind of cloth which is quite good as per the climate of Ladakh. The women wear goat skin on their back, which looks beautiful. Taday, the scenario has totally changed. I remember very well, that some three decades back we were having 7 to 10 horses, 5 to 6 camels, 4 to 5 donkeys, 8 to 10 cows, a pair of dzos and a dog, but today there is none. Instead we are having 4 to 5 big and small vehicles, one JCB and other small machines. Sowing, harvesting and grinding everything is made through machines. The domesticated animals are disappearing gradually. A day will come that we will have to take our children at the cattle farm to show these animals. Where from we will procure wool, pashmina, milk, butter and meat? Previously Ladakhis were self sufficient to produce the requirements locally.

Horticulture

According to Moorcroft, when he visited Leh in 1837, 600 maunds of dried apricots were exported to Lhasa every year. Now the border trades have been ceased since 1950. The dry apricots are mostly consumed in India itself. The tourists are very fond of it and purchase it to present to their friends and relatives. Apart from civilians from outside Ladakh the army and paramilitary forces are the largest buyers of dry fruits. Moreover the local people consumed it in large number during the functions. After September the apples can be stored for months together without fridge or cold storage.

The lower Leh and some parts of lower Shayok valley in Nubra, Sanjak, Hardas, Karke-Chhu, Pashkum, dah-hanu, Garkon and Chhani-gund, etc. are very popular in producing fine apricots and apples. On the other hand, the rest of the areas of Ladakh like Dras, Durbuk, Panamik, Suru Valley, Wakha Nyoma, Zangskar, Chumathang and upper Leh are very poor in horticulture. During the childhood I came to know from my forefathers and other senior citizens that fruit plants like apricot and apples, etc. cannot grow at such places where Glaciers are visible. They never did efforts to grow fruit plants. But in the course of time it proved totally wrong. Today the people of Indus belt like Chushot, Thiksay, Ranbirpura, Shay, Spituk, Choglamsar, Stagna, Sanjak and Phey, etc. are producing a large quantity of apricot and apples. In this regard, the Horticulture Department Leh had done a commendable job. They distributed fruit plants and saplings among the needy people and promoted the process of horticulture. They also made the public aware of taking care and secure the plants from insects and other disease. The fruits in Ladakh I knew till 1963 were only walnut, apricot and apple. People were ignorant about the fruits of the plain areas, like mango, grapes, cherry, banana, peas, pomegranate, watermelon, and pineapple, etc. But today all kinds of fruits are available in Ladakh and some are grown here. The fruit trees start flowering in April and May and get the fruit in August-September. Some of the apricot varieties ripe early. In the past, there was no fridge or other machine, therefore the local people put the apples with grain in the bags and preserved for a long time, it did not spoil because of cold. Today, it is a boon of modern technology that jam and juices are being made locally and apples are preserved for months together. A kind of bush which is called Seabukthorn is found on the bank of rivers and deserts where water is available. It is found in Nubra on the bank of river Shayok in large number. It bears a very small orange coloured fruit which is called berry. The Leh berry juice is very popular in Ladakh, which is having a large quantity of vitamin C. Shampoo and some other herbal medicines are also prepared with seabukthorn.

Plantation

The most of the parts of Ladakh is desert and greenery is very rare. The climate of Ladakh is severe with aridity; therefore the region is extremely dry. Today, one experiences intense heat under direct sunshine and biting cold in shade. It has affected the growth of plants and trees. That is why Cunningham has stated in his book that he has seen only one tree at Choglamsar. Here is a Mohla in Kargil town called "Changchik" meaning one tree. Similarly, a Mohla in Chumathang is known as "Changma-chan" meaning having tree. It indicates that in the past there were very less number of trees in Ladakh. People were using certain type of wild grasses like "Burtsey", "Ayuk", etc. as fuel and the bushes found on the bank of rivers. It is true that in the past because of intense cold trees and plants could not grow easily. But we cannot deny the contributions of the Dogra's, especially Mehta Basti Ram and Mehta Manggal, who did keen efforts to convert Ladakh into a greenery belt, they planted trees in different places of the region, wherever, water was available. They planted popular trees on the road side right from Leh Bazaar to Zorawar fort. Some of the "Baghs" are still in a good position, like Saspol Bagh, Manggal Bagh Skara, Rani Bagh, Hemya, Partapura Bagh, Karzoo Bagh, Nemo Bagh, etc. But unfortunately most of the Bagh's like Wazir Bagh Leh, Ranbirpura Bagh, Skara Bagh, Tehsil Bagh, Manggal Bagh, Rampur Bagh and Kigue Bagh, etc. have been destroyed by the then administrators of Leh for fuel purposes during winter because there was no system of importing wood for fuel from other regions like Kashmir. Thus what the Dogra administrator did during 1860's to promote the greenery and economy of Ladakh, were destroyed by the then Ladakhi administrators during 1960 onwards. However, the forest department Leh did a remarkable job by planting siblings on the meadows on the bank of rivers and the land under the command areas both in Kargil and Leh. Moreover, they motivated and encouraged the public by granting incentives on the basis of the quantity of plants. Therefore after 1980, the greenery of the Ladakh has increased and it has certainly affected the ecological phenomena of the region. Moreover after the completion of the Kurbathang, Lagjung, Igoo-Phey and many more canals, the people took keen interest in plantation. Recently the people of Leh under the aegis of Drukchen Rinpoche planted 53,000 plants within 30 minutes near Hemis which made a Guinness record. Later Philppine planted 64,091 saplings in an hour by breaking the Ladakh record. On 29th October 2012 Ladakh again created history by breaking the previous world record of planting most saplings in one hour. The plantation drive was organized by "Live to love" organization at Tunkey-lato near Changga village where 9,814 people drawn from all over Ladakh planted 99,013 saplings simultaneously in 53 minutes on 26 acres of land. But we have to see how much it becomes successful and grow properly. "Live to love" organization Chairman, Gyalwang Drukpa Rinpoche in his address appreciated the participants and organizers for registering Ladakh's name in Guinness Book of World Records. He said "it is a proud moment for all of us as such plantation drives are important for safeguarding the nature and environment besides they being beneficial for the overall development of every beings." He further added that such endeavour is not aimed only at breaking the world record but also to benefit for the world as a whole. He urged the people to plant trees as much as possible in other areas of Ladakh in order to contribute for protection of environment and ecology in the wake of growing threats of global warming. This was done on the eve of 4th Drukpa council, held at Hemis.

Food Habit

The soil of Ladakh is sandy and the agricultural lands are situated at the height of 900 to 1500 feet from the sea level and are mostly dependent on river and stream water for irrigation. That too is possible between April to November. Therefore because of cold and limited agricultural season they grow wheat, barley, and peas only. The vegetables like cabbage, cauliflower, carrot, brinjal, potato, turnip, and onion, etc. are grown. The soil is not fit for rice. Thus the ancient Ladakhis were taking mostly the locally available diet prepared by wheat and barley flour. With the wheat flour they prepare various type of dishes like "Skyu, Chhu-tagi, Tapu, Paktsa-Marku, Momok, Lowa-momok, Bread and Thuhgpa, etc. The breads are of many kinds, like chapatti, buskuruk, khameri, thaltak, tsapkur, tenten and kulcha, etc. similarly, they have many types of Thugpas like gyathug, timstuk, chat-thuk, rguthuk, and rhultuk, etc. With barley flour, the Ladakhis prepare Kholak, Paba and Namtuk, etc. Almost meat is a part of all these dishes, subject to the availability. Instead oil the ancient Ladakhis preferred soup, and used peas and locally available vegetables. Rice was imported from Kashmir and used occasionally at the time of festivals and functions. Later the government also made the rationing system, which was not frequent like today. The people would get 2 kg of rice and one kg of sugar during Eid, Losar and other festivals. The diets of ancient Ladakhis were very simple and hygienic. The Yarkendi, Tibetans and Kashmiri introduced some dishes in Ladakh. For example, the Yarkendi introduced polao, momok, baqir-khawni bread and meat samosa. Gyatuk and lova-momok by Tibetans and the central Asian dishes like rogan-josh, yakhni, goshtaba, and kabab, etc. reached Ladakh through Kashmir. The author remembers when the old Ladakhis in the past used to admire about the taste and quality of the Yarkendi polao and samosa. The Ladakhis are habitual of taking "gur-gur" tea at least 5 to 10 cups within a limited time. Most of the Buddhists take "chhang", which is prepared by barley, but the young generation is trying to avoid it. The Punjabi introduced different kinds of sweets and halwa which is liked very much by the children. Today many types of Chinese and western foods are cooked and served in the Ladakhi hotels. Many people especially the educated, and young generation have adopted the Indian or western type of food like breakfast, lunch and dinner, etc.

Dress

The Ladakhi male and female both wear "Gowncha". The male Gowncha is called Gyazo; whereas the female Gowncha is called "Sulma". Gyazo is combination of two words. Gya and Zo. Gya means China and Zo means style. Thus the "Goncha" is of Chinese style. One looks very attractive and smart in Ladakhi dress. One can attend parties and go office in Goncha, whereas it is not the case with Kashmiri "Phiran". The Goncha is being presented to the VIPs, whenever they come on official tour. Ladakhis have presented Goncha to Mrs. Indira Gandhi, Rajiv Gandhi and young leader Rahul Gandhi. In the past Ladakhi themselves weaved rough kind of woolen cloth and Gonchas were prepared, so as to protect oneself from the severe cold. But now most of the Ladakhis wear feather Jackets and woolen garments. Jeans pants, t-shirts, and suits. Instead of Papu shoe which is made of woolen thread, people use Chinese shoes and high quality Indian shoes. Now the dresses are becoming universal. It is very difficult to differentiate between a Ladakhi and outsiders. Here is a legend about the invention of Kantop cap, Tsaru (ear flap) and Tsakta sulma. According to Cunningham, "Once a Tobra of a Turkish soldier fell down from his horse and found by a Ladakhi. He used the same as cap and became fashion in the society." It is said that a Ladakhi prince married with a princes of a neighbouring country. She was wearing a Perak, which was a new ornament for this land. Later the wives of the nobles also adopted the "Perak". The wall paintings of courtiers at Tsemo Palace Leh and Bazgo palace indicate that the nobles wore round turban and the Rani is shown wearing "perak" without Charu, Hashmatullah is of the opinion that the Charu (earflap of lamb's skin) was invented at a later stage. Some historian says that once a Ladakhi Rani was suffering from ear problems, she kept lamb skin under her "perak"on both side of the ears. The wives of the nobles imitated it and it became fashion in the society. May be it is true. But Hashmatullah does not agree to this statement. According to him, the Charu (earflap) and Stakta Sulma were invented in memory of Kushok Stagtsang Raspa and Gyalpo Singgay Namgyal. Since the period of Gyalpo Singgay Namgyal and Lama Stagtsang Raspa is considered a golden period of Buddhism in Ladakh, in respect of constructions of Gonpas, propagation of Buddhism and preaching of moral and aesthetic values. Singgay means Lion and Stakta means Tiger. Hence "Charu" refers to Lion's ear and the stakta as tiger's skin. It seems to be very much correct. Still, the professional dancers use the stakta while performing dances. And Charu (earflap) is common in Ladakh. Ladakhi women are fond of "perak" and other ornaments. They wear the perak occasionally. However, the Muslim women have avoided wearing perak. It is said that the Dogra Wazir Syed Akbar Ali (1866-71) advised them to be in Taharat and use chadar as "purdha". Since then they are not wearing perak. The other ornaments are common in both the community. The Firaq and Shalwar are common in South Asian countries. It is a noble dress and the Ladakhi women also like to wear this dress. In the past Ladakhi women were wearing white goat skin with long hair on the back called Lokpa but now the young generation has avoided wearing it. Since the Kashmiri Shawl is very famous in the world for its good finishing and beauty, for which the raw material is being produced from Ladakh. According an estimate the Ladakhi Changpas produce about 16,000 kg of pashmina wool every year. But they continue to be exploited by the middlemen and traders from Leh, Srinagar and Kulu, etc. Now the government has decided that the wool Board would procure pashmina directly from Changthang to save pashmina growers from middlemen.

Road and Transport

Leh was connected with track routes from Srinagar, Nubra, Durbuk, Nyoma, Kargil and Manali since ancient period. Many invaders and travelers from different quarter reached Leh through these routes. There were some small bridges over the Rivers Indus, Suru and Shayok to connect Leh with other destinations, like Andho Bridge at Kargil, Khalsey Bridge at Balu Khar, Choglamsar Bridge, Zamghog Bridge at Igoo, Koyak Bridge over Shayok at Nubra, and Tsostang Bridge at Bogdang. History reveals us that during the reign of

King Delek Namgyal (1666-95 AD) about 6,000 strong Mughal army passed through Andho and Khalsey Bridge and came for the rescue of the king as per his request. The bridges were so small that only men and animal can pass through these bridges. Even a Tonga could not pass through it. The Srinagar-Leh road was completed and made jeepable in the year 1962, under the supervision of Engineer Sonam Nurboo. Therefore Government of India conferred him the award of "Padma Shri" for his outstanding performance. Later, Unimok and mini buses reached in Leh from Srinagar. The Ladakhis are of the opinion, that the Chinese aggression in 1962, proved like a boon, which forced the Indian Government to extend the road to Nyoma, Nubra and Chushul, etc. to boost the security of the country. Now these major roads are broad and almost 95 per cent villages have been linked with motorable road and transport facilities are there. Previously, the nomadic people of Chanthang called "Changpas" used to bring salt on the back of sheep and goats in small "Khurjuns". And in return they were taking back grains from here. The journey took months together. But today they have mobile ration store at their door steps and procure essential commodities through trucks within one day. Today Ladakh is linked with Delhi, Chandigarh, Jammu, and Srinagar through aeroplanes. It was Air-Commodore Mehar Singh, who landed the first aeroplane at the Leh airport on 24th of May 1948. That was a red letter day for the Ladakhis. It is said that an old lady reached at the airport taking grass on her back for the aeroplanes. It indicates that the old people were very innocent and ignorant. In August 1950, a jeep was brought to Leh through Army aeroplanes, which was in the use of the top army Officers within Leh city and neighbouring villages. An old man and his son were at the airport, when 2 jeeps were brought in the army aircraft. The old father said to his son, these are the children of the aeroplane, now feathers will grow in due course of time and they would fly. Ladakhis are very fond of cars and motors. Most of the people keep car and even some families have individual car for every member and the problem of parking is increasing in the town day by day. The old horse and ponies are disappearing rapidly. Previously, it took 15 days to reach

Srinagar on ponies but today the journey can be performed within half hour in an aeroplane. In the past one had to go on foot or on ponies to Baltistan, Tibet and Yarkend, but today if political relation improves and the barriers are removed with the neighbouring countries we can utilize the modern means to travel.

Building

Some of the important buildings of the past are Singgay palace Leh, Chiktan Razi Khar, Shay palace, Hemis Gonpa, Thiksay Gonpa, Pethub Gonpa, Zorawar fort and other monasteries. It is said that the Chief mason of Singgay palace and Chiktan Razi Khar was a Balti architect called Shingkhan Chandan Ali of Khapulo. The Singgay palace and Hemis Gonpa were built during the period of Raja Singgay Namgyal and Lama Stagsang Raspa during (1610-45 AD). Though not a handful of cement and iron have been used in its construction, except mud and stone, yet still are in a good position. But the Chiktan Razi Khar is ruined because of the negligence of the people of Chiktan. People not only removed the logs and door and windows but also destroyed other valuable monuments. This has affected the tourist industry in Kargil. No doubt, today the people of the area have realized the cultural and historical importance of the old palaces and are demanding for restoration of their old position. In Ladakh the old houses of the common people are made of local mud bricks and mud plaster. Doors and windows are very small and without window pane and glasses. Logs, twigs and mud have been used for roofing. The rich people made the wooden flooring only in the living room. The ground floor is used for cattle and fodder store. Moreover the dry alfa-alfa grass is kept on the roof of the house to consume during the winter. People live at the first floor. Mostly the houses are only 2 storey's high. Some rich people built 3 storey houses. Dry latrine is separately constructed adjacent to the house. Similarly, some people built the cow-shed separately. Today much improvement has been made in construction. People have used the modern technology of engineering. Cement and iron, etc. are used in a big quantity. Two, three and four star hotels have been constructed. Instead of old mud houses the modern Ladakhis have constructed western type bungalows with modern facilities. Even common people got cement plastered on their mud houses. Kitchen and bathrooms are made on the modern line. Hygienic principles are kept in mind. In short, the living standards of the Ladakhis have improved rapidly.

Communication

In the past there were no radio, television, and telephone system or newspaper. The only source of news was the verbal narration of the travelers and traders. One of the important events in the history of Ladakh was the opening of the post office in 1875, and runners were appointed at every destination from Leh to Srinagar to carry the mail. Moreover, few prominent persons of the town used to receive Urdu news papers by post. The postal system was very dull and slow. This took 16 days and some time one month's time to reach from Srinagar to Leh through postal runners. After the establishment of post office, the literate persons began to use the facilities of writing letters but the common people, who neither could read nor write the letters. Thereby they had to go from door to door in search of a literate person. The problem was solved to some extent in 1964, when a fifty line telephone exchange was installed at Leh. Now an illiterate person could talk on telephone to his near and dears, who reside outside the state. Now the TV, radio, mobile and internet system brought revolution in the life of the people. The Radio Station Leh was commissioned in the year 1970 and the Doordarshan Leh was started on 7th September 1984. Electricity has been provided to the maximum people of Leh District through Stakna Hydel Project since June 1987. This proved a boon for the TV watchers. Today, the far flung and backward areas have been connected with TV and radio. Since then the two institutions are playing a vital role by bringing about awareness programmes and also historical, cultural, craft, agricultural, entertainment and developmental programmes in every walk of life. Now the people have up to date news. People have forgotten to write letters and use of telegraph message. They directly convey the message through mobile. There was a time that most of the Ladakhi youths married a girl, without seeing or talking her earlier because of shyness and hesitation. But mobile has solved this problem; it has removed all the old barriers once for all. The latest developments in the field of communication are Google, Facebook and Twitter, etc. but the Indian youths, at present are mostly affiliated with Facebook. One can have the information about employment, business, educational, cultural and social programmes, etc. It depends upon the use of the social networking sites like Facebook, for instance. If you use it for positive purpose, certainly, it will give positive result, on the other hand, if you use it for negative purpose it will give negative result.

Employment Opportunities

Earlier, the employment opportunities were nil in Ladakh. Only some influential persons were appointed in the royal court as ministers called Kalon and Lonpo and the representatives of the Raja in major villages. According to Wazir Hashmatullah, there was no regular army to defend the country from the enemies. At the time of emergencies and war every household had to provide a person along with food and clothing. That too without salary, and whenever the war was over they proceeded directly to their home. Most of the persons had to arrange the weapon, i.e. either a sword or a spear. Very few people were having "Match-lock Gun". But people were loyal to the king and enthusiastic to defend the country. During the Dogra period very less chances of employment were there for the Local Ladakhis. They brought the officers, clerks and soldiers from Jammu. Some of the local people were appointed as peon and helpers, and employment opportunities were worse than the old regime. After independence many illiterate Ladakhi youths were recruited in the army. At that time Ladakhis were not qualified for higher post, however they got the lower post like clerks, patwari, teachers, peon and chokidar, etc. A clerk called "Munshi" enjoyed a high status in the society. Some of the Munshi families both in Buddhists and Muslims even today enjoy a very high respect and regards in the society, because their forefathers were clerks. Similarly, when a peon called

"Choprasi" of the Tehsildar office went to a village to deliver a summon, people used to salute him, otherwise he would abuse or even slap them. The cruelty of a police constable was more than that. After independence the innocent, illiterate and poor girls from the remote areas came for job to Leh. Quite often they fell into the trap of youngmen from the Leh town who sexually exploited these girls. This has created a problem of illegitimate children. But this has been checked now because of economic development and good education. It is because of the noble efforts of our modern leaders, the "Kar-Begar", i.e. forced labour and other ills are abolished. They emphasized to send the children to schools and for higher education to Srinagar. Thus many people completed their graduation and postgraduation and were appointed on high posts. Mr. Dechen was the first Ladakhi D.C., Mr. E. Joldan the first Headmaster, Dr. Tsewang Smanla the first Doctor, Col. C. Rinchen Twice M.V.C. the first army officer, Mr. C. Phuntsog the first I.A.S. Officer and Ataullah Radhu was the first Ladakhi diplomat, and so on. Now many Ladakhis are getting high and quality education in Medical, Engineering, Science, Social Sciences, Arts, Commerce, Journalism and Mass Communication, etc. Today there are dozens of IAS, IFS, IES, and KAS officers, army officers, Pilot, Scientists, Educationists, Doctors, Engineers, Lecturers and Professors and other administrators. Ladakh is on the move in respect of employment. After the Chinese aggression the deployment of military and paramilitary forces has proved a blessing in disguise for the Ladakhis because the road construction speeded up and transportation facilities developed fast. Moreover thousands of Ladakhi youth are working in Army and Paramilitary forces, because army has generated employment opportunities for the locals. Today, 99 per cent District Officers and subordinate employees are local. But most of them are lacking in sincerity and dedication unlike the Dogra administrators. Corruption is at high scale in most of the departments. People are fading up with the local administrators. Take the example of Mehta Basti Ram and Mehta Manggal, who did welfare activities for the people, in spite of their limited resources. Mehta Manggal is still remembered by the people for his tree plantation, widening of Leh Bazaar, revenue settlements and rehabilitation of poor people at Rampur, Ranbirpur, Partapur, etc. People at large expect good governance in Ladakh which is in their overall interest.

Health and Hygiene

The ancient Ladakhis were dependent on Amchi system of treatment. Amchi is also called "Lharje". He was an important man. He used the traditional herbal medicines to cure the patients. He prepared the medicine with the locally available herbs. Some of the herbs were imported from other countries and became expensive. To a Ladakhi an Amchi was the immediate available curer of disease. There was no Dispensary in Ladakh till 1887, when Dr. Karl Marx, a member of the Moravian Missionaries reached from Germany in April 1887 and opened a Dispensary and Clinic at Leh. Missionary Doctors attended the patients with sympathy, sincerity and dedication. They treated thousands of patients every year. The Missionary Doctors used to tour the villages, so as to give treatment to the village patients. The author's grandfather was treated in a missionary dispensary also where he was fully recovered. Similarly hundreds of other senior citizens of Ladakh admire the missionary doctors for their good behaviour and treatments. It is said that Typhus was common in those days. Unfortunately, Dr. Shah and Dr. Karl Marx passed away because of infection, by treating Typhus patients. That was a great loss for the Ladakhis. Though the people of Leh town and the neighbouring villages were getting treatment from the Missionary dispensary but it was not possible for the people of far flung areas like Kargil, Nubra, Changthang, Zangskar and Rong Churgyut. In the past, the population was low but the death rate was high. Thousands of people die because of infectious diseases like smallpox, typhus, chickenpox, TB, cancer and other communicable diseases. Moreover the hygienic condition of the people was very poor. They hardly used the water to bath or washing clothes. But one thing was there that they were taking simple food without oil and did agricultural work manually; walked miles together and travelled on foot to reach the town. That is why they were healthy and not suffering from diabetes, hyper tension and other disease. But today people follow the hygienic principles. All sort of facilities are there. Moreover, they take oily food, never walk and use car to purchase bread or vegetable from the market, and never do exercise. The agriculture work is being done by the Gorkhas and Biharis labours. But how long? Just imagine, even a group IV employee uses the car to go to office. It indicates that the living standard of the people has improved but side by side it has brought tension and different problems. People are prey to different unknown diseases. As far as medical facilities are concerned, today Ladakh has 100 bedded hospitals fully equipped with modern facilities at District headquarters. There are small hospitals at Block headquarters, Dispensaries, medical aid centres and first aid centers, etc. The serious patients are referred to the district hospital. Asha workers are there, and the pregnant women are looked after properly. Every woman gives birth to her child at the hospital under the care and supervision of gynaecologist. Because of modern facilities and immunization many dreaded diseases have been eradicated from the soil. The population is high as compared to the last few decades but the death rate is low at the time being. However, the young generation needs to be very cautious about their health. They have to follow the health and hygienic principles by taking nutritious food, fruits and salad avoiding oily food, alcohol and smoking.

Tourism

Ladakh was opened for tourism in 1974. Since then the number of tourists, domestic as well as foreigners are increasing year by year. In the beginning, 527 tourists arrived in Leh during the year 1974. Out of which 500 were foreign tourists and only 27 were from home. The number jumped to 9621 in 1978. Out of which, 8748 were foreigner and 873 domestic. By 2010 the number of tourists increased to 77800, out of which 22115 were foreign tourists and 55685 were the domestic tourists. This figure shows, now the maximum tourists are Indian. The arrival of Indian tourists increased since 2008. In overall assessment the whole of Ladakh is now more exposed to alien people and their ways than ever before.

This has resulted in the employment of many locals in business related with travel agents, tourist guides, taxi operators, hotels and restaurants. Now the shops are opened to sell the Ladakhi, Kashmiri and Tibetan antiques, art and craft like thankas, carpets, necklaces, statues, and old utensils, etc. but most of these shops and pavement stalls are owned by the Tibetans and the Kashmiri traders. If both the government of India and China agree to open Kailash-Mansarovar road, then the inflow of tourists would be much higher than the present number. Ladakh has suffered its share of social evils. Outside influence has led to the abandonment of traditional values. Like a coin which has two sides; the impact of tourism in Ladakh has also two values, i.e. negative and positive values. The impact of tourism was so intense during the first 15 years of opening Ladakh to tourists. The cases of stealing statues, frescos and other religious goods have been reported from many villages and Gonpas. This was unthinkable for Ladakh before 1974. The state government opened an office in Leh for the registration of antiquities. But these government measures had little success and for a long time the antique business created a lot of problems for both the local people and the other lovers of art, culture and religion. Though tourism in Ladakh came as part of development package, thousands of hotels and restaurants have come up in the region. The hoteliers, transporters, shopkeepers, guides, helpers, trekkers, pony owners, camel owners and Gonpas, etc. get the benefit of tourism in one way or other. Yet, it would not be wrong to say that the Ladakhis are the least gainers of tourism development package. It is the none Ladakhis like Kashmiris, Tibetans, and others who owned the antique shops and run its business on Kashmiri and Tibetan Art and Craft getting a very handsome amount. The Airliners also get a major portion of tourist income. The negative impact of tourism is that some of the tourists introduced the drugs like charas, opium, alcohol, etc. among the youths. They also do inhuman acts like hugging, embracing and kissing the women in open in the main Bazaar and streets which has certainly harmed the moral and ethical values, and the young generations easily become the prey of these uncultured activities.

Social and Economic Boycott of Muslims and Formation of LAHDC

Ladakh remained a peaceful region for centuries together. Since the period of king Takpa Bum-Ldey Ladakhis, irrespective of religion and sects enjoyed a congenial and amicable relation. Matrimonial relation was there, not only among the common people but also in the royal families. Many Muslim princesses right from Rgyal Khatoon to Zahra Khatoon married with some of the Rajas of Namgyal dynasty. Similarly some Ladakhi Buddhist princesses like Mendok Rgyalmo, Shema Tashi Wangmo and some unknown princesses were married to the Muslim Rajas of Baltistan. Conflicts and disputes in the name of religion were quite unknown. However, during the end of 20th century, some confusion, doubts, resentment and grievances developed in the mind of the Buddhists of Ladakh. The Buddhists were of the opinion that conversion is being made by way of marriage with Buddhist women: that most of the important business in the town is dominated by the Muslims; that the minority Muslims of the town are getting the full favour from Kashmiri officers in dealing with different cases and allotment of contract, etc; attitude and behaviour of the Muslim youths towards the Buddhist girls is quite negative and with the power of muscle and money they indulge in adultery. Similarly the attitude of some traders like butchers and shopkeepers was not decent towards the common Buddhist and that the Shia Muslims are not taking the food prepared by a Buddhist. Above all their allegation was that the Kashmiri rulers show stepmotherly treatment towards the Ladakhi Buddhists. The people continue to think that they are economically deprived, discriminated and alienated by the state government. Agitation in Leh was not an abrupt rise. Things had not come to that end all of a sudden. The resentment had been brewing in the district over the years. It was being neglected on all counts. There was a great resentment against the discrimination of the J&K Government. The above cited causes show though the fire had been ignited internally but later it turned into a flame. Once, two groups of Muslim and Buddhist youths quarreled with one another at

Jiva Tsal, and Leh Bazaar and later it turned into a communal clash.

Congress Leaders involved in S.T. struggle are Honoured after releasing from Jail

The Buddhist youths came out of the Chokhang in a big procession, chanting slogans against the minority Muslims, and pelted stones at some of the important buildings and Muslim houses. Later in 1989, under the leadership of LBA President, Thufstan Tsewang, the Buddhist started agitation against the discrimination of Government of Jammu and Kashmir, and the majority community declared social and economic boycott against the Muslims. The communal gap widened between the two, who were living like brothers for centuries. This continued for a period of three years. The Muslims had to face many hardships during this period. The friends and relatives could not participate in each other's functions and funerals. Any member of the majority community who, if and when violates the norms and dared to do so was also punished and fined. Muslim taxis were not allowed to enter the Gonpa with tourists. Wind screen of many taxis, trucks and trippers were damaged. Some Muslim houses were burnt to ashes at village Shay, Matho, etc. When the situation was beyond the control of the administration, army was called out and curfew was imposed in Leh town on July 8, 1989. Thus the traditional value system, tolerance and humanism are on wane. The exemplary case of integrated society of Ladakh is fast becoming a thing of yester years. Now they see each other with indifference and doubt. Consequently, the old age traditional Buddhist-Muslim relationship of harmony, integration and tolerance continue to get impaired. When the situation became normal curfew was lifted on July 12, 1989. But the boycott continued. Most of the Buddhist brothers were not happy with this act. They opposed secretly and silently. Former Minister Sonam Wangyal was at the fore front. He agreed to support their all demands and requested for lifting the boycott and to maintain traditional harmonious relations with the Muslims. He said, "Since they are part and parcel of Ladakhi community for centuries together, hence we should maintain communal harmony." But unfortunately, his request was turned down and he was also boycotted and not allowed him to participate in the funeral ceremony and pay homage to his beloved wife Ugrian Dolma. That was a great tragedy for an old man. Though the Buddhists continued their agitation to achieve the Autonomous Hill Council status for Ladakh, but the Muslims kept themselves aside from the agitation. However, the then Home Minister of Government of India asked the Buddhist leaders to shun out the differences with the Muslims and maintain the traditional brotherhood and harmonious relation. He said, "Unless and until, the Muslims would not co-operate the cause, the government could not consider your demand". Consequently, the LBA lifted the social boycott against the Muslims during a tripartite talk in New Delhi, between Government of India, State Government and the Ladakhi representatives, on November 29, 1992, and the Muslims of Ladakh under the aegis of LMA president M. Akbar Ladakhi, agreed to co-operate the struggle to achieve the Hill Council Status for Ladakh. Consequently, a coordination committee for Leh Autonomous Hill Development Council came into being. This comprised of LBA and LMA and they jointly fought for the cause. Later several rounds of talks had been taken place at State and Central level and finally S.B. Chavan, then Home Minister, the Government of India agreed in principle to grant "Hill

Council Status" to Ladakh. The State Government then made a draft of Autonomous Hill Development Council of Ladakh and sent it to New Delhi for approval. The draft was received by the Law Ministry Government of India. After thorough study of the draft by the Law and Home Ministries it was sent to cabinet for formal approval, before submitting it to the President of India for his consent. Finally, on May 9, 1995 the President of India approved the "Ladakh Autonomous Hill Development Council Act." Under the act the District Council is to comprise 30 members, out of whom 26 shall be elected. The remaining 4 shall be nominated by the Governor from the principal minorities and women in the District. The Members of the Council shall elect a chairman, who will also be the Chief Executive Councillor. The four other executive councillors shall be nominated by the Chief Executive Councillor.

After the election of the councillors, the swearing in ceremony took place at Polo ground Leh under the supervision of the Governor of J&K on 3rd of September, 1995. Thufstan Tsewang was elected as first Chairman and Chief Executive Councillor of LAHDC Leh. As far as the District Kargil was concerned they were suspicious about the system and refused to form the council at that time. Later, they formed it in 2000, and Mr. Qamar Ali Akhon was elected as first Chairman and Chief Executive Councillor of the LAHDC Kargil. The Chief Executive Councillors of LAHDC Leh had been 1. Thufstan Tsewang, 2. Rigzin Spalbar, 3. Tsering Dorjay Lakruk. Whereas the Executive Councillors till date were 1. Er. Sonam Dawa, 2. Tundup Sonam Timisgam, 3. Mr. M. Akbar Ladakhi, 4. Nawang Rigzin Jora, 5. Rigzin Spalbar, 6. Mr. Ashraf Ali Barcha, 7. Mr. Ghulam Abbas Aabedi, 8. Mr. Ghulam Mohammad Khan, 9. Tsultim Dorjay Diskit, 10. Nurboo Gyalchan Advocate, 11. Skarma Stanzin Tukchupa, 12. Tsering Angchuk, Panamik, 13. Nurboo Lampa, 14. Tsewang Rigzin Khardong, 15. Stanzin Delek Tigar, 16. Tsewang Tundup Ney, 17. Phunchok Tashi Skurbuchan, 18. Dorjay Moutup Hemya, 19. Dorjay Stanzin Lonpo Durbuk, 20. Dr. Sonam Angchuk Hunder, 21. Advocate Sonam Dorjay Tia, 22. Tsering Gurmat Korzok. The Chairmen and Chief

Executive Councillors of Kargil District were 1. Mr. Qamar Ali Akhon, 2. Haji Azgar Ali Karbalai and 3. Kacho Ahmad Ali Khan. Similarly, the Executive Councillors are 1. Mr. Nasir Munshi, 2. Kacho Gulzar Hussain, 3. Kacho Ahmad Ali Khan, 4. Sonam Namgyal, 5. Haji Mohammad Ishaq, 6. Haji Aamir, 7. Mr. Abdul Majid Nago, 8. Phuntsog Tashi, 9. Agha Syed Kazim. During Farooq Abdullah's regime the due powers were not delegated to the council but when the coalition Government of PDP and Congress came in power in J&K in 2000, it was Mufti Mohammad Sayeed, Chief Minister of J&K who granted cabinet status to the CEC and Deputy Minister Status to the EC's. Presently, the people of both the districts are looking forward towards the LAHDC's for speedy developments in every field and proper upliftment of the backward region. Since now people have their own Government the responsibility for lapses can not be fixed on any body else. The LAHDC's proved very fruitful for the two districts of Ladakh. Now councillors at village and sub-block level have got the power to propose the schemes and projects for their concerned blocks. It is discussed in the general council meeting and if genuine, it is approved and kept in the plan. Now construction of roads, buildings, bridges, schools, hospitals, veterinary centers and other developmental works are taking place all over the region.

It is not out of place to mention here that some 60 Muslim families from Leh, Chushot and Thiksay were socially boycotted by the majority of Muslims during 1970's. This was the first of its kind done by the Muslims to the members of their own community and it continued for about 7 years. This inhuman act was done because of the bifurcation of the National Congress Party, which proved harmful for the masses in general and Muslims in particular. The two factions of the Congress-A and Congress-B drew their support from different areas and communities. Congress-A was popular in Leh Tehsil, where Buddhists dominate, while Congress-B was popular in Kargil Tehsil where Shia Muslims are in majority. During parliamentary election compaign there was hardly agenda on economic grievances. Sonam Wangdus Lachumir was projected as saviour of Muslims in Leh and called "Sheikh Aman"—peace loving person by some people to lure the voters of Kargil and K.G. Bakula as an enemy and opponent of Islam. Ninety per cent Muslims both Shia and Sunni from Leh were supporting the Congress-B. Their main aim was to strengthen the Congress-B by hook or crook. Therefore, they imposed boycott socially as well as religiously on the supporters of Congress-A headed by K.G. Bakula. According to Quraan, Sura, Baqra, Aya No. 114, any person has no right to ban a Muslim to enter a mosque for prayer. But they dared to do so and their opponents were not allowed to enter Imam-Barah and mosqus for prayer and were tortured mentally and physically. Supporters of Congress-A Muslims were entrapped in fabricated Police cases. They were nick-named as "Gaddar" and were never allowed to condole the death of their nearest relatives. Finally, about seven years later boycott was lifted without any outcome or without the achievement of any goal. The boycott was a great blunder in the history of Islam in Leh. A Muslim is required to maintain good relationship with his relatives and neighbours. As the prophet Muhammad (SAW) has said, "Be good and kind to your parents and your children will be good and kind to you." Islam enjoins us not only to be good to those who are good to us, but also to be good to those who are not good to us. The essence of Islam is thus to serve God and do good to our fellow creatures, including the animals. So the Islamic laws of morality and decency must be observed. Once the Prophet (SAW) asked, "Do you know what the rights of neighbours are?" And then he went on to give a list, "Help him if he asks for your help. Give him relief if he seeks relief from you. Give him a loan if he needs one. Show him concern if he is distressed. Nurse him when he is ill. Attend his funeral if he dies. Congratulate him if he meets with any good. Sympathise him if any calamity befalls him." He further says, "Nobody can be a believer, if his neighbour passes the night hungry, while he has his stomach full." The Hadith tells us that nobody can be a true believer unless his neighbours feel secured from his hands and tongue. We are urged to be good and helpful to our neighbours in particular for they, being near, have more right to our goodness and assistance.

Bibliography

Aabedin, Aabedi Zainul, *Emergence of Islam in Ladakh*, 2009.

Aabedi, Mohammad Hussain, Autobiography, 1990.

Cunningham, Alexander, *Ladakh Physical and Historical*, 1977.

Dughlat, Mirza Haider, *Tarikh-e-Rashidi.*

Col. Basti Ram, *Ladakh*, 1846.

Franke, A.H., *A History of Western Tibet.*

——, *The Mysterious Land*, 1980.

Gergan, S.S., *Ladakh: The Land of Gonpas*, 1980.

Jina, Prem Singh and Zainul Aabedin, *Islam in Ladakh*, 2001.

Jina, Prem Singh, *Religious History of Ladakh*, 2001.

——, *The Impact of Tourism on Ladakh*, 1995.

Joldan, Eliezer, *Harvest Festivals of Darads in Ladakh*, 1985.

Khan, Hashmatullah, *Tarikh-e-Jammu*, 1939.

Khan, Kacho Sikander, *Qadim Ladakh*, 1987.

Koul, H.N., *Rediscovery of Ladakh*, 1998.

Luciano, Petech, *The Kingdom of Ladakh*, 1977.

Mohammad Hasan Hasrat, *Baltistan Tehzeeb-o-Saqafat*, 1995.

Naqashi, Ganga Ram, *His Note to Maharaja Gulab Singh*, 1846.

Rather, Ali Mohammad, *Ethnography of Mons.*

Rizvi, Janet, Ladakh: Crossroads of High Asia, 1985.

——, *Trans-Himaliyan Carvan*, 1999.

Sharma, Suresh & Usha Sharma, *Kashmir Through the Age*, 1998.

Sheikh, Abdul Ghani, *Ladakh Muhaqqiquu Aur Sayahuu ki Nazar me.*

Sheikh, Abdul Ghani, *Ladakh Tahzib-o-Saqafat*, 2006.

——, *Reflections of Ladakh, Tibet and Central Asia.*

Younghusband, Francis, *Travel in Kashmir.*

Zakaullah, *Tarikhe Hind.*

(2) 304